AF745928

UNIVERSITY OF BRISTOL
UNIVERSITY LIBRARY
TYNDALL AVENUE
BRISTOL, BS8 1TJ

Date due for return (unless recalled earlier)

NOT FOR LOAN
BEFORE
20 APR 1994

30.JUN.1997

30-SEP-97

02.JAN.2002

Issues in Business Taxation

Edited by
JOHN POINTON
Business Taxation Research Unit
Plymouth Business School
University of Plymouth

Avebury

Aldershot · Brookfield USA · Hong Kong · Singapore · Sydney

© The Contributors, 1994

All rights reserved. No part of this publication may be reproduced, stored in a retrieval system, or transmitted in any form or by any means, electronic, mechanical, photocopying or otherwise without the prior permission of the publisher.

Published by
Avebury
Ashgate Publishing Limited
Gower House
Croft Road
Aldershot
Hants GU11 3HR
England

Ashgate Publishing Company
Old Post Road
Brookfield
Vermont 05036
USA

HD 2753 ISS

British Library Cataloguing in Publication Data

Issues in Business Taxation
I. John Pointon
336.2

ISBN 1 85628 419 0

Printed and Bound in Great Britain by
Athenaeum Press Ltd, Newcastle upon Tyne.

UNIVERSITY
OF BRISTOL
LIBRARY

Contents

Figures and tables

Acknowledgements

Many thanks are due to Paul Adams for his assistance with the survey on controlled foreign companies and his help with the production of the chapters. The editor would also like to express his thanks to the trustees of the Nuffield Foundation for their financial support, under the Small Grants Scheme in the Social Sciences, for two projects: Finance Lease Evaluation in the UK (SOC/181(1881)) and A Comparative Study of European Taxation and Corporate Investment (SOC/181(2256)). Chapters Two, Four and Five are based upon these externally funded projects. Nick Wiseman provided guidance on Chapter Six, Zofjia Wills processed the background papers to Chapter Five and Jean Jones provided administrative support. Their help is much appreciated.

The editor and contributors have tried to ensure that the contents of this book are accurate. However, if our interpretations and analyses prove to be in any way incorrect or misleading, please let us know and accept our sincere apologies. We, and indeed the publishers, accept no responsibility for any losses which may occur due to reference to this publication.

Preface

He saw a man named Matthew, sitting at the tax collector's booth.
"Follow me".

New York International Bible Society (1978),
The Holy Bible: New International Version,
Matthew, Chapter 9, Verse 9,
Hodder and Stoughton, London.

Introduction

The aim of this book is to examine a number of domestic and international issues in business taxation. Part One, incorporating Chapters One to Three, relates to the UK context.

In Chapter One, the combined effects of corporate and personal taxation on the risk-return relationship of capital projects is evaluated. Incentives and disincentives are determined.

An important form of finance is from leasing. In Chapter Two the theory of leasing is discussed with and without tax considerations. An empirical survey is reported in an attempt to answer key issues in lease evaluation. These include the degree of importance of taxation in the finance lease decision, how respondents treat tax effects in the discount rate, and the treatment of tax lags and tax losses.

For a particular company, the relevant tax environment is the firm as a whole. But the tax effects of a particular project can impact upon other potential projects. A formal approach to a solution is through mathematical programming. In Chapter Three, such a model is developed, incorporating constraints to deal with the setoff of advance corporation tax, losses and leasing.

Part Two, comprising Chapters Four to Seven, widens the tax horizon to other European countries. In Chapter Four, comparisons are made of the tax treatment of dividends, depreciation, capital gains, losses, stocks, interest, foreign source income and value-added tax. Examples are also shown of non-deductible items.

In Chapter Five, a model is derived to accommodate risk, personal and corporate tax rates, imputed credits and tax depreciation methods. Comparisons are made, for countries within the European Community, between the pre-tax equilibrium rates of return for different asset categories and risk levels under a post-tax model and the respective rates under a tax-free model. Relative incentives and disincentives are evaluated.

A controversial issue in financial economics is whether the differing tax treatments of debt and equity finance affect the total value of the firm. In Chapter Six, the existing evidence is reviewed and new research is undertaken to examine European capital structure patterns and differentials and to search for the determinants of capital structure patterns across Europe.

Chapter Seven outlines the concepts of fiscal neutrality and the harmonization of corporation tax systems. A putative case is set out for a harmonized system within the European Community, including the elimination of welfare reducing production distortions and related administration and compliance costs. The merits of a decentralized market-led route are contrasted with a rational centralized solution.

Part Three, incorporating Chapters Eight and Nine, deals with specific multinational aspects. Chapter Eight aims at producing a framework for UK companies operating outside the UK to avoid being subjected to UK corporation tax on their full overseas profits, as a result of an Inland Revenue direction. Potential key issues are tested for their degree of importance by surveying a number of major UK international and multinational companies.

As well as different national tax systems, the financing and capital budgeting decisions of the multinational can be distorted by exchange controls, political risks, international market segmentation, foreign exchange risks and the organizational structure of the multinational enterprise. In Chapter Nine the importance of taxation and other factors are determined from survey data of UK and US multinational.

Part I

THE UK

1 UK taxation and capital investment

John Pointon

Introduction

The UK corporate tax system broadly follows accounting principles and so is primarily based on profits rather than cash flow. However, instead of accounting depreciation there is a system of capital allowances. But, except for buildings in enterprise zones, the allowances spread the cost in some way over the asset life. To maximize wealth, projects need to be evaluated in terms of cash flows and so deviations away from cash flows in the tax base can create incentives or disincentives. Recommendations for a cash flow tax system have been made by Brown (1948) and Meade (1978). However, there are doubts whether such a system can raise revenue, (MacDonald, 1980). The tax saving initially is a proportion of the outlay, whilst tax payments later are constant proportions of the inflows. In equilibrium, the expected returns should be zero and so for the central government, the net present value of the tax effects are also zero, under a cash flow tax system.

Alternatively, the tax system could be based upon true economic income, with deductions for true economic depreciation and interest. In practice, capital allowances can be significantly different from economic depreciation. In any event, the economic values of assets at different points in time are subjective and peculiar to how each firm plans to utilize them.

Empirical studies of how tax is treated in practice in project appraisal reveal significant results. Hodgkinson (1989) concluded from her postal survey, interview studies and computer simulations, that tax is often not properly dealt with in the evaluation of capital projects. Around 20 per cent of top UK companies ignore tax in project appraisal, not necessarily tax loss companies. The full effects of transferring capital allowances between members of a group are also not always fully evaluated. Morgan (1987) also found discrepancies between theory and practice.

The intention in this chapter is to evaluate the combined effects of corporate and personal tax on the risk-return relationship of capital projects. An analysis by Pointon (1980) was based on the question that if the market returns are always expressed on an after-tax basis, then what would be the effects of a particular capital investment if its corporation tax effects are ignored? The present chapter is motivated from a different standpoint. Suppose there is a tax-free world in which the overall market rate of return and the risk-free rate are known. The systematic risk of a project can change on account of the particular system of capital allowances. However, with taxation, the market returns as a whole change and so does the slope of the security market line, depending upon whether investors can lend, and therefore pay tax on interest, or borrow on personal account, and not be allowed tax relief. It will be shown that the combined effects of personal and corporate tax can create incentives, disincentives or rarely neutral effects on capital projects.

A number of other authors have examined models of the effect of tax on project appraisal, such as King (1977), Berry and Dyson (1979), Devereux and Mayer (1984), Moon and Hodges (1989), and Mole (1990) and the effects of tax on the capital asset pricing model, for example Ashton (1989) and Dempsey (1991). Rather than attempting to reconcile the individual contributions made by different authors, instead the analysis in this chapter begins from first principles hoping to provide a single coherent analysis.

Interactions between corporation tax and income tax

The capital budgeting decision can be evaluated by discounting the relevant cash flows at the appropriate discount rate. Taxation can change both the cash flows and the discount rate.

As far as the cash flows are concerned, tax payments reduce the cash flows, and tax savings through capital allowances increase them. The tax base in the UK is primarily based upon profit, except that capital allowances for tax purposes replace depreciation. But profit before depreciation is broadly equivalent to the net cash flows from operations plus the periodic investment in net working capital. Profit before depreciation of £10m converts into a cash flow of only £6m, if £4m is represented by the increase in working capital. So a tax of, say, 33 per cent on £10m is £3.3m, which is actually 55 per cent of the cash flow of £6m. Capital projects usually require a build-up of working capital in the early years and a reduction in working capital in later years. Thus, the tax rate is effectively increased during the early years and reduced in later years. The net result is a tax disincentive effect, as far as the periodic investment in net working capital is concerned, over the life of a capital project.

The net operating cash flow X is used to pay interest R_d, dividends, D_{IV}, advance corporation tax on dividends and net mainstream corporation tax. It is assumed that gross mainstream corporation tax is based on the net operating cash flow less interest, thus ignoring the working capital effects. Capital allowances will be evaluated separately. Net mainstream corporation tax takes account of advance corporation tax already paid.

We can therefore model the mean net operating cash flow X^* by:

$$X^* = R_d^* + D_{IV}\left(\frac{b}{1-b}\right) + n\left\{\left(X^* - R_d^*\right)T - D_{IV}\left(\frac{b}{1-b}\right)\right\}. \qquad (1.1)$$

where:

b = the basic rate of income tax

$\frac{b}{1-b}$ = the rate of advance corporation tax

n = the discount factor for the tax lag

R_d^* = the mean interest payments

This assumes a maximum dividend payout. Net mainstream corporation tax is paid nine months after the year-end. The small delay between the dividend payment and the payment of advance corporation tax is ignored.

The relationship can be re-expressed in terms of the advance corporation tax payment:

$$D_{IV}\left(\frac{b}{1-b}\right) = \left[\frac{\left(X^* - R_d^*\right)(1-Tn)b}{1-bn}\right]. \qquad (1.2)$$

The sum of the advance corporation tax and the discounted net mainstream corporation tax is:

$$\frac{\left\{[Tn(1-b) + b(1-n)]\left(X^* - R_d^*\right)\right\}}{1-bn}.$$

Hence, an incremental change in the taxable profit, $\Delta\left(X^* - R_d^*\right)$, produces an effective discounted marginal tax rate of T_E such that:

$$T_E = \left[\frac{Tn(1-b) + b(1-n)}{1-bn}\right]. \qquad (1.3)$$

Ignoring discounting, n equals one and T_E equals T, the corporate tax rate. The net dividend is given by:

$$D_{IV} = \left(X^* - R_d^*\right)\left(1 - T_E\right). \tag{1.4}$$

It equals the underlying cash flow after interest less the effective tax.

A numerical illustration should help to clarify the factors at work. The underlying cash flow after interest is £10m. The rate of advance corporation tax is 25/75, consistent with a basic rate of income tax of 25 per cent. The discount rate is 10 per cent and the tax lag is 1.25 years, *i.e.*, six months from mid-year to the year-end plus nine months. The rate of corporation tax is 33 per cent.

$$n = \frac{1}{(1.1)^{1.25}} = 0.887685536.$$

$$T_E = \frac{0.75(0.33)(0.8876855) + 0.25(1 - 0.8876855)}{1 - 0.25(0.8876855)} = 0.3184521.$$

The effective tax on £10m is £3,184,521. Hence, the amount available for the dividend is:

$$£10,000,000 - £3,184,521 = £6,815,479.$$

The advance corporation tax is:

$$\frac{25}{75}(£6,815,479) = £2,271,826.$$

The gross mainstream corporation tax is:

$$0.33(£10,000,000) = £3,300,000.$$

Hence, the net mainstream corporation tax is:

$$£3,300,000 - £2,271,826 = £1,028,174.$$

The discounted net mainstream corporation tax is:

$$£1,028,174\left[\frac{1}{(1.1)^{1.25}}\right] = £912,695.$$

The total discounted cash outflows are therefore:

£6,815,479 (div.)+£2,271,826(ACT) +£912,695 (disc.NMCT) = £10m.

As far as the shareholder is concerned, for a net dividend of £1 the gross dividend is $\frac{£1}{1-b}$. Around nine months after the end of the fiscal year a tax payment is due, at a net rate equal to the excess of the marginal rate h_s over the basic rate b. A net dividend of £1 results in a discounted net benefit to the shareholder of:

$$1-\left(\frac{n_s(h_s-b)}{1-b}\right)$$

where, n_s is the discount factor for taxes paid on the gross equivalent of $\frac{£1}{1-b}$ after accounting for the basic rate credit.

If the effective discounted shareholder tax rate on the net dividend is T_{PS}, then:

$$T_{PS}=n_s\left(\frac{h_s-b}{1-b}\right). \tag{1.5}$$

For the debenture holder, the net discounted cash flow for every £1 of gross interest is:

$$1-b-n_D(h_D-b).$$

where, n_D is the discount factor for debenture-holders.

The effective discounted debenture-holder tax rate on the gross interest is T_{PD} such that:

$$T_{PD}=b+n_D(h_D-b). \tag{1.6}$$

If the shareholder were to invest in a risk-free asset, as well as in shares, then if income tax is deducted at source the effective discounted tax rate on the risk-free asset is T_{PSF}, such that:

$$T_{PSF}=b+n_s(h_s-b). \tag{1.7}$$

which is similar to that for the debenture-holder.

A zero-one variable will now be introduced. If interest on the risk-free asset is taxed then $a = 1$, if not $a = 0$. Thus the effective tax rate is aT_{PSF}, which is either T_{PSF} or zero. For a negative investment, for instance, if it represents borrowing, interest may not be tax deductible, in which case aT_{PSF} = zero. The shareholder's after-tax risk-free rate of interest is therefore:

$$k_{SF} = r_f\left(1 - aT_{PSF}\right). \tag{1.8}$$

where, r_f is the before-tax risk-free rate, or

$$k_{SF} = r_f\left\{1 - a\left[b + \frac{(h_s - b)}{(1 + k_{SF})^t}\right]\right\}. \tag{1.9}$$

where t is the tax lag. This can be solved iteratively. For example, if $r_f = 0.1$, $a = 1$, $b = 0.25$, $t = 0.75$ and $h_s = 0.40$, then:

$$k_{SF} = 0.1\left[1 - 0.25 - \frac{0.15}{(1 + k_{SF})^{0.75}}\right]. \tag{1.10}$$

Plugging $k_{SF} = 0.07$ into the right-hand side of the equation produces a value of 0.061. Using 0.061 instead produces 0.061 as a result, so k_{SF} is 6.1 per cent.

Let r_j^* = the mean rate of return before corporation tax. For a perpetuity, the mean rate of return after corporation tax is:

$$r_j^*\left(\frac{1 - T_{Ej}}{1 - c_j T_{Ej}}\right).$$

The cash flows are taxed at the effective discounted rate of T_{Ej}. As far as the outlay is concerned, capital allowances may be claimed but c_j, the discounted value of allowances for every £1 of outlay, may be less than 100 per cent, that is $0 \leq c_j \leq 1$. The after-corporation tax return is used to pay dividends, so the after-personal tax mean rate of return is:

$$r_j^*\left[\frac{(1 - T_{Ej})(1 - T_{PS})}{1 - c_j T_{Ej}}\right].$$

For simplicity, let

$$z_j = \left[\frac{\left(1-T_{Ej}\right)\left(1-T_{PS}\right)}{1-c_j T_{Ej}}\right]. \tag{1.11}$$

Capital allowances

Over the years there have been changes in the allowances available on plant and machinery. At the time of writing, there is a 40 per cent allowance in the first year, followed by a 25 per cent allowance each year based on a reducing balance method. The allowances form a geometric progression. Discounting at k to the first tax payment date on which the first tax saving arises, the present value is:

$$0.4 + \frac{0.25(1-0.4)}{1+k} + \frac{0.25(1-0.4)(0.75)}{(1+k)^2} + \frac{0.25(1-0.4)(0.75)^2}{(1+k)^3} + \ldots$$

Using the fact that, for a convergent geometric progression, the sum to infinity equals the first term divided by (1 - the common ratio), then for a ratio of $\frac{0.75}{1+k}$, the value is:

$$0.4 + \frac{0.15}{0.25+k}.$$

This assumes that there is a zero scrap value. For plant and machinery with an expected life of more than 5 years, the written down values are pooled and the proceeds of sale are normally deducted from the pool balance.

Assets can be declared as short-life assets and separated from the pool. In this instance, if the disposal takes place within 5 years, a balancing allowance or charge is created. For example, suppose the asset is sold for 20 per cent of its original cost in the fourth year. The written down value was 33.75 per cent of cost at the beginning of this year, so there is an extra 13.75 per cent to be written off. This is allowable in the fourth year. Alternatively, if the asset is sold for 50 per cent of cost in the fourth year, this is 16.25 per cent more than its written down value at the beginning of the year. Thus, 16.25 per cent of the cost is treated as a taxable item in the fourth year.

Industrial buildings are given a 20 per cent initial allowance plus a 4 per cent annual allowance, including one in the first year. By the end of the first year, 24 per cent is normally written off, leaving 76 per cent. Thus, there are 19 further allowances at 4 per cent to be claimed.

The present value of the allowances, discounted to the first tax payment date is:

$$0.24+\frac{0.04}{1+k}+\frac{0.04}{(1+k)^2}+\ldots+\frac{0.04}{(1+k)^{19}}.$$

For a convergent geometric progression, this conveniently reduces to:

$$0.24+\left\{\frac{0.04\left[1-\frac{1}{(1+k)^{19}}\right]}{k}\right\}.$$

There are special rules for buildings not acquired new. Commercial buildings, such as offices and shops, do not normally qualify for allowances. However, where there is expenditure on industrial on commercial buildings in enterprize zones, then 100 per cent allowances are given in the first year. The values discounted to the first tax payment dates are given in Table 1.1.

A nil disposal proceeds is assumed. Chargeable gains can also arise on the disposal of assets, but these are ignored.

Table 1.1
The present value of capital allowances, for every £1 of outlay, discounted to the first tax payment date

Category of investment	Discount rate	
	(8 %)	(10 %)
Plant and machinery, 1 year life	1.00	1.00
Plant and machinery, 2 year life	0.96	0.95
Plant and machinery, 3 year life	0.92	0.91
Plant and machinery, 4 year life	0.90	0.88
Plant and machinery, long life	0.85	0.83
Industrial building, not in enterprize zone	0.62	0.57
Commercial building, not in enterprize zone	0	0
Building in enterprize zone	1.00	1.00

Tax and risk

The after-tax portfolio mean rate of return P_{jm} for an investment of a fraction x in security j and $(1-x)$ in the market yields:

$$P_{jm} = xr_j^* z_j + (1-x) r_m^* z_m \tag{1.12}$$

where, z_m reflects the representative tax position for the market portfolio as a whole. The variance of the portfolio is:

$$V_{jm}^e = x^2 z^2 \operatorname{var}(r_j) + (1-x)^2 z_m^2 \operatorname{var}(r_m) + 2x(1-x) z_j z_m \operatorname{cov}(r_j, r_m) \tag{1.13}$$

Extending the work of Sharpe (1964), a UK tax adjusted capital asset pricing model can be derived.

The change in the portfolio rate of return per unit variance is:

$$\frac{dP_{jm}}{dV_{jm}^e} = \left(\frac{dP_{jm}}{dx}\right)\left(\frac{dx}{dV_{jm}^e}\right). \tag{1.14}$$

As x tends to zero,

$$\frac{dP_{jm}}{dV_{jm}^e} = \frac{z_j r_j^* - z_m r_m^*}{2 z_j z_m \operatorname{cov}(r_j, r_m) - 2 z_m^2 \operatorname{var}(r_m)}. \tag{1.15}$$

For a portfolio comprising a fraction x invested in a risk-free asset and $(1-x)$ in the market, we have:

$$P_{fm} = xr_f(1 - aT_{PSF}) + r_m^* z_m (1-x). \tag{1.16}$$

The variance of the portfolio is:

$$V_{fm}^e = (1-x)^2 z_m^2 \operatorname{var}(r_m). \tag{1.17}$$

As x tends to zero:

$$\frac{dP_{fm}}{dV_{fm}^e} = \frac{r_f(1 - aT_{PSF}) - r_m^* z_m}{-2 z_m^2 \operatorname{var}(r_m)}. \tag{1.18}$$

Assuming a competitive market:

$$\frac{dP_{jm}}{dV^{e}_{jm}} = \frac{dP_{fm}}{dV^{e}_{fm}}. \tag{1.19}$$

It follows that:

$$z_j r_j^* = r_f\left(1 - aT_{PSF}\right) + \frac{\left[z_m r_m^* - r_f\left(1 - aT_{PSF}\right)\right]\operatorname{cov}\left(z_j r_j, z_m r_m\right)}{\operatorname{var}\left(z_m r_m\right)}. \tag{1.20}$$

This represents the post-personal tax capital asset pricing model. The post-tax beta is given by the covariance $\left(z_j r_j, z_m r_m\right)$ divided by the variance of the market after tax. If each investor has the same tax position, and all firms have the same tax positions relative to size, then $\left(z_j = z_m = z\right)$. In this case, the post-tax beta is:

$$\frac{\operatorname{cov}\left(z_j r_j, z_m r_m\right)}{\operatorname{var}\left(z_m r_m\right)} = \frac{z^2 \operatorname{cov}\left(r_j, r_m\right)}{z^2 \operatorname{var}\left(r_m\right)}$$

which equals the pre-tax beta.

The post-tax beta of the market is found by letting $z_j = z_m$ and $r_j = r_m$, in which instance:

$$\frac{\operatorname{cov}\left(z_j r_j, z_m r_m\right)}{\operatorname{var}\left(z_m r_m\right)} = z_m\left[\frac{\operatorname{cov}\left(r_m, r_m\right)}{z_m \operatorname{var}\left(r_m\right)}\right] = 1.$$

The post-tax beta for the efficient market is the same as its pre-tax beta. If it is assumed that the tax reduction factor z_j is the same in each state of nature, then β_j^A, the after-tax beta coefficient of project j is:

$$\beta_j^A = \frac{\operatorname{cov}\left(z_j r_j, z_m r_m\right)}{\operatorname{var}\left(z_m r_m\right)} = \left(\frac{z_j z_m}{z_m^2}\right)\left[\frac{\operatorname{cov}\left(r_j, r_m\right)}{\operatorname{var}\left(r_m\right)}\right]$$

$$\beta_j^A = \beta_j^B\left(\frac{z_j}{z_m}\right). \tag{1.21}$$

where β_j^B is the pre-tax beta.

The after-tax capital asset pricing model is dependent upon the effective personal tax rate T_{PS}, since this affects the after-tax risk-free rate. However, personal tax does not generally affect the beta.

$$\beta_j^A = \beta_j^B \left[\frac{(1-T_{Ej})(1-T_{PS})(1-c_m T_{Em})}{(1-T_{Em})(1-T_{PS})(1-c_j T_{Ej})} \right]$$

$$\beta_j^A = \beta_j^B \left[\frac{(1-T_{Ej})}{(1-c_j T_{Ej})} \bigg/ \frac{(1-T_{Em})}{(1-c_m T_{Em})} \right] \qquad (1.22)$$

The capital allowance factor c_j is related to the pre-tax and post-tax betas:

$$c_j = \left(\frac{1}{T_{Ej}} \right) - \left[\frac{\beta_j^B (1-T_{Ej})(1-c_m T_{Em})}{\beta_j^A (1-T_{Em}) T_{Ej}} \right]. \qquad (1.23)$$

Whether borrowing or lending applies depends upon whether the after-tax beta is greater than or less than one. By substituting for $\beta_j^A = 1$ in equation (1.23) the critical value of c_j, noted as c_j^* ,can be derived.

Assuming the market capital allowance factor is 0.7 and the market tax rate is 33 per cent then:

$$c_j^* = \left(\frac{1}{T_{Ej}} \right) - \left[\frac{0.769 \beta_j^B (1-T_{Ej})}{0.67 T_{Ej}} \right] \qquad (1.24)$$

If the post-tax beta is less than one, to obtain the same risk, the investor engages in some lending. If more than one, the investor borrows. Otherwise the investor invests solely in the market. Lending or borrowing does not preclude some investment in the market. The proportion depends upon the overall risk planned. These are features of the capital asset pricing model. The importance for tax purposes is the different tax treatment between personal borrowing and lending.

In Table 1.2, the critical values of the capital allowance factor c_j^* are computed, to determine whether borrowing or lending applies. For example, if the corporate tax rate is 33 per cent, then a pre-tax beta of 0.9 is converted into a post-tax beta of more than 1.0 if the capital allowance factor exceeds 0.933. A factor of more than 0.933 for a project can occur if the expenditure relates to buildings in enterprize zones or plant and machinery of 1 year life for any discount rate or a life of 2 years, if the discount rate is, for example, 12 per cent or less. Thus, if this occurs, although the pre-tax beta is less than one, instead of the investor lending, the investor borrows because the post-tax beta would exceed one. Conversely, if the investment is in a commercial building not in an enterprize zone, pre-tax betas of 1.1, 1.2, or 1.3 can be converted into post-tax betas of less than one. Despite the fact that the pre-tax beta exceeds one, the investor would lend since the post-tax beta would be less than one.

Table 1.2
Critical values of the capital allowance factor to determine borrowing or lending (c_j^*)

Corporate tax rate	Pre-tax beta 0.8	0.9	1.0	1.1	1.2	1.3
0.25	1.245	0.901	0.557	0.212	-0.132	-0.476
0.33	0.166	0.933	0.700	0.467	0.234	0.001
0.35	1.152	0.939	0.726	0.512	0.299	0.086

Capital investment incentives

Let us assume the following parameters:

* the pre-tax risk-free rate is 8 per cent per annum,
* the mean pre-tax rate of return on the efficient market portfolio is 14 per cent per annum,
* the capital allowance factor for the market is 0.7, and
* the corporate tax rate for the market is 33 per cent.

If $c_j \geq c_j^*$, then:

$$r_j^* = \frac{r_f\left(1 - c_j T_{Ej}\right)}{\left(1 - T_{Ej}\right)\left(1 - T_{PS}\right)} + \beta_j^B\left[r_m^* - \frac{r_f\left(1 - c_m T_{Em}\right)}{\left(1 - T_{Em}\right)\left(1 - T_{PS}\right)}\right]. \qquad (1.25)$$

Thus, *Model A*, for $\beta_j^A \geq 1$, is:

$$r_j^* = \frac{0.08(1 - c_j T_{Ej})}{(1 - T_{Ej})(1 - T_{PS})} + \beta_j^B \left[0.14 - \frac{0.09182}{(1 - T_{PS})} \right]. \tag{1.26}$$

If $c_j < c_j^*$, then:

$$r_j^* = \left[\frac{r_f (1 - T_{PSF})(1 - c_j T_{Ej})}{(1 - T_{Ej})(1 - T_{PS})} \right] + \beta_j^B \left\{ r_m^* - \left[\frac{r_f (1 - T_{PSF})(1 - c_m T_{Em})}{(1 - T_{Em})(1 - T_{PS})} \right] \right\}. \tag{1.27}$$

So, *Model B*, for $\beta_j^A < 1$, is:

$$r_j^* = \frac{0.08(1 - T_{PSF})(1 - c_j T_{Ej})}{(1 - T_{Ej})(1 - T_{PS})} + \beta_j^B \left[0.14 - \frac{0.09182(1 - T_{PSF})}{(1 - T_{PS})} \right]. \tag{1.28}$$

Table 1.3
Capital allowance factors for different risk categories

Parameters						
Pre-tax beta	0.8	0.8	1.0	1.0	1.2	1.2
Corporate tax rate	0.33	0.25	0.33	0.25	0.33	0.25
Discount rate	8.6	9.6	9.4	10.5	10.2	11.4
Categories						
I Building in enterprize zone	1.0	1.0	1.0	1.0	1.0	1.0
II Plant and machinery, 4 year life	0.8970	0.8869	0.8889	0.8780	0.8809	0.8694
III Plant and machinery, long life.	0.8464	0.8335	0.8360	0.8225	0.8261	0.8121
IV Industrial building	0.6081	0.5837	0.5883	0.5638	0.5702	0.5458
V Commercial building	0	0	0	0	0	0

The discount rate for the capital allowance factor is the post-corporation tax rate. Tax allowances are of lower risk than the tax on the returns from a project. If the tax rate is given and sufficient taxable profits exist, the allowances are fairly risk-free.

However, there is a risk associated with the sufficiency of profits against which to offset the allowances. Also, the tax rate can change. An approximation to the appropriate discount rate is the after-corporation tax cost of debt, for a predetermined tax rate and a given project beta. Although not strictly correct, it seems a reasonable yardstick in the absence of fuller information.

For a low beta of 0.8, a tax-free market rate of 14 per cent and a tax-free risk-free rate of 8 per cent, the tax-free capital asset pricing model produces a rate of 12.8 per cent. The post-tax rate is thus 12.8(1 - 0.33) = 8.6 per cent or 12.8(1 - 0.25) = 9.6 per cent, for tax rates of 33 per cent and 25 per cent, respectively.

The capital allowance factors for different risk categories are given in Table 1.3. Simulations can now be made of the effects of personal and corporate tax on capital investment.

Example (i): *A low-risk building project in an enterprize zone*

Parameters: $T_{Ej} = 0.33$ (full corporate rate) $b = 0.25$ (basic rate)
$c_j = 1$ (100 % allowance) $T_{PS} = 0.20$ (implied)
$T_{PSF} = 0.40$ (higher tax rate) $\beta^B = 0.8$ (low risk)

Following *Model B*, $c_j < c_j^* = 1.166$, for $\beta^B = 0.8$ the pre-tax rate of return required to obtain an equilibrium post-tax rate is: $r_j^* = 11.69$ per cent. In a tax-free world, the required rate is: 0.08 + 0.8 (0.14 - 0.08) = 12.8 per cent. Hence, the tax system creates an incentive to invest in this project. If the expected rate is less than 11.69 per cent, however, there is a disincentive to invest.

Example (ii): *An average risk building project in an enterprize zone*

Parameters: $T_{Ej} = 0.33$ (full corporate rate) $b = 0.25$ (basic rate)
$c_j = 1$ (100 % allowance) $T_{PS} = 0.20$ (implied)
$T_{PSF} = 0.40$ (higher tax rate) $\beta_j^B = 1$ (average risk)

Since c_j exceeds the critical value of 0.7 for a pre-tax beta of 1.0 (see Table 1.2), then the post-tax beta exceeds 1. Risk is increased. Hence, *Model A* is used, *i.e.*, tax relief on personal interest on borrowing is disallowed. The equilibrium pre-tax rate is 12.5 per cent and the tax-free rate is 14.0 per cent (for a beta of 1). Hence, there is an incentive to invest.

Alternative tax scenarios are given in Table 1.4. From this, 60 simulations are provided in Table 1.5. Low, medium and high risk are defined as pre-tax betas of 0.8, 1.0 and 1.2 respectively.

Table 1.4
Alternative tax scenarios

Tax Scenarios:	*S1*	*S2*	*S3*	*S4*
Parameters:				
Corporate tax rate, T_{Ej}	0.33	0.33	0.25	0.25
Basic rate, b	0.25	0.25	0.25	0.25
Higher income tax rate, T_{PSF}	0.40	0.25	0.40	0.25
Implied rate, T_{PS}	0.20	0.00	0.20	0.00

Based on the parameters given, there are tax incentives to invest in buildings in enterprize zones, and plant and machinery. For the levels of tax-free beta, *i.e.*, in a world in which there is no taxation, the tax-free rates of return required for the level of risk are greater than the equilibrium rates of return in a post corporate and personal tax model.

As far as industrial buildings are concerned, there are disincentives to invest in average risk projects, where companies pay the full corporate tax rate. Companies with small profits investing in average risk industrial building projects, would find that the post-tax rate of return required for the post-tax level of risk is the same as the rate of return required in a tax-free world. This is a situation of tax neutrality for the company with small profits. High profit companies investing in low risk industrial building projects are also in a tax neutral position. However, for low profit companies investing in low risk industrial building projects, there are tax incentives: the post-tax required rate for the level of post-tax risk is less than the tax-free rate for the level of risk in a tax-free world. For both high and low profit companies investing in high risk industrial building projects, there are incentives to invest.

Finally, for investments in commercial buildings for which there are no allowances, there are disincentives to invest, regardless of the tax scenario chosen, and regardless of the level of risk.

Conclusion

Given the parameters chosen, tax incentives exist in buildings in enterprize zones and plant and machinery, whilst there are disincentives to invest in commercial buildings, not in enterprize zones. As for industrial buildings, there can be tax neutrality, incentives or disincentives, depending upon the level of risk, and the level of profits.

Table 1.5
Tax incentives to capital investment

Description	No.	Tax scenario	c_j	Risk	Model	Equilibrium rate	Tax-free rate	Result
Building in enterprize zone	1	S1	1	low	B	11.7	12.8	Incentive
	2	S2	1	low	B	11.7	12.8	Incentive
	3	S3	1	low	B	11.7	12.8	Incentive
	4	S4	1	low	B	11.7	12.8	Incentive
	5	S1	1	ave.	A	12.5	14.0	Incentive
	6	S2	1	ave.	A	12.8	14.0	Incentive
	7	S3	1	ave.	A	12.5	14.0	Incentive
	8	S4	1	ave.	A	12.8	14.0	Incentive
	9	S1	1	high	A	13.0	15.2	Incentive
	10	S2	1	high	A	13.8	15.2	Incentive
	11	S3	1	high	A	13.0	15.2	Incentive
	12	S4	1	high	A	13.8	15.2	Incentive
	13	S1	0.8970	low	B	12.0	12.8	Incentive
	14	S2	0.8970	low	B	12.0	12.8	Incentive
	15	S3	0.8869	low	B	11.9	12.8	Incentive
	16	S4	0.8869	low	B	11.9	12.8	Incentive
	17	S1	0.8889	ave.	A	13.1	14.0	Incentive
	18	S2	0.8889	ave.	A	13.1	14.0	Incentive
	19	S3	0.8780	ave.	A	12.9	14.0	Incentive
	20	S4	0.8780	ave.	A	13.1	14.0	Incentive
	21	S1	0.8809	high	A	13.6	15.2	Incentive
	22	S2	0.8809	high	A	14.3	15.2	Incentive
	23	S3	0.8694	high	A	13.5	15.2	Incentive
	24	S4	0.8694	high	A	14.1	15.2	Incentive
Long-life asset (plant and machinery)	25	S1	0.8464	low	B	12.1	12.8	Incentive
	26	S2	0.8464	low	B	12.1	12.8	Incentive
	27	S3	0.8335	low	B	12.0	12.8	Incentive
	28	S4	0.8335	low	B	12.0	12.8	Incentive
	29	S1	0.8360	ave.	A	13.3	14.0	Incentive
	30	S2	0.8360	ave.	A	13.5	14.0	Incentive
	31	S3	0.8225	ave.	A	13.1	14.0	Incentive
	32	S4	0.8225	ave.	A	13.3	14.0	Incentive
	33	S1	0.8261	high	A	13.9	15.2	Incentive
	34	S2	0.8261	high	A	14.5	15.2	Incentive
	35	S3	0.8121	high	A	13.7	15.2	Incentive
	36	S4	0.8121	high	A	14.3	15.2	Incentive

(Table 1.5 continued)

Description	No.	Tax scenario	c_j	Risk	Model	Equilibrium rate	Tax-free rate	Result
Industrial building	37	S1	0.6081	low	B	12.8	12.8	Neutral
	38	S2	0.6081	low	B	12.8	12.8	Neutral
	39	S3	0.5837	low	B	12.5	12.8	Incentive
	40	S4	0.5837	low	B	12.5	12.8	Incentive
	41	S1	0.5883	ave.	B	14.3	14.0	Disincentive
	42	S2	0.5883	ave.	B	14.3	14.0	Disincentive
	43	S3	0.5638	ave.	A	14.0	14.0	Neutral
	44	S4	0.5638	ave.	A	14.0	14.0	Neutral
	45	S1	0.5702	high	A	15.1	15.2	Incentive
	46	S2	0.5702	high	A	15.1	15.2	Incentive
	47	S3	0.5458	high	A	14.5	15.2	Incentive
	48	S4	0.5458	high	A	15.0	15.2	Incentive
Commercial building	49	S1	0	low	B	14.6	12.8	Disincentive
	50	S2	0	low	B	14.6	12.8	Disincentive
	51	S3	0	low	B	13.7	12.8	Disincentive
	52	S4	0	low	B	13.7	12.8	Disincentive
	53	S1	0	ave.	B	16.1	14.0	Disincentive
	54	S2	0	ave.	B	16.1	14.0	Disincentive
	55	S3	0	ave.	B	15.1	14.0	Disincentive
	56	S4	0	ave.	B	15.1	14.0	Disincentive
	57	S1	0	high	B	16.5	15.2	Disincentive
	58	S2	0	high	B	16.5	15.2	Disincentive
	59	S3	0	high	A	16.4	15.2	Disincentive
	60	S4	0	high	A	16.4	15.2	Disincentive

References

Ashton, D.J. (1989), 'The Cost of Capital and the Imputation Tax System', *Journal of Business Finance and Accounting*, Vol.16, No.1, Spring, pp.75-88.

Berry, R.H. and Dyson, R.G. (1979), 'A Mathematical Programming Approach to Taxation-Induced Interdependencies in Investment Appraisal', *Journal of Business Finance and Accounting*, Vol.6, No.4, Winter, pp.425-441.

Brown, E.C. (1948), 'Business Income Taxation and Investment Incentives', in *Income, Employment and Public Policy: Essays in Honor of Alvin Hansen*, New York, Norton.

Dempsey, M.J. (1991), 'Modigliani and Miller Again Revisited: The Cost of Capital Under the Assumption of Non-equal Borrowing and Lending Rates', *Accounting and Business Research*, Vol.21, No.83, Summer, pp.221-226.

Devereux, M.P. and Mayer, C.P. (1984), *Corporation Tax: The Impact of the 1984 Budget*, Institute for Fiscal Studies Report Series, No.11, June.

Hodgkinson, L. (1989), *Taxation and Corporate Investment*, London, Chartered Institute of Management Accountants.

King, M.A. (1977), *Public Policy and the Corporation*, London, Chapman and Hall.

MacDonald, G. (1980), 'Can a Corporation Tax Under an Expenditure Tax Regime be Non-Distortionary ?' *Accounting and Business Research*, Vol.11, No.41, Winter, pp.66-70.

Meade, J.E. (1978), *The Structure and Reform of Direct Taxation*, London, Institute for Fiscal Studies.

Mole, R. (1990), 'Post-Tax Capital Investment Appraisal: Plant and Machinery', *Accounting and Business Research*, Vol.20, No.78, Spring, pp.123-134.

Moon, P. and Hodges, S. (1989), 'Implications of the Recent Tax Changes for Corporate Capital Investment', *Journal of Business Finance and Accounting*, Vol.16, No.1, Spring, pp.25-39.

Morgan, E.J. (1987), *Corporate Taxation and Investment: The Implications of the 1984 Tax Reform*, Aldershot, Gower.

Pointon, J. (1980), 'Investment and Risk: The Effect of Capital Allowances', *Accounting and Business Research*, Vol.10, No.40, Autumn, pp.432-439.

Sharpe, W.F. (1964), 'Capital Asset Prices: A Theory of Market Equilibrium Under Conditions of Risk', *Journal of Finance*, Vol.19, No.3, September, pp.425-442.

2 UK taxation and finance leasing

John Pointon and Emma Welsh

Introduction

Finance leasing provides for the lessee the rewards of ownership during the expected useful life of an asset, without obtaining a legal title. Not only is it a popular method of finance, but the leasing business has grown, and the growth has survived seemingly adverse changes in accounting and fiscal policies.

The thrust of the empirical component of this chapter is an attempt to answer several key issues in lease evaluation. Are finance leases seriously being considered in this era of capitalized leases and decelerated capital allowances? Does the disclosure requirement affect the finance lease decision? What is the relationship between disclosure and borrowing capacities? Is the tax factor important in the finance lease decision and is it significantly different for unquoted companies? How do respondents deal with the effects of taxation on the discount rate? At what level of sophistication are practitioners conversant with some of the more esoteric aspects of the finance lease evaluation, namely the derivation of discount rates with tax lags and tax losses? Has the general level of sophistication , in lease evaluation techniques applied in practice, changed over the last ten years? To what extent are respondents educated or trained in finance lease evaluation?

Leasing theory in a perfect market

If we had a perfect capital market in its strong form (Fama, 1970), including perfect information flows, investors would in theory be aware of finance leases even before they were retrospectively disclosed on a balance sheet. Now, if lessees and lessors are in identical tax positions, with regards to marginal tax rates and tax payment dates in particular, then under perfect capital markets and symmetrical tax positions, we can consider the elegant analysis of Miller and Upton (1976). Then, by relaxing these two assumptions we can gain an insight into the implications of non-symmetrical taxation and changes in accounting disclosure requirements on the finance lease decision.

Miller and Upton's theory shows that if the lessee and lessor are in identical tax positions, the discounted cost to the lessee of the leasing rentals after tax relief should be equal to the present value to the lessor of the leasing rentals after tax. But, since competition between leasing firms should eliminate excess returns, the present value to the lessor of the leasing rentals after tax should be equal to the discounted purchase cost after tax and eventual disposal. Thus, the lease or buy decision should be financially equivalent in a perfect capital market with symmetrical tax positions.

Imperfections

Since the above analysis demonstrates that the lease or buy decision should be one of indifference, is the leasing decision of any significance?
The answer is that it is important in practice for two reasons:

1 The leasing market may not be highly competitive. The lessor company needs to ensure that it is not undercharging. The lessee company needs to ensure that the lessor is not overcharging. The lessor's rentals are too low for the lessor if:
(a) the present value of the leasing rentals received by the lessor after tax is less than:
(b) the purchase cost, plus
(c) the tax savings to the lessor from the capital allowances, plus
(d) the present value from the future disposal after tax.

2 The tax position for the lessor and potential lessee are not normally identical.
(a) The user may pay tax at the small company rate, or at the higher marginal rate applicable between the lower and higher profit thresholds.
(b) If the user has restricted set-off of advance corporation tax, then, since the patterns of tax deductible items, leasing rentals or capital allowances, differ for the lease or buy decision, then the net incremental effects on advance corporation tax set-off can be significant.
(c) If the user is a new unincorporated business, then leasing may be preferred since leasing rentals reduce taxable profits which may be

assessed in more than one tax year, through the opening year rules of assessment. In this situation, leasing should be preferable to buying.

(d) An interesting development in the UK taxation treatment of finance leasing is that in April 1991, the Inland Revenue issued a statement of tax practice, SP 3/91, to the effect that the tax treatment for lessees will follow Statement of Standard Accounting Practice No. 21. However, lessors will pay taxes on rentals regardless of the fact that the rentals comprise both a finance charge and a revenue component. So let us briefly examine the accounting statement.

Statement of Standard Accounting Practice 21 and the discount rates

'Accounting for leases and hire purchase contracts' was issued in August 1984.Broadly, where assets are leased for their useful life they are capitalized on the balance sheet. Depreciation is charged on the asset. A liability is created at the start of the lease. Rental payments are deducted from the liability account, whereas the finance component for each period is added to the liability account and charged to the profit and loss account. Hence, the effect on the profit and loss account for the lessee is that the profit is reduced by the depreciation charges and the finance charges.

Therefore, for tax purposes, lessees now claim tax deductions for depreciation and finance charges relating to assets under finance leases. There are no capital allowances for the lessee.

By contrast, the lessor does claim capital allowances on leased equipment but pays tax on the full rental. Before we provide an illustration, let us determine the appropriate discount rate.

Now, fixed leasing rentals represent a commitment very similar to debt and so the discount rate should be the cost of debt. Interest on debt is a charge against taxable profits, so the opportunity cost is the after-tax cost of debt. The after-tax cost of debt for a nine month period involves interest in nine months' time. If this occurs three months before the year-end, then with taxes payable nine months after the year-end, the tax lag is one year. By contrast, for interest payable at the end of an assessable year, the tax lag is only nine months. Thus, the annual percentage after-tax cost of debt varies according to the tax lag and the fraction of the accounting period under consideration. A method to assess this has been derived by Pointon (1993).

The annual percentage rate for the nine months after the year end is given by y such that;

$$y = \left[\frac{2RT}{a - c}\right]^{\frac{4}{3}} - 1$$

where,

R = the pre-tax borrowing rate
T = the tax rate
$a = 1 + R + Tr - T$
$r = (1+R)^{0.25}$
$c^2 = a^2 - 4RTr$

For example, if the pre-tax rate is 12 per cent per annum, and the tax rate is 33 per cent:

$r = 1.028737345$
$a = 1.129483324$
$c = 1.054884157$
$y = 8.3066\%.$

The annual percentage rate for the whole year is i such that:

$$i = R\left[1 - \frac{T}{(1+y)^{0.75}}\right] = 0.12\left[1 - \frac{0.33}{(1.083066)^{0.75}}\right] = 8.27\%.$$

Let us use percentage discount rates of 8.31 and 8.27, respectively. The reader may note that where there are tax losses, the discount rate can change from year to year. A method of evaluation is given by Franks and Hodges (1978).

Consider the following example of a finance lease. An asset costs £56,160 on 1 January 1993. The annual rentals are £20,800 for three years, beginning immediately. The asset life is simply three years. The lessor has a 31 March year-end, whereas the potential lessee's year-end is 31 December. The pre-tax borrowing rate is 12 per cent per annum for both the lessee and the lessor. The tax rate is 33 per cent for each and the tax lag is 9 months after the year-end.

The lessor claims capital allowances as shown in Table 2.1. The first allowance falls in the year-ended 31 March 1993 and so the tax saving on this occurs at the end of the first calendar year. In Table 2.2 the tax savings from capital allowances are discounted at the annual rate of 8.27 per cent for complete years. The first rental occurs on 1 January and so it is not discounted. For tax purposes the rental is apportioned to the period to which it relates. Hence, for the lessor, in the year-ended 31 March 1993, only a quarter of the rental, namely £5,200, is taxable initially. Tax is paid on 31 December and therefore is discounted for a complete year.

We can observe from Table 2.2 that the lessor's net present value is positive, which signifies that it is attractive to the lessor.

Table 2.1
Capital allowances for the lessor (£)

Cost	56,160
25% allowance-year 1	(14,040)
Net	42,120
25% allowance-year 2	(10,530)
Net	31,590
Balancing allowance	(31,590)
Disposal proceeds	0

Table 2.2
Net present value for the lessor (£)

Cost:	(56,160)
Tax savings from capital allowances:	
$14{,}040[0.33/(1.0827)]$	4,279
$10{,}530\left[0.33/(1.0827)^2\right]$	2,964
$31{,}590\left[0.33/(1.0827)^3\right]$	8,214
Rentals:	
20,800	20,800
$20{,}800/(1.0827)$	19,211
$20{,}800/(1.0827)^2$	17,744
Taxes on rentals:	
$5{,}200[0.33/(1.0827)]$	(1,585)
$20{,}800\left[0.33/(1.0827)^2\right]$	(5,855)
$20{,}800\left[0.33/(1.0827)^3\right]$	(5,408)
$15{,}600\left[0.33/(1.0827)^4\right]$	(3,746)
Net present value	458

Let us now turn our attention to the lessee. Given the rentals of £20,800 and an outright purchase price of £56,160, this implies a finance charge at the rate of 11.55 per cent per annum compounded annually, as demonstrated in Table 2.3. Remembering that the lessee's year-end is 31 December, the first finance charge of £4,086 reduces taxable profits for the year-ended 31 December 1993, resulting in a tax saving occurring on 30 September 1994. The annual discount rate for the nine months' lag after the year-end is 8.31 per cent, whereas the annual discount rate for the first year is 8.27 per cent.

Table 2.3
The lessee's liability account (£)

Opening balance	56,160	39,444	20,797
Less: rental	(20,800)	(20,800)	(20,800)
Subtotal	35,360	18,644	(3)
Add: interest @ 11.55%	4,084	2,153	-
Closing balance	39,444	20,797	-
Adjustment to interest for rounding error:	2	1	-
Adjusted finance charge	4,086	2,154	-

The lessee also claims depreciation deductions, following Statement of Standard Accounting Practice 21, which we assume to be on a straight-line basis at £18,720 per annum for 3 years. The discounted cost of leasing is given in Table 2.4 and that of buying in Table 2.5.

Table 2.4
Discounted cost of leasing (£)

Rentals:	
20,800	20,800
$20{,}800/(1.0827)$	19,211
$20{,}800/(1.0827)^2$	17,744
Tax savings on the finance charges:	
$4{,}086\left\{0.33\big/\left[(1.0827)(1.0831)^{0.75}\right]\right\}$	(1,173)
$2{,}154\left\{0.33\big/\left[(1.0827)^2(1.0831)^{0.75}\right]\right\}$	(571)
Tax savings on depreciation:	
$18{,}720\left\{0.33\big/\left[(1.0827)(1.0831)^{0.75}\right]\right\}$	(5,374)
$18{,}720\left\{0.33\big/\left[(1.0827)^2(1.0831)^{0.75}\right]\right\}$	(4,964)
$18{,}720\left\{0.33\big/\left[(1.0827)^3(1.0831)^{0.75}\right]\right\}$	(4,585)
Net discounted cost	41,088

Leasing is therefore cheaper than buying, even though the lessor makes a positive net present value from the exercise. Whether it is attractive to lease, however, must of course depend upon the discounted after-tax benefits of asset usage, regardless of whether the asset is bought or leased. If these benefits have a present value of at least £41,088, then leasing is worthwhile. One important point to observe is that the discounted purchase cost after capital allowances is cheaper for the lessor than for the lessee because of the differences in year-end dates. If the potential lessee were to buy instead of lease, the tax savings from capital allowances would be discounted for an extra 9 months, because the lessee's year-end occurs 9 months later than the date for the lessor.

Table 2.5
Discounted cost of buying (£)

Cost	56,160
Tax savings from capital allowances:	
$14{,}040\left\{0.33\Big/\left[(1.0827)(1.0831)^{0.75}\right]\right\}$	(4,031)
$10{,}530\left\{0.33\Big/\left[(1.0827)^{2}(1.0831)^{0.75}\right]\right\}$	(2,792)
$31{,}590\left\{0.33\Big/\left[(1.0827)^{3}(1.0831)^{0.75}\right]\right\}$	(7,736)
Net discounted cost	41,601

A neglected aspect of the lease or buy literature appears to be the opportunity costs that arise from the indexation of capital gains for the general effects of inflation. There are specific tax rules pertaining to the tax treatment of chattels, *i.e.* tangible movable property. Wasting chattels are those which have an estimated useful life of less than 50 years. Equipment and vehicles are good examples. Wasting business chattels are exempt from capital gains tax, or corporation tax on chargeable gains, if the gross disposal proceeds are less or equal to a prescribed amount, which is £6,000 for 1992/93 In this instance, there is no chargeable gain and no allowable loss. For wasting business chattels, which are not exempt, the allowable cost is given by the original cost, for assets acquired after 31 March 1982, less any capital allowances, after any balancing allowance or charge. The indexation allowance is based on the allowable cost.

For all business chattels, there are marginal rules such that if the disposal price exceeds the prescribed limit, the chargeable gain cannot exceed 5/3 times the difference between the proceeds and the prescribed limit. For 1992/93, this will not operate when the consideration exceeds £15,000. In brief, if the sale proceeds are expected to be less than the prescribed limit for wasting business chattels for capital gains tax purposes, then there is no chargeable gain or loss. However, if this is not the case then there should be an allowable loss equal to the indexation allowance. Since the allowable cost should equal the sale proceeds,then the expected loss should normally equal:

1 the sale proceeds times the indexation factor, or

2 nil, if the sale proceeds are less than the prescribed limit.

UNIVERSITY
OF BRISTOL
LIBRARY

As far as chargeable gains and allowable losses are concerned, the lease or buy decision should take account of the anticipated inflation rate until disposal, and whether the disposal proceeds are likely to exceed the prescribed limit for wasting business chattels.

At the end of the primary period of the finance lease, the asset may be sold and the balance shared between the lessor and the lessee, depending on the contract. For the lessor there may be a balancing allowance or charge if it is a short-life asset. For a high value asset, there may be a tax loss under the capital gains legislation.

Empirical studies of leasing

A number of studies have been undertaken to evaluate the effects of leasing disclosures. In a US study, Cheung (1982), evaluated the effect of a firm's lease disclosure on its systematic risk, *i.e.*, its sensitivity of the share price to changes in returns on an efficiently diversified portfolio. In this instance, the disclosures were by way of footnotes providing details of finance leases which were not capitalized. He found some evidence of an imperfection in information flows. Elam (1975), who used a multiple discriminate model, found that including capitalized leases in financial ratios did not improve the predictive ability of bankruptcy. There were, however, some technical objections to this, in that Altman (1976) argued that a quadratic model would have been preferable to a linear model.

Ro (1978) found from empirical tests in the US that the Security and Exchange Commission's decision to require the disclosure of non-capitalized finance leases had an impact on share prices. Then, US research by Finnerty *et al* (1980) showed that the SEC's requirement and the Financial Accounting Standards Board's statement on leasing had little effect on the systematic risk of companies before and after June 1973. However, Bowman (1980) found that the debt to equity ratio and leases to equity ratio were highly correlated and so when the multicollinearity problem was controlled, leases made a significant contribution to the tests on market risk.

Wilkins and Zimmer published two studies of Singaporean officials. In one, (Wilkins and Zimmer, 1983a), sixty financial analysts were presented with financial statements of two hypothetical companies which differed materially only in respect of gearing levels. The hypothesis that their earnings predictions and share valuations are the same regardless of the method of accounting for finance leases was rejected. However, in their other study (Wilkins and Zimmer, 1983b), of bank loan officers, credit evaluations and decisions were not affected by the method of accounting for finance leases or by whether a term loan or finance lease was used. In the work of Bazley *et al* (1985), voluntary disclosure by Australian lessees was shown to be related to industry, firm size and a lessee's foreign parent company.

Abdel-Khalik (1981) found that full disclosure of finance leases in the US resulted in attempts to avoid capitalization through the use of operating leases instead. UK commentators have highlighted similar dangers [Fawthrop (1986), Blake (1989), Lennard (1985) and Stevens (1986)]. However, Macmillan (1988), a director of a software house that released (no pun intended) leasing software, has emphasized the economic justifications for leasing at the decision stage, rather than the SSAP 21 requirements. But what have the previous UK empirical studies shown?

In a field test of 23 UK companies, Ashton (1985) found that voluntary lease capitalization did not have a significant effect on the main indicators of financial performance. Taylor and Turley (1985) reported managers' attitudes, before the leasing disclosure became operative, and demonstrated that 41 per cent believed that leasing would be less attractive and 34 per cent believed that the volume of leasing would be affected. There was evidence to suggest some shift towards operating leases to avoid capitalization. However, Drury and Braund (1989) reveal that SSAP 21 was perceived to have little effect on leasing activity.

Capital market imperfections were considered by Hull and Hubbard (1980). They stated that an imperfection would be evidenced if lessees paid a rate of interest on displaced debt which is higher than that paid by lessors. In fact, just over half of their respondents stated that, for them, one reason for leasing was that it did not affect other borrowing sources. In an earlier study by Fawthrop and Terry (1975) leasing was often regarded as an integral part of an informally planned financing mix.

The identification of significant discrepancies between theory and practice in the treatment of taxation in capital investment decisions has been investigated in depth by Hodgkinson (1987). Before the 1984 UK tax reform, Morgan (1987) found that tax exhausted firms were more likely to lease than tax paying firms. Mayes and Nicholas (1988) emphasised the importance of taxation in the leasing decisions of small firms. Curiously, Hull and Hubbard (1980) did not find that taxation was a significant reason for leasing even though their study was conducted before the phased reduction in capital allowances. however, in Drury and Braund's study (1989), taxation was considered to be an important factor in the leasing decision.

With regards to the techniques of lease evaluation, Hull and Hubbard (1980) found that only half of their respondents used DCF techniques and even if they did, half of those used the wrong discount rate. Drury and Braund (1989) reported less than half using the wrong discount rate in the evaluation procedure.

In an econometric study by Mayes and Nicholas (1988), they report that leasing appears to have contributed to economic growth. However, they state that this is contradicted by their questionnaire survey of firms, which indicates that lessees frequently undertake financing and investment decisions separately and so any tax-induced relatively cheap form of finance through leasing would not normally lead to a faster rate of investment. Furthermore, their survey indicates that firms in the South West Economic Planning Region did not generally expect to increase the amount of leasing following the 1984 Budget. This result was consistent with the National Institute of Economic and Social Research survey of panel firms.

With the financial support of the Nuffield Foundation, the Business Taxation Research Unit despatched, during the summer of 1989, 400 questionnaires split equally between quoted companies and unquoted companies. The sample of quoted companies was selected at random from the Times 1,000 (1988-89). The vast majority of covering letters were addressed to the finance director. The unquoted companies were selected from 10,000 in Macmillan's Unquoted Companies 1989. Second reminders were sent two or three weeks later and a limited telephone follow-up was conducted approximately one month after the second reminders were sent. Overall, there were 104 replies (26 per cent) of which 83 were usable. Included in the replies were three who gave their responses to the questionnaire over the telephone.

A few directors, or their colleagues, were asked by telephone why they had not yet responded to the survey. Of the five replies that gave reasons for a non-response, they indicated that the reasons were:

1 the pressure of work,
2 a lack of time,
3 that the questions seemed long and that the finance lease decision was a group decision,
4 there was no intention to participate,
5 that the firm was not engaged in finance leases.

These responses were not too dissimilar to those who explained by letter their reasons for not completing the questionnaire.

Finance leasing had been considered in the past by 84 per cent of respondents. This compares with 56 per cent who were presently considering finance leasing and 86 per cent who stated that they intend to consider finance leasing in the future. Although the proportion of unquoted companies not currently considering finance leases was greater than the proportion for the unquoted companies, the difference was not statistically significant at the 5 per cent level of significance. The chi-squared statistic was 2.04 compared with a critical level of 3.84.

One company responded that "the administrative burden of finance leasing, both in accounting, and in dealing with secondary rentals, and keeping track of which machines are still in use, is significant although unquantifiable." Although this view is consistent with the Taylor and

Turley study (1985) of the likely effect of the disclosure requirement before the standard became operative, it appears to be untypical of the response, now that the standard is in force. For example, in Table 2.6 we set out the replies of the 76 respondents who answered a question on the importance of the disclosure requirement factor in the finance lease decision. Only 22 per cent (17 out of 76) thought that the disclosure requirement factor was important, or very important, in the finance lease decision. This result compares with 53 per cent (40 out of 76) who thought that it was unimportant or very unimportant.

Table 2.6
The importance of the lease disclosure requirement factor in the finance lease decision (76 responses)

Very important	2
Important	15
Neither	19
Unimportant	29
Very unimportant	11

Table 2.7
The gearing ratio of the company, defined as the ratio of long-term debt to the total of long-term debt and shareholders' equity (83 responses)

0 - 24%	49
25 - 49%	17
50 - 74%	14
75 - 99%	3

It was stated earlier that in theory finance leasing displaces debt. Thus, we were interested in the gearing ratio of the firm, and the sensitivity of the borrowing capacity of the firm . In Table 2.7 we set out the gearing ratios of the respondents. We then discovered that the sensitivity of the borrowing capacities were statistically related to the level of gearing. In Table 2.8 we show the number of respondents who stated whether finance lease contracts currently affected the firm's borrowing capacity, and analyse this in relation to the level of gearing of the respondents. The figures in brackets indicate the expected number, to the nearest decimal point, if the null hypothesis were true, *i.e.*, if there were no relationship between gearing and the sensitivity of borrowing capacity to finance lease contracts. The null hypothesis was rejected at the 5 per cent level of significance, since the chi-squared statistic was found to be 8.54, approximately, compared with a critical level of 3.84. This demonstrates that, for those who responded, there is a statistically significant relationship at the 5 per cent level of significance between the level of a firm's gearing and whether finance lease contracts affect a firm's borrowing capacity. The researchers then made a distinction between the current borrowing capacity and the borrowing capacity of the firm before finance lease contracts were disclosed on the balance sheet. We found no statistically significant difference at the 5 per cent level of significance between the level of gearing and whether finance lease contracts affected a firm's borrowing capacity before finance lease contracts were disclosed on the balance sheet, as shown in Table 2.9.

On this basis, the disclosure requirement factor may have had a perceived detrimental effect on the borrowing capacity of the firm, unless firms experienced substantial changes in gearing levels since the disclosure under SSAP 21. Hence, although many firms did not believe that SSAP 21 was important to the finance lease decision, there is some evidence to suggest that it may have had a detrimental effect on the firm's borrowing capacity. This is consistent with an imperfect capital market in that borrowing capacities were not affected by former undisclosed leases, at the 5 per cent level of statistical significance.

We now turn our attention to the taxation implications of the finance lease decision. 80 per cent of respondents (out of 75) assessed a finance lease decision on an after-tax basis compared with 15 per cent on a before-tax basis (including two who used both!). The remainder mentioned other criteria such as group policy and company strategy. One firm stated that "when capital expenditure is being considered the option to lease is always considered to see how it fits into the general company strategy. As such, 'after-tax' most closely applies but it is only one of several factors". Taxation was normally considered to be an important factor in the lease or buy decision by 64 per cent of respondents (out of 74). A test was performed to examine whether there was a difference in responses by quoted and unquoted companies. As shown in Table 2.10, a statistically significant difference was found at the 5 per cent level of significance. However, although taxation was more important for quoted companies than unquoted companies, the sample size of unquoted companies was only small.

One reason for the lack of importance of the taxation factor in the finance lease decision might have been that most of the unquoted companies were not expecting to pay mainstream corporation tax over the next few years. However, this was not shown to be true. Details of whether respondent firms were expecting to pay mainstream corporation tax over the next few years are given in Table 2.11, which reveals that most of the quoted and unquoted firms expected to be in tax-paying position. One company stated that "finance leasing was only undertaken by our US subsidiary which has tax losses. It is used as a method of accelerating tax relief. Our profitable UK operation does not use finance leasing."

Table 2.8
A significant relationship between gearing and whether a firm considers that finance lease contracts affect its borrowing capacity

	Low geared (< 25 %)		High geared (> 25 %)	
Disclosure affects borrowing capacity	8	(10.8)	11	(8.2)
Disclosure does not affect borrowing capacity	34	(31.2)	21	(23.8)

Statistical significance at 5% level: chi-squared = 8.54 approx.
(critical level = 3.84)

Table 2.9
No significant relationship between gearing and whether a firm considers that finance lease contracts affected its borrowing capacity, before finance lease contracts were disclosed on the balance sheet (expected responses in brackets)

	Low geared (< 25 %)		High geared (> 25 %)	
Disclosure affects borrowing capacity	4	(6.3)	8	(5.7)
Disclosure does not affect borrowing capacity	32	(29.7)	25	(27.3)

No statistical significance at 5% level: chi-squared = 2.14 approx.
(critical level = 3.84)

Table 2.10
The importance of taxation in finance leasing for quoted and unquoted companies

	Important		Not important	
Quoted	37	(31.1)	12	(17.9)
Unquoted	10	(15.9)	15	(9.1)

Statistical significance at 5%: chi-squared = 6.8, approx.
(critical level = 3.84)

The importance of discounted cash flow analysis has already been highlighted in our brief review of the theory of lease evaluation. In our survey we discovered that 79 per cent of companies (58 out of 73) used discounted cash flow analysis in the finance lease decision. A number of respondents who did not use DCF gave further details of their procedures.

Their replies included the following statements made on their returned questionnaires.

1 "A pre-tax break-even rate on the after-tax cash flows."
2 "Payback" (mentioned by two respondents).
3 "I view discounted cash flows as a dangerous tool particularly when applied to a cash flows which include an element of interest payable or receivable. Since we are considering whether at the end of the day we are better or worse off from leasing, it is simplest to work out the probable cash flows and see whether we are better or worse off at the end of the lease period, taking tax into account. There are several other factors we would like to take into account; available facilities, terms of the lease, etc., but in view of the fact that the time value of money is not relevant as interest is being paid in both alternatives, we do not use DCF."
4 "Leasing forms only a small proportion of our funding requirement. We pay most attention to the overall (gross) interest cost and our view of what interest rates will be over the (5 year) period of the lease. Do not also forget additional administration costs and the dangers of early terminations."
5 "Group policy."
6 "Equivalent interest rate method."
7 "A commercial decision based upon cash flow effect and deferred payment terms."
8 "Cash availability."
9 "Cheapest actual rate."
10 "Cash flow requirement regarding budgeted shop refurbishment and/or acquisition ."
11 "Cash flow."

For those that used DCF in lease evaluation, they were asked to state whether the rate to discount the leasing rentals was the before-tax cost of debt, the after-tax cost of debt, the weighted average cost of capital or some other rate. The results which are shown in Table 2.12 indicate that although the after-tax cost of debt was popular, eleven chose the weighted average cost of capital and one chose the return on capital employed, both of which are incorrect. Additionally, fifteen firms used the before-tax cost of debt and yet their responses to an earlier question indicated that they were in a taxpaying position.

We attempted to discover the extent to which the derivation of the theoretically correct after-tax discount rate could be determined by respondents based upon a one year tax lag (as an approximation). Few respondents could determine the correct rate.

Table 2.11
The tax paying capacity of quoted and unquoted firms

	1989	1990	1991	1992
Expecting to pay mainstream corporation tax				
Quoted	45	45	47	47
Unquoted	23	24	25	26
Not expecting to pay MCT				
Quoted	5	5	3	3
Unquoted	3	2	1	0

It is not surprising, however, that the practice of lease evaluation lags behind the theory. In fact, the academic literature on leasing has taken a number of wrong turns during its development, of which an incisive review is published by Burrows (1988). Nevertheless, substantial improvements have been made in the techniques used in practice. For example, in the 1979 study by Hull and Hubbard (1980), 29 per cent of respondents were still using payback and 10 per cent used an accounting rate of return. In our survey, ten years later, only 3 per cent used payback and 1 per cent used return on capital employed. In this context any lack of precision in adjusting the discount rate for tax lags, identifies a relatively small improvement needed.

Data was also collected to determine to what extent respondents had received any formal education or training in lease evaluation techniques. Of the 73 respondents that held professional qualifications, only 38 stated that their training had included lease evaluation techniques. Furthermore, of the 16 graduates that held a relevant degree, *i.e.*, with a business or accountancy element, only 8 had studied the techniques of lease evaluation, although of the 4 respondents with a relevant postgraduate degree, 3 had studied leasing. Additionally, leasing had been studied on a number of short-courses by 4 respondents on in-house training courses and 10 reported their attendance on external courses. There appears to be a clear need for training in lease evaluation. A test was set up to determine whether respondents with professional qualifications completed during the 1980's were more accurate (to the nearest one percentage point) in the derivation of the after-tax cost of debt, than those who had completed their professional qualifications before the 1980's. Another chi-squared test was performed according to whether respondents indicated that their professional training had included lease evaluation techniques. We performed another test to compare relevant first and higher degree holders with non-relevant postgraduate and non-relevant first degree holders. A test was also set up to compare graduates (including postgraduates) with non-graduates.

Table 2.12
The choice of rate to discount the leasing rental payments
(59 responses)

Before-tax cost of debt	18
After-tax cost of debt	22
After-tax net cost of capital (26% gross, 17% net)	1
After-tax interbank discount rate	1
Weighted average cost of capital	11
Both the before-tax cost and the after-tax cost	2
Cost of borrowing*	1
Cheapest actual borrowing rate*	1
Opportunity cost*	1
Return on capital employed*	1

*. The researchers were not sure whether these rates were intended to be before or after tax.

We also compared relevant graduates with non-graduates. Finally, we discriminated between the responses to the after-tax cost of debt calculation made by directors with others. The only factor which we found to be statistically significant at the 5 per cent level of significance was whether the respondent held a relevant degree. In such cases the discount rate was closer to the correct rate, although few understood the full ramifications.

Although the choice of the discount rate we believe is important in the finance lease evaluation, we do not necessarily infer that finance executives who do not hold relevant degrees are making incorrect lease or buy decisions. Indeed, many executives now use computer software. It does indicate, however, that lease evaluation is an area of study not properly understood by most finance executives, regardless of qualifications, seniority and prior training.

Conclusions

We began by an examination of the theory of leasing and then considered some of the tax imperfections that may arise. Lessors pay taxes on rentals and claim capital allowances, whereas lessees claim tax deductions for depreciation and the finance charge components of the rentals. The after-tax cost of debt, which is used as the opportunity cost of capital can vary as an annual percentage rate depending upon the period under consideration. We also examined the indexation effects on valuable capital losses for "big ticket" leasing.

Previous empirical studies on leasing were then reviewed before reporting on our own empirical work undertaken in 1989. The following main conclusions were reached :

1 Finance leasing is actively being considered by many respondents.
2 The disclosure requirement under SSAP 21 is not normally important in the finance lease decision.
3 There is a relationship between the level of gearing and whether finance lease contracts affect a firm's borrowing capacity. Before SSAP 21 this relationship was not significant. This suggests that there was an imperfect capital market.
4 Most respondents take tax into account in the finance lease decision and it is normally considered to be an important factor, although less important for unquoted companies. Most companies expect to be in a tax paying position during the next four years.
5 Most respondents use discounted cash flow analysis in finance lease evaluation.
6 Although the after-tax cost of debt was popular as a discount rate, and indeed theoretically correct for a tax paying company, many respondents are incorrectly choosing the wrong rate.
7 The full effects of taxation are not properly understood. In particular, few respondents understand how to discount the tax savings from interest deductibility in an after-tax cost of debt calculation.
8 However, lease evaluation procedures are substantially superior to those revealed by studies undertaken ten years previously.

References

Abdel-Khalik, A.R. (1981), The Economic Effects on Lessees of FASB Statement No.13, *Accounting for Leases*, Financial Accounting Standards Board.

Altman, E.I. (1976), Capitalization of Leases and the Predictability of Financial Ratios: A Comment? *Accounting Review*, April, pp.408-411.

Ashton, R.K. (1985), 'Accounting for Finance Leases: A Field Test', *Accounting and Business Research*, Summer, pp.233-238.

Bazley, M., Brown, P. and Izan, H.Y. (1985), 'An Analysis of Lease Disclosures by Australian Companies', *Abacus*, Vol.21, No.1, pp.44-62.

Bierman, H. Jnr. and Smidt, S. (1966), *The Capital Budgeting Decision*, 2nd. ed. Macmillan.

Blake, J. (1989), 'SSAP 21 - Accounting for Leases and Hire Purchase Contracts', *Accountants Record*, June, pp.9-14.

Bowman, R.G. (1980), 'The Debt Equivalence of Leases: An Empirical Investigation', *Accounting Review*, Vol.60, No.2, April, pp.227-233.

Burrows, G.H. (1988), 'The Evolution of a Lease Solution', *Abacus*, Vol.24, No.2, pp.107-119.

Cheung, J.K. (1982), 'The Association Between Lease Disclosure and the Lessee's Systematic Risk', *Journal of Business Finance and Accounting*, Vol.9, No.3, pp.297-305

Clark, T.M. (1978), *Leasing*, McGraw-Hill, London.

Drury, C. (1989), 'Evaluating the Lease or Purchase Decision', *Managerial Finance*, Vol.15, No.1/2, pp.26-35.

Drury, C. and Braund, S. (1989), 'A Survey of UK Leasing Practice', *Management Accounting*, April, pp.26-35.

Elam, R. (1975),'The Effect of Lease Data on the Predictive Ability of Financial Ratios', *Accounting Review*, January, pp.25-43.

Fama, E.F. (1970), 'Efficient Capital Markets: A Review of Theory and Empirical Work', *Journal of Finance*, Vol.25, No.2, May, pp.343-417

Fawthrop, R. (1986), Equipment Leasing', in *Issues in Finance*, edited by Firth, M. and Keane, S.M. Phillip Allan, Oxford.

Fawthrop, R.A. and Terry, B. (1975), 'Debt Management and the Use of Leasing Finance in UK Corporate Financing Strategies', *Journal of Business Finance and Accounting*, Vol.2, No.3, Autumn, pp.295-314.

Finnerty, J.E., Fitzsimmons, R.N. and Oliver, T.W. (1980), 'Lease Capitalization and Systematic Risk', *Accounting Review*, Vol.55, No.4, October, pp.631-639.

Franks, J.R. and Hodges, S.D. (1978), 'Valuation of Financial Lease Contracts: A Note', *Journal of Finance*, Vol.33, No.2, May, pp.657-669.

Hodgkinson, L. (1987), *The Impact of Taxation on the Capital Budgeting Decision of Corporate Groups*, PhD Thesis, CNAA.

Hull, J.C. and Hubbard, G.L. (1980), Lease Evaluation in the UK: Current Theory and Practice', *Journal of Business Finance and Accounting*, Vol.7, No.4, Winter, pp.619-637.

Lennard, A. (1985), 'Classifying leases: more guidance needed', *Accountancy*, November, pp.486-488.

Macmillan, G. (1988), 'Leasing: Sales patter pitfalls', *Certified Accountant*, July, pp.40-41.

Mayes, D.G. and Nicholas, C.S. (1988), *The Economic Impact of Leasing*, Macmillan, Basingstoke.

Miller, M.H. and Upton, C.W. (1976), 'Leasing, Buying and the Cost of Capital Services', *Journal of Finance*, Vol.31, No.3, June, pp.761-786.

Myers, S.C., Dill, D.A. and Bautista, A.J. (1976), 'Valuation of Financial Lease Contracts', *Journal of Finance*, Vol.31, No.3, June, pp.799-819.

Morgan, E.J. (1987), 'Investment Behaviour and the 1984 Tax Reform: A Managerial Perspective', *Business Economist*, Vol.19, No.1, Winter pp.31-39.

Pointon, J. (1993), 'A Note on Taxation and the Leasing Discount Rates', *Journal of Business Finance and Accounting*, Vol.20, No.4, June, pp.599-603.

Ro, B.T. (1978), 'The Disclosure of Capitalized Lease Information and Stock Prices', *Journal of Accounting Research*, Vol.16, No.2, Autumn, pp.315-340.
Stevens, R. (1986), 'Accounting for Leases: Too Many of the Wrong Sums?', *Certified Accountant*, December, pp.14-15.
Taylor, P. and Turley, S. (1985), 'TheViews of Management on Accounting for Leases', *Accounting and Business Research*, Winter, pp.59-67.
Wilkins, T. and Zimmer, I. (1983a), 'The Effects of Alternative Methods of Accounting for Leases - An Experimental Study', *Abacus*, Vol.19, No.1, pp.64-75.
Wilkins, T. and Zimmer, I. (1983b), 'The Effects of Leasing and Different Methods of Accounting for Leases on Credit Evaluations', *Accounting Review*, Vol. 58, No. 4, October, pp. 749-764.

3 Taxation and capital investment appraisal: A mathematical programming approach

Suzanne Farrar

Introduction

It is a fundamental principle of project appraisal that all relevant cash flows must be taken into account, including taxation. The relevant tax environment is that of the firm as a whole since its overall tax position determines its marginal tax rate, the advance corporation tax setoff provisions, and the sufficiency of profits against which to set off capital allowances granted in respect of new investments. Project appraisal should therefore be carried out in this context. But the tax effects of a particular incremental project may have an impact on the tax effects of existing activities or other potential investment projects being considered at the same time, creating interdependencies where none may have existed on a pre-tax basis. The result of this interdependency may be that a project which appeared attractive when evaluated in isolation has a negative incremental net present value when superimposed on the firm's existing activities, or when it is undertaken at the same time as another project. The distortion may also, of course, work in the other direction.

Recognition of this problem has led many authors to agree that it is necessary to consider all combinations of incremental projects and the firm's existing activities jointly in the decision process (for instance, Grundy and Burns (1979), Berry and Dyson (1979). Optimization models for project selection on a post-tax basis have been developed by Berry and Dyson (1979), Ashford, Berry and Dyson (1986) and Pointon (1981, 1991).

To demonstrate the impact of taxation on project appraisal, the most relevant features of the UK corporate tax system will be described and illustrated by numerical examples. In the second part of the chapter a mathematical programming model will be developed which incorporates the tax rules relating to the setoff of advance corporation tax and losses, and includes constraints relevant to lease evaluation.

Features of the UK corporate tax system

Capital allowances

A firm's profits assessable for corporation tax will depend partly on the amount of capital allowances it can claim. In calculating taxable profit, accounting depreciation is added back to the accounting profit and capital allowances deducted. The pattern of capital allowances for plant and machinery is based on the concept of 'pools' of expenditure on which a writing down allowance (WDA) of 25 per cent on the reducing balance method is granted. A WDA is calculated on the basis of the opening pool balance plus expenditure on new assets during the year, less the disposal value of assets sold during the year. An adjustment or 'balancing charge' will be made if the disposal value is more than the qualifying expenditure. At the time of writing, a temporary 40 per cent WDA was available in the first year for plant and machinery.

Most items of plant and machinery may, if the firm chooses, be 'depooled' and treated in a separate pool as a short life asset irrespective of its actual life. If the asset is sold within five years an adjustment is made so that the balancing allowance or balancing charge on the asset for that year is the asset's residual pool balance, that is after deducting the sale proceeds. The effect of this provision is to align the tax relief on capital expenditure more closely with an asset's life. Because of the time value of money there will generally be an advantage in depooling, unless the disposal value is expected to be significant.

Losses

Where there are insufficient profits to absorb the available capital allowances, a trading loss will result. Unrelieved debenture interest carried forward may also result in a loss. Trading losses may be offset against total profits, including capital gains, of the same year. Since the Finance Act 1991 losses can be carried back against total profits of the previous three years, with priority being given to more recent years in priority to earlier ones, or carried forward and set against future years' liabilities as soon as possible. In a group structure trading losses may be set off against the total profits of companies in the same 75 per cent group. Generally it is of more value to carry back the loss and claim a rebate, obtaining a cash inflow at the present time which may be used for further investments or to improve liquidity. Where the tax rate is expected to be significantly higher in future years, the option of carrying the loss forward may be preferable.

Marginal tax rates

The structure of the UK corporation tax rates is illustrated in Figure 3.1. A reduced rate of corporation tax, T_s, applies to companies whose taxable profits fall below the lower marginal limit M_l. Above the upper marginal limit M_u the full rate of corporation tax, T_f, applies. Between the marginal limits profits are taxed at a higher marginal rate T_m where

$$T_m = (T_f M_u - T_s M_l) / (M_u - M_l)$$

Figure 3.1. The corporate tax function

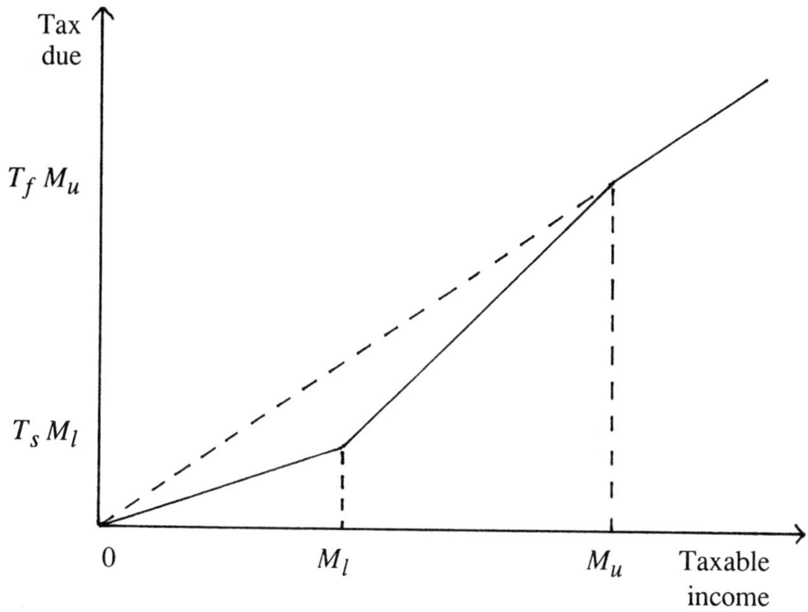

Currently:

M_l = £250,000
M_u = £1,250,000
T_s = 25%
T_f = 33%
T_m = 35%.

Where a firm has taxable profits above M_u, heavy capital allowances from additional projects under consideration may reduce the taxable profit to a level where the higher marginal rate applies, particularly if the income from the additional projects is low in the early stages when capital allowances are at their highest. The offset of losses from other years may have the same effect. Conversely, the impact of the incremental projects may be in the other direction so that the firm moves out of the higher marginal rate. Similar effects will occur around the M_l threshold. As a result, if projects are assessed sequentially, suboptimal decisions may be made (Grundy and Burns, 1979). An individual project may have a positive NPV at a 25 per cent tax rate, but not at 33 per cent or 35 per cent, while a project which appears unattractive in isolation may become attractive if the tax effects of other projects reduce the relevant tax rate. Another potential difficulty is that the firm's overall tax rate may change over a project's life.

The impact of the system of tax rates on project appraisal may be illustrated by means of an example (Table 3.1). A firm is considering a project which involves an initial outlay of £1m on plant and machinery and is expected to generate future cash inflows of £65,000, £700,000 and £500,000 arising midway through years one, two and three respectively. The scrap value of the machinery at the end of the three years is nil. Capital allowances are available at 25 per cent on the reducing balance basis, with a balancing adjustment in year three. The amounts of the allowances in the three years will therefore be £250,000, £187,500 and £562,500. Mainstream corporation tax is payable nine months after the year end. The firm's cost of capital is 10 per cent.

Columns (i) and (iii) represent the firm's tax situation with and without the additional project. The project will increase taxable profit in each year by the value of the additional cash inflow less the additional capital allowance. Columns (ii) and (iv) show the present value of the relevant tax effects. The final column gives the changes in the present values of the cash flows which result from undertaking the project. The sum of these gives the post tax incremental net present value of the project, which is negative.

But if the firm has £1m of losses brought forward and set off against profits in year one, so that the taxable profit for that year is now £700,000 (Table 3.2), the project's post tax NPV becomes positive. The reason for the difference is simply that the taxable profit for year one now falls into the marginal tax band so that relief for the additional capital allowance is at a 35 per cent rate of tax, rather than 33 per cent as before. The extra relief of £3,132 switches a negative NPV of £1,315 to a positive value of £1,816, allowing for a rounding error of £1.

Table 3.1
Incremental project value after tax (£)

	Before incremental project	Present value	After incremental project	Present value	Incremental value
	(i)	(ii)	(iii)	(iv)	(iv) - (ii)
Initial outflow				(1m)	(1m)
Year 1					
Additional cash inflow			65,000	61,975	61,975
Net taxable income for year	1,700,000		1,515,000		
Gross CT liability	561,000	474,816	499,950	423,145	51,671
Year 2					
Additional cash inflow			700,000	606,749	606,749
Net taxable income for year	1,700,000		2,212,500		
Gross CT liability	561,000	431,651	730,125	561,781	(130,130)
Year 3					
Additional cash inflow			500,000	393,993	393,993
Net taxable income for year	1,700,000		1,637,500		
Gross CT liability	561,000	392,410	540,375	377,983	14,427
Incremental NPV					(1,315)

UNIVERSITY OF BRISTOL LIBRARY

Table 3.2
Effect of tax relief at marginal rate (£)

	Before incremental project	Present value	After incremental project	Present value	Incremental value
	(i)	(ii)	(iii)	(iv)	(iv) - (ii)
Initial outflow				(1m)	(1m)
Year 1					
Additional cash inflow			65,000	61,975	61,975
Net taxable income for year	700,000		515,000		
Gross CT liability	220,000	186,202	155,250	131,400	54,803
Year 2					
Additional cash inflow			700,000	606,749	606,749
Net taxable income for year	1,700,000		2,212,500		
Gross CT liability	561,000	431,651	730,125	561,781	(130,130)
Year 3					
Additional cash inflow			500,000	393,993	393,993
Net taxable income for year	1,700,000		1,637,500		
Gross CT liability	561,000	392,410	540,375	377,983	14,427
Incremental NPV					1,816

Advance Corporation Tax

Under the UK imputation tax system, a part of the firm's tax liability is treated as a prepayment of personal tax on dividends paid to shareholders. Dividends are paid net of the shareholder tax credit at the rate s on the gross equivalent. The firm pays the shareholder tax to the Inland Revenue on its shareholders' behalf shortly after the dividend payment is made. This amount of tax, known as Advance Corporation Tax, may be offset against the firm's mainstream corporation tax liability subject to the restriction that the amount of ACT setoff must be no greater than the taxable profits for the relevant year multiplied by the basic rate of personal tax. The effect of this rule is to ensure that shareholders cannot get credit against their income tax liability on dividends received unless the firm has actually paid at least an equivalent amount of tax. If the firm has insufficient taxable profit to offset its ACT in full then a part of it will be unrelieved, or 'surplus'. Surplus ACT may be recovered in one or more of several ways, which may be summarised as follows:

(i) part or all of it may be carried back against tax liabilities on total profits, including capital gains, for the previous six years, with offset being made in more recent years as far as possible;
(ii) it may be carried forward without time restriction and set off against profits of future years as soon as possible;
(iii) where a group structure exists, it may be surrendered to one or more 51 per cent subsidiaries.

The ACT setoff restrictions may interact with the rules concerning the carry back of trading losses. Where a loss is carried back and offset against profits of a previous year, part or all of the ACT offset in that year may be displaced. This occurs because the maximum amount which may be offset is a proportion of taxable profits, which will be reduced by the loss carry back claim. Surplus ACT created by this displacement will be carried forward.

Where there is surplus ACT which must be carried forward, its present value will be reduced. The tax rules concerning ACT can therefore be significant for project appraisal (Buckley, 1975). The impact of the ACT setoff restrictions may be demonstrated by extending the example developed above. Assume that in each year the firm pays gross dividends of £1.6m, equivalent to £1.2m net of ACT, with the associated ACT payments falling due at the end of June. (The ACT rate, s, is assumed here to be 25 per cent. At the time of writing, there are proposals for this to be reduced in stages to 20 per cent.) Table 3.3 shows the relevant cash flows.

The incremental net present value of minus £2,950 indicates that the project is more unattractive than before.

Table 3.3
Surplus ACT arising from project acceptance (£)

Incremental	Before incremental project	Present value	After incremental project	Present value	value
	(i)	(ii)	(iii)	(iv)	(iv) - (ii)
Initial outflow				(1m)	(1m)
Year 1					
Additional cash inflow			65,000	61,975	61,975
Net taxable income for year	1,700,000		1,515,000		
Gross CT liability	561,000		499,950		
Dividends (gross)	1,600,000		1,600,000		
ACT	400,000	381,385	400,000	381,385	
ACT setoff	400,000		378,750		
Net MCT	161,000	136,266	121,200	102,581	33,686
Unrelieved ACT	0		21,250		
Year 2					
Additional cash inflow			700,000	606,749	606,749
Net taxable income for year	1,700,000		2,212,500		
Gross CT liability	561,000		730,125		
Dividends (gross)	1,600,000		1,600,000		
ACT	400,000	346,714	400,000	346,714	
ACT setoff	400,000		400,000		
Relief for surplus ACT	0		21,250		
Net MCT	161,000	123,879	308,875	237,658	(113,780)
Balance of unrelieved ACT	0		0		
Year 3					
Additional cash inflow			500,000	393,993	393,993
Net taxable income for year	1,700,000		1,637,500		
Gross CT liability	561,000		540,375	377,983	
Dividends (gross)	1,600,000		1,600,000		
ACT	400,000	315,194	400,000	315,194	
ACT setoff	400,000		400,000		
Relief for surplus ACT	0		0		
Net MCT	161,000	112,617	140,375	98,190	14,427
Balance of unrelieved ACT	0		0		
Incremental NPV					(2,950)

Table 3.4
Project value with no surplus ACT (£)

	Before incremental project	Present value	After incremental project	Present value	Incremental value
	(i)	(ii)	(iii)	(iv)	(iv) - (ii)
Initial outflow				(1m)	(1m)
Year 1					
Additional cash inflow			65,000	61,975	61,975
Net taxable income for year	1,700,000		1,515,000		
Gross CT liability	561,000		499,950		
Dividends (gross)	1,500,000		1,500,000		
ACT	375,000	357,548	375,000	357,548	
ACT setoff	375,000		375,750		
Net MCT	186,000	157,426	124,950	105,755	51,671
Unrelieved ACT	0		0		
Year 2					
Additional cash inflow			700,000	606,749	606,749
Net taxable income for year	1,700,000		2,212,500		
Gross CT liability	561,000		730,125		
Dividends (gross)	1,600,000		1,600,000		
ACT	400,000	346,714	400,000	346,714	
ACT setoff	400,000		400,000		
Relief for surplus ACT	0		0		
Net MCT	161,000	123,879	330,125	254,009	(130,130)
Balance of unrelieved ACT	0		0		
Year 3					
Additional cash inflow			500,000	393,993	393,993
Net taxable income for year	1,700,000		1,637,500		
Gross CT liability	561,000		540,375		
Dividends (gross)	1,600,000		1,600,000		
ACT	400,000	315,194	400,000	315,194	
ACT setoff	400,000		400,000		
Relief for surplus ACT	0		0		
Net MCT	161,000	112,617	140,375	98,190	14,427
Balance of unrelieved ACT	0		0		
Incremental NPV					(1,315)

By comparison with Table 3.4, it may be shown that this deterioration arises as a result of the net decrease in taxable profit in year one if the project is undertaken, so that £21,250 of unrelieved ACT arises which is not relieved until year two. Table 3.4 shows the tax situation where a slightly lower dividend of £1.5m gross (£1.125m net of ACT) is paid in year one, so that surplus ACT does not arise. In this case the project's incremental NPV, minus £1,315, is the same result that was obtained in table 3.1 where dividends were ignored. The two outcomes in Tables 3.3 and 3.4 may be reconciled by the timing difference in the discounted relief on ACT of £21,250:

$$£[21{,}250/(1.10)^{1.75} - 21{,}250/(1.10)^{2.75}] = £1{,}635$$

Even if no surplus ACT arises, the project is still unattractive. If, however, the effects of loss offset are taken into account, the situation may change dramatically. Tables 3.5 and 3.6 show the impact of a loss offset of £1m in year one which reduces taxable profit to £700,000. Surplus ACT will arise whether or not the project is undertaken, although the amounts will differ. It is assumed that any surplus ACT which remains unrelieved after year three will be relieved in year four. In this situation, acceptance of the project will increase the present value of the firm after tax by £8,197 regardless of whether year one's gross dividend is £1.6m (Table 3.5) or £1.5m (Table 3.6).

The outcome in Table 3.5 may be reconciled with Table 3.2 by considering the pattern of relief of surplus ACT with and without the incremental project. If the project is not undertaken, £225,000 of surplus ACT will arise in year one of which £25,000 will be offset in year two, £25,000 in year three and £175,000 in year four. If no dividend had been paid, that £225,000 would have been paid as mainstream corporation tax on year one's taxable income. Allowing for the nine month tax lag, the effect of the delayed offset in present value terms is:

$$£[25{,}000/(1.10)^{2.75} + 25{,}000/(1.10)^{3.75} + 175{,}000/(1.10)^{4.75} \\ -225{,}000/(1.10)^{1.75}] = £42{,}430.$$

Similarly, if the project is undertaken, £271,250 of surplus ACT will arise in year one. The amounts offset in years two, three and four will be £153,125, £9,375 and £108,750 respectively. The present value of the delayed offset will be:

$$£[153{,}125/(1.10)^{2.75} + 9{,}375/(1.10)^{3.75} + 108{,}750/(1.10)^{4.75} \\ -271{,}250/(1.10)^{1.75}] = -£36{,}049.$$

Table 3.5
Effect of loss offset (£)

	Before incremental project	Present value	After incremental project	Present value	Incremental value
	(i)	(ii)	(iii)	(iv)	(iv) - (ii)
Initial outflow				(1m)	(1m)
Year 1					
Additional cash inflow			65,000	61,975	61,975
Net taxable income for year	700,000		515,000		
Gross CT liability	220,000		155,250		
Dividends (gross)	1,600,000		1,600,000		
ACT	400,000	381,385	400,000	381,385	
ACT setoff	175,000		128,750		
Net MCT	45,000	38,087	26,500	22,429	15,658
Unrelieved ACT	225,000		271,250		
Year 2					
Additional cash inflow			700,000	606,749	606,749
Net taxable income for year	1,700,000		2,212,500		
Gross CT liability	561,000		730,125		
Dividends (gross)	1,600,000		1,600,000		
ACT	400,000	346,714	400,000	346,714	
ACT setoff	400,000		400,000		
Relief for surplus ACT	25,000		153,125		
Net MCT	136,000	104,643	177,000	136,189	(31,547)
Balance of unrelieved ACT	200,000		118,125		
Year 3					
Additional cash inflow			500,000	393,993	393,993
Net taxable income for year	1,700,000		1,637,500		
Gross CT liability	561,000		540,375		
Dividends (gross)	1,600,000		1,600,000		
ACT	400,000	315,194	400,000	315,194	
ACT setoff	400,000		400,000		
Relief for surplus ACT	25,000		9,375		
Net MCT	136,000	95,130	131,000	91,632	3,497
Balance of unrelieved ACT	175,000		108,750		
Value of relieved ACT (yr 4)		111,282		69,153	(42,128)
Incremental NPV					8,197

Table 3.6
Effect of loss offset and lower dividend payment (£)

	Before incremental project (i)	Present value (ii)	After incremental project (iii)	Present value (iv)	Incremental value (iv) - (ii)
Year 1					
Additional cash inflow			65,000	61,975	61,975
Net taxable income for year	700,000		515,000		
Gross CT liability	220,000		155,250		
Dividends (gross)	1,500,000		1,500,000		
ACT	375,000	357,548	375,000	357,548	
ACT setoff	175,000		128,750		
Net MCT	45,000	38,087	26,500	22,429	15,658
Unrelieved ACT	200,000		246,250		
Year 2					
Additional cash inflow			700,000	606,749	606,749
Net taxable income for year	1,700,000		2,212,500		
Gross CT liability	561,000		730,125		
Dividends (gross)	1,600,000		1,600,000		
ACT	400,000	346,714	400,000	346,714	
ACT setoff	400,000		400,000		
Relief for surplus ACT	25,000		153,125		
Net MCT	136,000	104,643	177,000	136,189	(31,547)
Balance of unrelieved ACT	200,000		93,125		
Year 3					
Additional cash inflow			500,000	393,993	393,993
Net taxable income for year	1,700,000		1,637,500		
Gross CT liability	561,000		540,375		
Dividends (gross)	1,600,000		1,600,000		
ACT	400,000	315,194	400,000	315,194	
ACT setoff	400,000		400,000		
Relief for surplus ACT	25,000		9,375		
Net MCT	136,000	95,130	131,000	91,632	3,497
Balance of unrelieved ACT	175,000		83,750		
Value of relieved ACT (yr 4)		95,384		53,256	(42,128)
Incremental NPV					8,197

The difference of £6,381 accounts for the difference between the project's incremental value in Table 3.2, where no dividend is paid, and in Table 3.5.

By comparison, Table 3.6 shows what happens when the gross dividend payment in year one is £1,500,000. It can be seen that the incremental net present value is exactly the same as in Table 3.5. The explanation is that, with or without the additional project, the unrelieved ACT arising in year one is now reduced by £0.25(1,600,000-1,500,000), or £25,000. As a result, the amount of surplus ACT relieved in year four is £25,000 less than in the previous example whether or not the project is undertaken. The net incremental effects are therefore the same as in Table 3.5.

The above analysis shows that ACT setoff restrictions can create an interaction between dividend policy and capital budgeting decisions where the surplus ACT would arise only as a result of undertaking a particular project, or combination of projects. Where the firm's existing activities would lead to a surplus of ACT in any case, this interaction may not occur.

Leasing

Lease finance can provide a preferable alternative to buying, depending on the lessee's tax position. However, the tax rules regarding leasing have changed recently. Prior to April 1991 in the UK, a lessee was able to claim a trading deduction for the lease rentals incurred. Depreciation and the finance charge component of the lease agreement were added back to accounting profit and the rentals paid deducted. Finance lease agreements could be drafted in such a way that much higher rentals were paid in the early part of the lease, but this manipulation is now no longer possible. Tax relief is available for the amount of the finance charge and the accounts depreciation charge is deductible. In the straightforward case of level rental payments where the primary period reflects the asset's useful life, the new rules accelerate the incidence of tax relief. Where the asset's life is significantly longer than the primary lease period, the timing of relief will be deferred.

The tax effects of the lease/purchase decision can be illustrated with an example. A firm is evaluating a project involving an investment in a machine costing £90,500. The project is expected to generate cash inflows of £49,000, £54,000 and £25,000 midway through years one, two and three respectively. The firm is in a full taxpaying position in each year and acceptance of the project would not alter this. The cash inflows and associated tax payments are discounted at a risk adjusted rate of 15 per cent.

Table 3.7
The lease/purchase decision (£)

Purchase alternative

Year	0	1	2	3	Total
Purchase cost	(90,500)				(90,500)
Cash inflows		49,000	54,000	25,000	
Discounted value		45,693	43,787	17,628	107,108
Tax on inflows		16,170	17,820	8,250	
Discounted value		12,227	11,717	4,717	(28,661)
Capital allowances		22,625	16,969	50,906	
Tax savings		7,466	5,600	16,799	
Discounted value of tax savings		6,360	4,403	12,191	22,955
Net present value					10,901

Leasing alternative

Year	0	1	2	3	Total
Cash inflows		49,000	54,000	25,000	
Discounted value		45,693	43,787	17,628	107,108
Tax on inflows		16,170	17,820	8,250	
Discounted value		12,227	11,717	4,717	(28,661)
Rental payments	33,210	33,210	33,210	0	
Discounted value	33,210	30,652	28,291	0	(92,153)
Finance charges		5,987	3,142	0	
Discounted value of tax savings		1,683	815	0	2,499
Depreciation		30,167	30,167	30,167	
Discounted value of tax savings		8,481	7,827	7,224	23,532
Net present value					12,324

The tax savings from capital allowances have a similar risk to that of debt finance and are discounted at the after tax cost of debt r^* (Myers, Dill and Bautista, 1976) which is derived from the pre-tax cost of debt, r, from the formula:

$$r^* = r - [rT / (1 + r^*)] \qquad \text{(see Appendix 3.1)}$$

The firm's pretax cost of debt is 12 per cent and so r = 8.345 per cent approximately. A tax lag of one year is assumed for the sake of simplicity. (An analysis of the implications of a nine month tax lag for the after tax cost of debt is contained in Chapter 2 of this volume.)

The alternative to purchasing the asset is to lease it over the three years of the project's life at an annual rental of £33,210, with the payments falling due on the first day of each year. The implicit rate of interest in the lease, i, may be determined from:

$$£[33{,}210 + 33{,}210 / (1+i) + 33{,}210 / (1+i)^2] = £90{,}500$$

so that i = 10.45 per cent approximately. The rental payments, the associated finance charge tax savings and depreciation tax savings are discounted at the after tax cost of debt. Table 3.7 shows that the NPV of leasing is higher than that of purchasing by £(12,324-10,901), so that £1,423 may be described as the net advantage of leasing.

Table 3.8 shows the situation where the firm has no taxable profits in years one and two but expects to return to a full taxpaying situation in year three. The taxes on the cash inflows in years one to three will be paid at the end of year four and are all discounted by a factor of $1/(1.15)^4$. The present value of the tax shield on all the capital allowances, obtained in year four, is derived by discounting at an after tax cost of debt which takes into account the time lag (see Appendix 3.1 for derivation). This same discount rate is used for the relief on the financing charges and accounting depreciation. The rentals are discounted at the appropriate after tax cost of debt to reflect the timing of the payments (Appendix 3.1).

The net advantage of leasing in this situation is £887 (£14,852-13,965), a decrease of £536 compared to the full taxpaying case in Table 3.7, but still substantial.

Summary

It is evident that tax distortions will be particularly important for the firm which is temporarily in a non-taxpaying situation because of a lack of taxable profits. Tax exhaustion has been a significant problem in the UK over the last ten to fifteen years (Devereux, 1987; Young, 1992). While

Table 3.8
The lease/purchase decision for a temporary non-taxpayer (£)

Purchase alternative

Year	0	1	2	3	Total
Purchase cost	(90,500)				(90,500)
Cash inflows		49,000	54,000	25,000	
Discounted value		45,693	43,787	17,628	107,108
Tax on inflows		16,170	17,820	8,250	
Discounted value					(24,151)
Capital allowances		22,625	16,969	50,906	
Tax savings		7,466	5,600	16,799	
Discounted value of tax savings					21,508
Net present value					13,965

Leasing alternative

Year	0	1	2	3	Total
Cash inflows		49,000	54,000	25,000	
Discounted value		45,693	43,787	17,628	107,108
Tax on inflows		16,170	17,820	8,250	
Discounted value					(24,151)
Rental payments	33,210	33,210	33,210	0	
Discounted value	33,210	30,498	28,075	0	(91,783)
Finance charges		5,987	3,142	0	
Tax savings on finance charges		1,976	1,037	0	
Discounted value of tax savings					2,170
Depreciation		30,167	30,167	30,167	
Tax savings on depreciation		9,955	9,955	9,955	
Discounted value of tax savings					21,508
Net present value					14,852

this situation persists, losses created due to unabsorbed capital allowances may be carried forward, which will reduce their present value unless the marginal tax rate increases substantially. When the firm regains a taxpaying position, its taxable profits may progress through the marginal limits so that the losses carried forward may be relieved at the lower small companies rate or the higher marginal rate between the marginal limits, rather than at the full rate.

But tax losses will also create surplus ACT which, unless it can be carried back and offset against previous years' tax liabilities, must be carried forward. This will increase the effective cost of paying a dividend. On the other hand the after tax cost of debt will be increased, since the present value of the tax savings from interest deductibility will be reduced as the unrelieved interest is carried forward. This may have significant consequences for the evaluation of alternative forms of finance which carry obligations similar to debt, such as leasing. Also, reduced taxable profits as a result of heavy capital allowances may distort the marginal tax rate at which relief is finally obtained on debenture interest. There is therefore a need for the firm's total investment programme and financing policy to be considered jointly. In the remaining part of this chapter a mixed integer programming model is developed which aims to fulfil this function. The complete mathematical model is presented in Appendix 3.2.

The mathematical programming model

Purchased assets

Assuming that an asset is purchased at the start of the year and capital allowances are obtained one year later, then the written down value of the asset at the end of year t will be:

$$WDV_{j_t} = C_j (1 - \alpha'_j)(1 - \alpha)^{t-1} \tag{1}$$

where C_j is the asset cost at time 0, α'_j is the proportion of that cost which is the capital allowance available in the first year and α is the writing down allowance available on a reducing balance basis in the second and subsequent years of the asset's life.

The writing down allowance (WDA) in the first year will be:

$$WDA_{j_{t=1}} = \alpha' C_j \tag{2}$$

and in any subsequent year t:

$$WDA_{j_{t>1}} = \alpha C_j (1-\alpha'_j)(1-\alpha)^{t-2}. \tag{3}$$

Representing incremental projects being considered at t by $j = 1,....,J$, then capital outlay at the start of t will be:

$$\sum_{j=1}^{J} C_{j_t} \delta_j$$

where δ_j is a binary variable which has the value 1 if project j is accepted and 0 if it is rejected.

The closing balance on the capital allowance pool at the end of year t, CP_t, will be:

$$CP_t = (1-\alpha)(CP_{t-1} - S_t) + (1-\alpha')\sum_{j=1}^{J} C_{j_t} \delta_j \tag{4}$$

where S_t represents asset disposals made in t.

The total of capital allowances obtained at the end of the year will be:

$$WDA_t = \alpha\left[\max(CP_{t-1} - S_t),0\right] + \alpha'\sum_{j=1}^{J} C_{j_t} \delta_j \tag{5}$$

If the disposal value in t exceeds the 'qualifying expenditure' then a balancing charge BC_t will arise. Assuming that the disposal proceeds are less than the cost of the assets, then:

$$BC_t = \max\left[(S_t - CP_{t-1} - \sum_{j=1}^{J} C_{j_t} \delta_j),0\right] \tag{6}$$

Where an asset is treated as a short life asset (SLA) then a balancing allowance may arise on disposal:

$$BA_{j_t} = \max\left[(WDV_{j_t} - S_{j_t}),0\right]$$

that is, the excess if any of the written down value of asset j at the start of the year t in which it is sold, over its sale price. The balancing allowance for year t will be:

$$BA_t = \sum_{j=0}^{J} \max\left[(WDV_{j_t} - S_{j_t}),0\right]\delta_{j*} \tag{7}$$

where $j=0$ represents the firm's ongoing projects at the start of t and δ_{j*} is a binary variable which takes the value 1 if the asset is 'depooled' and 0 if it is not.

Leased assets

Lease rentals R_{j_L} will result in a cash outflow at the start of each year of the term of the lease on asset j. Assuming a straight line basis of depreciation, the accounting depreciation in year t on a leased asset j_L will be:

$$D_{j_{L_t}} = C_{j_L} / n_j \tag{8}$$

where n is the number of years of the asset's life.

The finance charge in year 1 of the leased asset's life will be:

$$F_{j_{L_{t=1}}} = i_{j_L}(C_{j_L} - R_{j_L}) \tag{9}$$

where i_{j_L} is the rate of interest implicit in the lease.

In year 2:

$$F_{j_{L_{t=2}}} = i_{j_L}\left[(C_{j_L} - R_{j_L})(1+i_{j_L}) - R_{j_L}\right]$$

and in year 3:

$$F_{j_{L_{t=3}}} = i_{j_L}\left\{\left[(C_{j_L} - R_{j_L})(1+i_{j_L}) - R_{j_L}\right](1+i_{j_L}) - R_{j_L}\right\}$$

so that in general, the finance charge in each year after year 1 will be:

$$F_{jL_t} = [(F_{jL_{t-1}} / i_{jL})(1+i_{jL}) - R_{jL}]i_{jL}$$
$$= F_{jL_{t-1}}(1+i_{jL}) - R_{jL}i_{jL}. \qquad (10)$$

For any asset j which may be either leased or purchased, a decision to accept at most one of these alternatives in the optimal solution may be forced by imposing the constraint:

$$\delta_j + \delta_{jL} \leq 1. \qquad (11)$$

(Where 'depooling' the asset would be considered if the asset were purchased, the constraint must be $\delta_j + \delta_{j*} + \delta_{jL} \leq 1$).

Taxable profit

Schedule D trading profit in t is given by

$$P_t = \max\{[(N_{j_t} - D_{jL_t} - F_{jL_t})_{j=0} + \sum_{j=1}^{J} N_{j_t}\delta_j - \sum_{j=1}^{J} D_{jL_t}\delta_{jL_t}$$
$$-\sum_{j=1}^{J} F_{jL_t}\delta_{jL} - WDA_t + BC_t - BA_t], 0\} \qquad (12)$$

where N_{j_t} = net operating cash flows from project j in t, ignoring any changes in working capital.

Conversely the trading loss in t will be:

$$L_t = \max\{-[(N_{j_t} - D_{jL_t} - F_{jL_t})_{j=0} + \sum_{j=1}^{J} N_{j_t}\delta_j - \sum_{j=1}^{J} D_{jL_t}\delta_{jL_t}$$
$$-\sum_{j=1}^{J} F_{jL_t}\delta_{jL} - WDA_t + BC_t - BA_t], 0\}. \qquad (13)$$

If a trading loss is made in t then provided the firm has no other income, the debt interest carried forward from t, X_t, will be:

$$\sum_{j=0}^{J} b_{j_t}$$

representing the total debt interest payments made in t.

If a trading profit is made in t, then the interest on debt which is carried forward will be:

$$\max\left[-(P_t - \sum_{j=0}^{J} b_{j_t}),0\right].$$

So,

$$X_t = \max\left[-(P_t - \sum_{j=0}^{J} b_{j_t}),0\right]\delta_{x_t} + \sum_{j=0}^{J} b_{j_t}(1-\delta_{x_t}) \tag{14}$$

where $\delta_{x_t} = 1$ if $P_t > 0$, otherwise $\delta_{x_t} = 0$.

Assessable profits, π_t,will be given by the Schedule D Case I profits less debt interest for the period:

$$\pi_t = \max\left[(P_t - \sum_{j=0}^{J} b_{j_t}),0\right].$$

π_t will be adjusted for any losses carried forward from previous years, $L_{F,t}$, giving:

$$\pi_t' = \max\left[(P_t - \sum_{j=0}^{J} b_{j_t} - L_{F,t}),0\right]. \tag{15}$$

The remainder, if any, of these losses will be carried forward to $t+1$:

$$L_{F_{t,t+1}} = \max\left[-(P_t - \sum_{j=0}^{J} b_{j_t} + X_t - L_{F,t}),0\right]. \tag{16}$$

The corporation tax payment in respect of year t will be calculated on the basis of π_t'. The structure of the tax function has been described earlier in the chapter.

The tax payment may be calculated as follows:

If $\pi_t' > M_{u_t}$, then $T_{\pi_t'} = T_{f_t}\pi_t'$.

If $M_{l_t} < \pi_t' \leq M_{u_t}$, then $T_{\pi_t'} = T_{f_t}\pi_t' - \frac{(M_{u_t} - \pi_t')}{(M_{u_t} - M_{l_t})}(T_{f_t} - T_{s_t})M_{l_t}$.

If $0 < \pi'_t \le M_{l_t}$, then $T_{\pi'_t} = T_{f_t}\pi'_t - (T_{f_t} - T_{f_t})\pi'_t$
$= T_{f_t}\pi'_t - (\pi'_t / M_{l_t})(T_{f_t} - T_{s_t})M_{l_t}$.

Combining these gives:

$$T_{\pi'_t} = T_{f_t}\pi'_t - \{ [(\pi'_t / M_{l_t})(1-\delta_m) + \frac{(M_{u_t} - \pi'_t)}{(M_{u_t} - M_{l_t})}\delta_m] (T_{f_t} - T_{s_t})M_{l_t} \} (1-\delta_f) \tag{17}$$

where

$\delta_m = 1$ if $\pi'_t \ge M_{l_t}$, otherwise $\delta_m = 0$
$\delta_{ft} = 1$ if $\pi'_t \ge M_{u_t}$, otherwise $\delta_{f_t} = 0$

Losses may be carried back or carried forward. The profits of $t-1$, $t-2$ and $t-3$ will be adjusted to absorb L_{t_B}, the amount carried back. Adjusted profit figures will then arise for those years and these may be denoted by $\pi'_{A_{t-1}}$, $\pi'_{B_{t-2}}$ and $\pi'_{C_{t-3}}$ respectively.

Any one year's profits will be adjusted three times in total. The adjusted profit for $t-1$ after carrying back a loss from t is:

$$\pi'_{A_{t-1}} = \pi'_{t-1} - L_{t,t-1}$$

where

$$L_{t,t-1} \ge 0.$$

Similarly:

$$\pi'_{B_{t-2}} = \pi'_{A_{t-2}} - L_{t,t-2}$$

$$\pi'_{C_{t-3}} = \pi'_{B_{t-3}} - L_{t,t-3}.$$

The following constraints ensure that the carry back is made, as far as possible, against more recent periods first:

$$L_{t,t-1} = \min[L_t, \pi'_{t-1}] \tag{18}$$

$$L_{t,t-2} = \min[(L_t - L_{t,t-1}), \pi'_{A_{t-2}}] \tag{19}$$

$$L_{t,t-3} = \min\left[(L_t - \sum_{i=1}^{2} L_{t,t-i}), \pi'_{B_{t-3}}\right] \tag{20}$$

The amount of the loss in t which is carried forward to $t+1$ will be:

$$L_{t_{F,t+1}} = L_t - \sum_{i=1}^{3} L_{t,t-i} \tag{21}$$

Combining (14), (16) and (21) gives the total amount of losses carried forward to $t+1$:

$$L_{F,t+1} = L_{F_{t,t+1}} + L_{t_{F,t+1}} + X_t \tag{22}$$

This includes debt interest carried forward, which is treated in the same way as trading losses carried forward.

A rebate in respect of tax paid in earlier years may arise as a result of the offset of losses. The rebate at t, B_t, will be:

$$B_t = \left(T\pi'_{t-1} - T\pi'_{A_{t-1}}\right) + \left(T\pi'_{A_{t-2}} - T\pi'_{B_{t-2}}\right) + \left(T\pi'_{B_{t-3}} - T\pi'_{C_{t-3}}\right)$$
$$- \sum_{i=1}^{3} SACT_{L_{t,t-i}}. \tag{23}$$

The final term is an adjustment to take into account ACT restrictions, which will be dealt with in detail in the next section. In practice the tax rebates may be adjusted for interest at the statutory rate.

Setoff of ACT

The initial ACT offset capacity in t is $s\pi'_t$, where s is the basic rate of income tax. After taking into account the ACT relating to W_t, the dividend distributions in t, any remaining 'unused' capacity will be given by:

$$U_t = \max\left[(s\pi'_t - sW_t/(1-s)), 0\right]. \tag{24}$$

If U_t is positive then any surplus ACT brought forward to t from previous years, $SACT_{F,t}$, may be offset against U_t. The amount of this surplus which is offset in t will be:

$$\min(SACT_{F,t}, U_t).$$

Any $SACT_{F,t}$ remaining after this offset will be carried forward to $t+1$. The amount carried forward will be:

$$SACT_{F,t} - \min(SACT_{F,t}, U_t).$$

If $sW_t/(1-s)$ exceeds $s\pi_t'$, then U_t will be zero and surplus ACT will arise in t as a result of the dividend distributions made in t. This surplus, $SACT_{W_t}$, is given by:

$$SACT_{W_t} = \max\left[-(s\pi_t' - sW_t/(1-s)),0\right] \tag{25}$$

$SACT_{W_t}$ may be carried back and offset against previous years' unutilized ACT capacity. The capacity in $t-1$ which is available to absorb $SACT_{W_t}$, U_{t-1}^t, will be determined by the adjusted profit figure resulting from the possible carry back of losses from t:

$$U_{t-1}^t = \max\left[(s\pi_{A_{t-1}}' - sW_{t-1}/(1-s) - \min(SACT_{F,t-1}, U_{t-1})),0\right] \tag{26}$$

Since $\pi_{A_{t-1}}'$ will be smaller than π_{t-1}' if losses from t have been carried back to $t-1$, surplus ACT may be created.

$$SACT_{L_{t,t-1}} = \max\left[-(s\pi_{A_{t-1}}' - sW_{t-1}/(1-s) - \min(SACT_{F,t-1}, U_{t-1}) + SACT_{W_{t-1}}),0\right] \tag{27}$$

This surplus will be carried forward from t and may be offset in subsequent years.

Similarly, the unutilized offset capacity in $t-2$ which is available for absorption of $SACT_{W_t}$ will be:

$$U_{t-2}^t = \max\left[(s\pi_{B_{t-2}}' - sW_{t-2}/(1-s) - \min(SACT_{F,t-2}, U_{t-2}) - SACT_{W_{t-1,t-2}}),0\right] \tag{28}$$

taking into account the effect of losses carried back from t to $t-2$, and any surplus ACT carried back from $t-1$ to $t-2$.

Surplus ACT created as a result of the loss carried back from t to $t-2$ will be:

$$SACT_{L_{t,t-2}} = \max\left[-(s\pi'_{B_{t-2}} - sW_{t-2} / (1-s) - \min(SACT_{F,t-2}, U_{t-2}) + SACT_{W_{t-2}} + SACT_{L_{t-1,t-2}} - SACT_{W_{t-1,t-2}}), 0\right] \tag{29}$$

Similarly in $t-3$:

$$U^t_{t-3} = \max\left[(s\pi'_{C_{t-3}} - sW_{t-3} / (1-s) - \min(SACT_{F,t-3}, U_{t-3}) - \sum_{i=1}^{2} SACT_{W_{t-i,t-3}}), 0\right] \tag{30}$$

$$SACT_{L_{t,t-3}} = \max\left[-(s\pi'_{C_{t-3}} - sW_{t-3} / (1-s) - \min(SACT_{F,t-3}, U_{t-3}) + SACT_{W_{t-3}} + \sum_{i=1}^{2} SACT_{L_{t-i,t-3}} - \sum_{i=1}^{2} SACT_{W_{t-i,t-3}}), 0\right] \tag{31}$$

At $t-4$, $t-5$ and $t-6$ there is no further possibility of carrying back losses from t, and so no further surplus ACT will be created in those years.

$$U^t_{t-4} = \max\left[(s\pi'_{C_{t-4}} - sW_{t-4} / (1-s) - \min(SACT_{F,t-4}, U_{t-4}) - \sum_{i=1}^{3} SACT_{W_{t-i,t-4}}), 0\right]$$

or,

$$U^t_{t-4} = \max\left[(U^{t-1}_{t-4} - SACT_{W_{t-1,t-4}}), 0\right] \tag{32}$$

Similarly:

$$U^t_{t-5} = \max\left[(U^{t-1}_{t-5} - SACT_{W_{t-1,t-5}}), 0\right] \tag{33}$$

$$U^t_{t-6} = \max\left[(U^{t-1}_{t-6} - SACT_{W_{t-1,t-6}}), 0\right]. \tag{34}$$

$SACT_{W_t}$ may be carried forward or carried back. A carry back claim may be restricted to part of the surplus ACT, but of the amount carried back, offset must be made in more recent years in priority to earlier ones. The following constraints ensure this:

$$SACT_{W_{t,t-1}} = \min[SACT_{W_t}, U_{t-1}^t] \tag{35}$$

$$SACT_{W_{t,t-2}} = \min[(SACT_{W_t} - SACT_{W_{t,t-1}}), U_{t-2}^t] \tag{36}$$

$$SACT_{W_{t,t-3}} = \min[(SACT_{W_t} - \sum_{i=1}^{2} SACT_{W_{t,t-i}}), U_{t-3}^t] \tag{37}$$

$$SACT_{W_{t,t-4}} = \min[(SACT_{W_t} - \sum_{i=1}^{3} SACT_{W_{t,t-i}}), U_{t-4}^t] \tag{38}$$

$$SACT_{W_{t,t-5}} = \min[(SACT_{W_t} - \sum_{i=1}^{4} SACT_{W_{t,t-i}}), U_{t-5}^t] \tag{39}$$

$$SACT_{W_{t,t-6}} = \min[(SACT_{W_t} - \sum_{i=1}^{5} SACT_{W_{t,t-i}}), U_{t-6}^t]. \tag{40}$$

The total amount of $SACT_{W_t}$ carried back will be claimed as recovered ACT:

$$ACT_{R_t} = \sum_{i=1}^{6} SACT_{W_{t,t-i}} \tag{41}$$

Any remainder will be carried forward to future years. The total surplus ACT which is carried forward from t to $t+1$ will be:

$$SACT_{F,t+1} = SACT_{F,t} - \min(SACT_{F,t}, U_t) + SACT_{W_t} - ACT_{R_t} + \sum_{i=1}^{3} SACT_{L_{t,t-i}} \tag{42}$$

Finally, mainstream corporation tax, MCT_t, will be:

$$MCT_t = T\pi_t' - \min[(sW_t/(1-s), s\pi_t')] \tag{43}$$

The objective function

The aim of this model is to maximize the post-tax net present value of the firm's portfolio of projects, including both ongoing activities and incremental projects, for all periods from $t = 1$ to the horizon time, H.

Maximize:

$$\sum_{t=1}^{H} [\sum_{j=1}^{J} N_{j_t} \delta_j / (1+k_t)^{t-0.5} + N_{j=0,t} / (1+k_t)^{t-0.5} - \sum_{j=1}^{J} C_{j_t} \delta_j / (1+k_t)^{t-1}$$

$$-\sum_{j=1}^{J} R_{j_{L_t}} \delta_{j_L} / (1+k_t)^{t-1} - R_{j=0,t} / (1+k_t)^{t-1} - \sum_{j=0,t}^{J} b_{j_t} / (1+k_t)^{t-1}$$

$$-(sW_t / (1-s)) / (1+k_t)^{t-0.5} - MCT_t / (1+k_t)^{t+0.75}$$

$$+(B_t + ACT_{R_t}) / (1+k_t)^{t+0.75}]$$

The assumptions made are:

(i) the horizon is sufficiently far away that the discounted value of the firm's activities at the horizon is negligible;

(ii) assets are purchased or leased at the start of the year;

(iii) the net operating cash inflows, debt interest payments and ACT payments occur midway through the year;

(iv) other tax effects occur nine months after the year end.

The derivation of the appropriate discount rate will be complex. k_t will vary in each period as a result of the changes in the investment and financing mix over time and the associated level of risk. Also, the optimal investment and financing decisions will depend on the value of k, so that an iterative approach may be necessary. Further work is planned in this important area.

Conclusion

The model developed above incorporates the most important tax rules concerning the carry back and carry forward of losses and surplus ACT, which can be highly significant in project appraisal, and includes constraints relevant to lease evaluation. It provides a basis for assessing the post tax net present value of a single incremental project or combination of projects in the context of the firm's overall tax situation. Suitable commercial packages are available to solve problems of this type within reasonable times and operational use of the model, using real or simulated data, is anticipated.

References

Ashford, R., Berry, R. and Dyson, R. (1986), 'Taxation Induced Interactions in Capital Budgeting', *Warwick Papers in Management*, No. 8, November.

Berry, R.H. and Dyson, R.G. (1979), 'A Mathematical Programming Approach to Taxation Induced Interdependencies in Investment Appraisal', *Journal of Business Finance and Accounting*, Vol. 6, No. 4.

Buckley, A. (1975), 'The Distorting Effect of Surplus ACT in Project Appraisal', *Accounting and Business Research*, Summer.

Devereux, M. (1987), 'Taxation and the Cost of Capital: The UK Experience', *Oxford Review of Economic Policy*, 3.

Grundy, G. and Burns, P. (1979), 'Taxation-Induced Interdependencies in Project Appraisal', *Accounting and Business Research*, Winter.

Myers, S.C., Dill, D.A. and Bautista, A.J. (1976), 'Valuation of Financial Lease Contracts', *Journal of Finance*, Vol. 31, no. 3.

Pointon, J. (1981), *Investment and Financing Decision Models Under the Imputation Tax System,* PhD Thesis, University of Warwick.

Pointon, J. (1991), *Programming for the Tax Interactivities of Capital Investment and Financing Decisions,* Research Paper, Business Taxation Research Unit, Polytechnic South West.

Williams, H.P. (1985), *Model Building in Mathematical Programming*, 2nd ed., Wiley.

Young, G. (1992), 'A New Approach to Modelling Corporation Tax', *NIESR Economic Review*, May.

Appendix 3.1

Derivation of the after tax cost of debt

If there is no delay in tax payment, the after tax cost of debt r^* is given by:

$$r^* = r - rT$$

where r is the pre-tax borrowing rate and T is the corporation tax rate. Where there is a delay of one time period this becomes:

$$r^* = r - rT / (1 + r^*)$$

so that if r = 0.12 and T = 0.33, r^* can be found by successive approximations to be 0.08345.

In the example in the text, the firm returns to a position of taxable profits in year three. The after tax cost of debt for year three, k_3, is 0.08345 because the tax deductibility of year three's debt interest occurs in year four. For year two, the tax saving is discounted for two years to reflect the delay between years two and four:

$$\begin{aligned} k_2 &= 0.12[1 - 0.33 / (1 + k_3)^2] \\ &= 0.12[1 - 0.33 / (1.08345)^2] \\ &= 0.08627. \end{aligned}$$

Similarly,

$$\begin{aligned} k_1 &= 0.12[1 - 0.33 / \{(1 + k_2)(1 + k_3)\}] \\ &= 0.12[1 - 0.33 / \{(1.08627)(1.08345)\}] \\ &= 0.08894. \end{aligned}$$

The rental payments are made at the start of each year and so the first payment is not discounted. The rental paid at the start of year two is discounted by the after tax cost of debt for year one, so the discount factor is given by $1/(1+k_1)$. Similarly the third rental payment, at the start of year three, is discounted by $1 / \{(1 + k_1)(1 + k_2)\}$ to reflect the delay of two years before it is paid. The discount factor which reflects the delay of four years before capital allowances, etc. are offset is given by $1 / \{(1 + k_1)(1 + k_2)(1 + k_3)(1 + k_4)\}$.

Appendix 3.2

The mathematical program

The constraints of the mixed integer programming model may be represented in a mathematical program, using binary variables to enforce the logical conditions (see, for example, Williams (1985). For instance, a constraint of the type

$$x - M\delta \leq 0$$

where M is a constant coefficient whose value is the known upper bound for x, forces δ to take the value 1 when $x > 0$. By combining this with the additional constraint

$$x\delta \geq 0$$

δ will take the value 1 if and only if x is non-negative.

The constraints of the model may be re-expressed in this format. In the following, the binary variables used to enforce these logical conditions apply in each of the time periods. The t subscripts are omitted for convenience.

1) $$WDV_{j_t} - C_j(1 - \alpha'_j)(1 - \alpha)^{t-1} = 0$$

2) $$WDA_{j_{t=1}} - \alpha' C_j = 0$$

3) $$WDA_{j_{t\triangleright 1}} - \alpha C_j \left(1 - \alpha'_j\right)(1 - \alpha)^{t-2} = 0$$

4) $$CP_t - (1 - \alpha)(CP_{t-1} - S_t) - (1 - \alpha') \sum_{j=1}^{J} C_{j_t} \delta_j = 0$$

5) $$WDA_t - \alpha(CP_{t-1} - S_t)\delta_1 - \alpha' \sum_{j=1}^{J} C_{j_t} \delta_j = 0$$

5a) $$(CP_{t-1} - S_t) - M\delta_1 \leq 0$$

5b) $$(CP_{t-1} - S_t)\delta_1 \geq 0$$

6) $$BC_t - (S_t - CP_{t-1} - \sum_{j=1}^{J} C_{j_t} \delta_j)\delta_2 = 0$$

6a) $$(S_t - CP_{t-1} - \sum_{j=1}^{J} C_{j_t} \delta_j) - M\delta_2 \leq 0$$

6b) $$(S_t - CP_{t-1} - \sum_{j=1}^{J} C_{j_t} \delta_j)\delta_2 \geq 0$$

7) $$BA_t - \sum_{j=0}^{J} (WDV_{j_t} - S_{j_t})\delta_3 \delta_{j*} = 0$$

7a) $$\sum_{j=0}^{J} (WDV_{j_t} - S_{j_t}) - M\delta_3 \leq 0$$

7b) $$\sum_{j=0}^{J} (WDV_{j_t} - S_{j_t})\delta_3 \geq 0$$

8) $$D_{j_{L_t}} - C_{j_L} / n_j = 0$$

9) $$F_{j_{L_{t=1}}} - i_{j_L}(C_{j_L} - R_{j_L}) = 0$$

10) $$F_{j_{L_t}} - F_{j_{L_{t-1}}}(1 + i_{j_L}) + R_{j_L} i_{j_L} = 0$$

11) $$\delta_j + \delta_{j_L} \leq 1$$

12) $$P_t - \Big[(N_{j_t} - D_{j_{L_t}} - F_{j_{L_t}})_{j=0} + \sum_{j=1}^{J} N_{j_t} \delta_j - \sum_{j=1}^{J} D_{j_{L_t}} \delta_{j_{L\,t}}$$

$$- \sum_{j=1}^{J} F_{j_{L_t}} \delta_{j_L} - WDA_t + BC_t - BA_t\Big]\delta_4 = 0$$

12a) $$[(N_{j_t} - D_{j_{L_t}} - F_{j_{L_t}})_{j=0} + \sum_{j=1}^{J} N_{j_t}\delta_j - \sum_{j=1}^{J} D_{j_{L_t}}\delta_{j_{L_t}} - \sum_{j=1}^{J} F_{j_{L_t}}\delta_{j_L} - WDA_t + BC_t - BA_t] - M\delta_4 \le 0$$

12b) $$[(N_{j_t} - D_{j_{L_t}} - F_{j_{L_t}})_{j=0} + \sum_{j=1}^{J} N_{j_t}\delta_j - \sum_{j=1}^{J} D_{j_{L_t}}\delta_{j_{L_t}} - \sum_{j=1}^{J} F_{j_{L_t}}\delta_{j_L} - WDA_t + BC_t - BA_t]\delta_4 \ge 0$$

13) $$L_t - [(N_{j_t} - D_{j_{L_t}} - F_{j_{L_t}})_{j=0} + \sum_{j=1}^{J} N_{j_t}\delta_j - \sum_{j=1}^{J} D_{j_{L_t}}\delta_{j_{L_t}} - \sum_{j=1}^{J} F_{j_{L_t}}\delta_{j_L} - WDA_t + BC_t - BA_t](\delta_4 - 1) = 0$$

14) $$X_t - (\sum_{j=0}^{J} b_{j_t} - P_t)\delta_5\delta_4 - \sum_{j=0}^{J} b_{j_t}(1-\delta_4) = 0$$

14a) $$(\sum_{j=0}^{J} b_{j_t} - P_t) - M\delta_5 \le 0$$

14b) $$(\sum_{j=0}^{J} b_{j_t} - P_t)\delta_5 \ge 0$$

15) $$\pi_t' - (P_t - \sum_{j=0}^{J} b_{j_t} - L_{F,t})\delta_6 = 0$$

15a) $$(P_t - \sum_{j=0}^{J} b_{j_t} - L_{F,t}) - M\delta_6 \le 0$$

15b) $(P_t - \sum_{j=0}^{J} b_{j_t} - L_{F,t})\delta_6 \geq 0$

16) $L_{F_{t,t+1}} - (-P_t + \sum_{j=0}^{J} b_{j_t} - X_t + L_{F,t})\delta_7 = 0$

16a) $(-P_t + \sum_{j=0}^{J} b_{j_t} - X_t + L_{F,t}) - M\delta_7 \leq 0$

16b) $(-P_t + \sum_{j=0}^{J} b_{j_t} - X_t + L_{F,t})\delta_7 \geq 0$

17) $T_{\pi'_t} - T_{f_t}\pi'_t + \{[(\pi'_t / M_{l_t})(1-\delta_8) + \frac{(M_{u_t} - \pi'_t)}{(M_{u_t} - M_{l_t})}\delta_8]$

$(T_{f_t} - T_{s_t})M_{l_t}\}(1-\delta_9) = 0$

17a) $(\pi'_t - M_{l_t}) - M\delta_8 \leq 0$

17b) $(\pi'_t - M_{l_t})\delta_8 \geq 0$

17c) $(\pi'_t - M_{u_t}) - M\delta_9 \leq 0$

17d) $(\pi'_t - M_{u_t})\delta_9 \geq 0$

18) $L_{t,t-1} - [L_t(1-\delta_{10}) + \pi'_{t-1}\delta_{10}] = 0$

18a) $(L_t - \pi'_{t-1}) - M\delta_{10} \leq 0$

18b) $(L_t - \pi'_{t-1})\delta_{10} \geq 0$

19) $L_{t,t-2} - [(L_t - L_{t,t-1})(1-\delta_{11}) + \pi'_{A_{t-2}}\delta_{11}] = 0$

19a) $(L_t - L_{t,t-1} - \pi'_{A_{t-2}}) - M\delta_{11} \leq 0$

19b) $(L_t - L_{t,t-1} - \pi'_{A_{t-2}})\delta_{11} \geq 0$

20) $L_{t,t-3} - \left[\pi'_{B_{t-3}}\delta_{12} + (L_t - \sum_{i=1}^{2} L_{t,t-i})(1-\delta_{12})\right] = 0$

20a) $(L_t - \sum_{i=1}^{2} L_{t,t-i} - \pi'_{B_{t-3}}) - M\delta_{12} \leq 0$

20b) $(L_t - \sum_{i=1}^{2} L_{t,t-i} - \pi'_{B_{t-3}})\delta_{12} \geq 0$

21) $L_{t_{F,t+1}} - L_t - \sum_{i=1}^{3} L_{t,t-i} = 0$

22) $L_{F,t+1} - L_{F_{t,t+1}} - L_{t_{F,t+1}} - X_t = 0$

23) $B_t - \left(T\pi'_{t-1} - T\pi'_{A_{t-1}}\right) - \left(T\pi'_{A_{t-2}} - T\pi'_{B_{t-2}}\right) - \left(T\pi'_{B_{t-3}} - T\pi'_{C_{t-3}}\right)$

$+\sum_{i=1}^{3} SACT_{L_{t,t-i}} = 0$

24) $U_t - \left[s\pi'_t - sW_t/(1-s)\right]\delta_{13} = 0$

24a) $\left[s\pi'_t - sW_t/(1-s)\right] - M\delta_{13} \leq 0$

24b) $\left[s\pi'_t - sW_t/(1-s)\right]\delta_{13} \geq 0$

25) $SACT_{W_t} - \left[-s\pi'_t + sW_t/(1-s)\right]\delta_{14} = 0$

25a) $\left[-s\pi'_t + sW_t/(1-s)\right] - M\delta_{14} \leq 0$

25b) $\left[-s\pi'_t + sW_t/(1-s)\right]\delta_{14} \geq 0$

26) $U_{t-1}^{t}-[s\pi'_{A_{t-1}}-sW_{t-1}/(1-s)-U_{t-1}\delta_{15}$

$-SACT_{F,t-1}(1-\delta_{15})]\delta_{16}=0$

26a) $[s\pi'_{A_{t-1}}-sW_{t-1}/(1-s)-U_{t-1}\delta_{15}$

$-SACT_{F,t-1}(1-\delta_{15})]-M\delta_{16}\leq 0$

26b) $[s\pi'_{A_{t-1}}-sW_{t-1}/(1-s)-U_{t-1}\delta_{15}-SACT_{F,t-1}(1-\delta_{15})]\delta_{16}\geq 0$

26c) $(SACT_{F_{t-1}}-U_{t-1})-M\delta_{15}\leq 0$

26d) $(SACT_{F_{t-1}}-U_{t-1})\delta_{15}\geq 0$

27) $SACT_{L_{t,t-1}}-[s\pi'_{A_{t-1}}-sW_{t-1}/(1-s)+SACT_{W_{t-1}}-U_{t-1}\delta_{15}$

$-SACT_{F,t-1}(1-\delta_{15})](\delta_{16}-1)=0$

28) $U_{t-2}^{t}-[s\pi'_{B_{t-2}}-sW_{t-2}/(1-s)-U_{t-2}\delta_{17}-SACT_{F,t-2}(1-\delta_{17})$

$-SACT_{W_{t-1,t-2}}]\delta_{18}=0$

28a) $[s\pi'_{B_{t-2}}-sW_{t-2}/(1-s)-U_{t-2}\delta_{17}-SACT_{F,t-2}(1-\delta_{17})$

$-SACT_{W_{t-1,t-2}}]-M\delta_{18}\leq 0$

28b) $[s\pi'_{B_{t-2}}-sW_{t-2}/(1-s)-U_{t-2}\delta_{17}-SACT_{F,t-2}(1-\delta_{17})$

$-SACT_{W_{t-1,t-2}}]\delta_{18}\geq 0$

28c) $(SACT_{F,t-2}-U_{t-2})-M\delta_{17}\leq 0$

28d) $(SACT_{F,t-2}-U_{t-2})\delta_{17}\geq 0$

29) $SACT_{L_{t,t-2}} - [s\pi'_{B_{t-2}} - sW_{t-2} / (1-s)-, U_{t-2}\,\delta_{17}$

$-SACT_{F,t-2}(1-\delta_{17}) + SACT_{W_{t-2}} + SACT_{L_{t-1,t-2}}$

$-SACT_{W_{t-1,t-2}}](\delta_{18}-1) = 0$

30) $U^{t}_{t-3} - [s\pi'_{C_{t-3}} - sW_{t-3} / (1-s) - U_{t-3}\,\delta_{19} - SACT_{F,t-3}(1-\delta_{19})$

$-\sum_{i=1}^{2} SACT_{W_{t-i,t-3}}]\delta_{20} = 0$

30a) $[s\pi'_{C_{t-3}} - sW_{t-3} / (1-s) - U_{t-3}\,\delta_{19} - SACT_{F,t-3}(1-\delta_{19})$

$-\sum_{i=1}^{2} SACT_{W_{t-i,t-3}}] - M\,\delta_{20} \leq 0$

30b) $[s\pi'_{C_{t-3}} - sW_{t-3} / (1-s) - U_{t-3}\,\delta_{19} - SACT_{F,t-3}(1-\delta_{19})$

$-\sum_{i=1}^{2} SACT_{W_{t-i,t-3}}]\delta_{20} \geq 0$

30c) $(SACT_{F,t-3} - U_{t-3}) - M\delta_{19} \leq 0$

30d) $(SACT_{F,t-3} - U_{t-3})\delta_{19} \geq 0$

31) $SACT_{L_{t,t-3}} - [s\pi'_{C_{t-3}} - sW_{t-3} / (1-s) - U_{t-3}\delta_{19} - SACT_{F,t-3}(1-\delta_{19})$

$-\sum_{i=1}^{2} SACT_{W_{t-i,t-3}} + SACT_{W_{t-3}} + \sum_{i=1}^{2} SACT_{L_{t-i,t-3}}](\delta_{20}-1) = 0$

32) $U^{t}_{t-4} - (U^{t-1}_{t-4} - SACT_{W_{t-1,t-4}})\delta_{21} = 0$

32a) $(U^{t-1}_{t-4} - SACT_{W_{t-1,t-4}}) - M\delta_{21} \leq 0$

32b) $(U_{t-4}^{t-1} - SACT_{W_{t-1,\,t-4}})\delta_{21} \geq 0$

33) $U_{t-5}^{t} - (U_{t-5}^{t-1} - SACT_{W_{t-1,\,t-5}})\delta_{22} = 0$

33a) $(U_{t-5}^{t-1} - SACT_{W_{t-1,\,t-5}}) - M\delta_{22} \leq 0$

33b) $(U_{t-5}^{t-1} - SACT_{W_{t-1,\,t-5}})\delta_{22} \geq 0$

34) $U_{t-6}^{t} - (U_{t-6}^{t-1} - SACT_{W_{t-1,\,t-6}})\delta_{23} = 0$

34a) $(U_{t-6}^{t-1} - SACT_{W_{t-1,\,t-6}}) - M\delta_{23} \leq 0$

34b) $(U_{t-6}^{t-1} - SACT_{W_{t-1,\,t-6}})\delta_{23} \geq 0$

35) $SACT_{W_{t,\,t-1}} - SACT_{W_t}(1-\delta_{24}) - U_{t-1}^{t}\delta_{24} = 0$

35a) $(SACT_{W_t} - U_{t-1}^{t}) - M\delta_{24} \leq 0$

35b) $(SACT_{W_t} - U_{t-1}^{t})\delta_{24} \geq 0$

36) $SACT_{W_{t,\,t-2}} - (SACT_{W_t} - SACT_{W_{t,\,t-1}})(1-\delta_{25}) - U_{t-2}^{t}\delta_{25} = 0$

36a) $(SACT_{W_t} - SACT_{W_{t,\,t-1}} - U_{t-2}^{t}) - M\delta_{25} \leq 0$

36b) $(SACT_{W_t} - SACT_{W_{t,\,t-1}} - U_{t-2}^{t})\delta_{25} \geq 0$

37) $SACT_{W_{t,\,t-3}} - (SACT_{W_t} - \sum_{i=1}^{2} SACT_{W_{t,\,t-i}})(1-\delta_{26}) - U_{t-3}^{t}\delta_{26} = 0$

37a) $(SACT_{W_t} - \sum_{i=1}^{2} SACT_{W_{t,\,t-i}} - U_{t-3}^{t}) - M\delta_{26} \leq 0$

37b) $(SACT_{W_t} - \sum_{i=1}^{2} SACT_{W_{t,t-i}} - U_{t-3}^{t})\delta_{26} \geq 0$

38) $SACT_{W_{t,t-4}} - (SACT_{W_t} - \sum_{i=1}^{3} SACT_{W_{t,t-i}})(1-\delta_{27}) - U_{t-4}^{t}\delta_{27} = 0$

38a) $(SACT_{W_t} - \sum_{i=1}^{3} SACT_{W_{t,t-i}} - U_{t-4}^{t}) - M\delta_{27} \leq 0$

38b) $(SACT_{W_t} - \sum_{i=1}^{3} SACT_{W_{t,t-i}} - U_{t-4}^{t})\delta_{27} \geq 0$

39) $SACT_{W_{t,t-5}} - (SACT_{W_t} - \sum_{i=1}^{4} SACT_{W_{t,t-i}})(1-\delta_{28}) - U_{t-5}^{t}\delta_{28} = 0$

39a) $(SACT_{W_t} - \sum_{i=1}^{4} SACT_{W_{t,t-i}} - U_{t-5}^{t}) - M\delta_{28} \leq 0$

39b) $(SACT_{W_t} - \sum_{i=1}^{4} SACT_{W_{t,t-i}} - U_{t-5}^{t})\delta_{28} \geq 0$

40) $SACT_{W_{t,t-6}} - (SACT_{W_t} - \sum_{i=1}^{5} SACT_{W_{t,t-i}})(1-\delta_{29}) - U_{t-6}^{t}\delta_{29} = 0$

40a) $(SACT_{W_t} - \sum_{i=1}^{5} SACT_{W_{t,t-i}} - U_{t-6}^{t}) - M\delta_{29} \leq 0$

40b) $(SACT_{W_t} - \sum_{i=1}^{5} SACT_{W_{t,t-i}} - U_{t-6}^{t})\delta_{29} \geq 0$

41) $ACT_{R_t} = \sum_{i=1}^{6} SACT_{W_{t,t-i}}$

42) $SACT_{F,t+1} - SACT_{F,t} + SACT_{F,t}(1-\delta_{30}) + U_t\delta_{30} - SACT_{W_t}$

$$+\sum_{i=1}^{6} SACT_{W_{t,t-i}} - \sum_{i=1}^{3} SACT_{L_{t,t-i}} = 0$$

42a) $(SACT_{F,t} - U_t) - M\delta_{30} \le 0$

42b) $(SACT_{F,t} - U_t)\delta_{30} \ge 0$

43) $MCT_t - T\pi'_t + (1-\delta_{31})sW_t/(1-s) + s\pi'_t\delta_{31} = 0$

43a) $(sW_t/(1-s) - s\pi'_t) - M\delta_{31} \le 0$

43b) $(sW_t/(1-s) - s\pi'_t)\delta_{31} \ge 0$

The objective function of the model will be unchanged.

Part II
EUROPE

4 A review of business taxation in Europe

Graham Clayton and Peter Harnett

Introduction

This chapter briefly covers the tax systems of the following European countries:

Belgium	Denmark	Eire	France	Germany
Greece	Italy	Luxembourg	Netherlands	Portugal
Spain	Sweden	Switzerland		

The United Kingdom is included as a "base case" in order to facilitate international comparisons. The reader should refer back to Part One for an analysis of the impact of corporate taxation on investment in the UK context.

This chapter provides, in tabular format, a summarised comparison of the treatment of similar business events in different European countries. These details provide the necessary information to assess correctly the true, comparative rates of tax on investments made in one country from another. These comparisons can be summarised in the measure known as the effective marginal tax rate (King and Fullerton, 1984) which takes into account all the divergent rates and treatments in different countries.

When considering a completely domestic investment project the effects of taxation on the project's cash flows must be considered if the correct decisions are to be made. These issues and techniques are covered in Part I. Likewise, when a company comes to consider investment proposals, all or part of which will be located in a country other than the company's country of residence, the international tax effects must be factored into the appraisal calculations. However, it is insufficient to consider merely the different 'headline' rates of tax in the countries under consideration. This is because the tax base, treatment of dividends and administration can be very different in different countries.

Domestic tax rates can only be regarded as the final tax rate where a company is resident in the country in which it invests. If this is not the case the final tax rate will also be affected by the treatment of foreign source income by the country of residency. Additionally, many countries levy withholding taxes on profits which are distributed by a company to its parent company in another country. Frequently the rates of withholding tax vary according to whether the distributions are made in the form of dividends or interest payments. The reader should note that withholding taxes are charged on top of the domestic corporation taxes. The rates of such withholding taxes vary according to bilateral tax treaties, the provisions of which differ depending on the two countries involved.

Cultural and political value systems have placed considerable emphasis on the goal of income redistribution in Europe and consequently post war rates of tax have been high across the continent. This was also due in part to the high costs of post-war reconstruction. From 1955 to 1983, tax, as a percentage of European GDP rose from 28.9 per cent to 39.7 per cent. In comparison, over the same period tax as a proportion of GDP in the USA rose from 23.6 per cent to 29 per cent.

There is currently wide variation in both tax rates and systems. Eire has a corporate tax rate of 10 per cent for companies operating in certain industries (mainly in the manufacturing sector, but including projects in the Shannonm Free Airport Development Area and the International Financial Services Centre) whereas Germany has a rate of 50 per cent (on undistributed profits). Some European countries operate a partial imputation / tax credit system for the taxation of dividends but a significant number have alternative systems. Countries such as Holland operate a classical system where the corporation is regarded as an entity entirely separate from its shareholders. Distributed income is therefore effectively taxed twice. Germany operates both a split rate and full imputation system and Belgium offers shareholders the choice of low rate double taxation or an imputation type system.

When distributions are received from an overseas subsidiary there may be a third level of taxation in some countries. A number of European countries simply exempt all foreign source income whereas others, including the UK operate a credit system. Under the credit system the amounts of tax actually paid on the distributed income are compared with the amounts that would have been paid if the income had been domestically generated. If more tax would have been paid if the income had been earned domestically the company becomes liable for the difference. Likewise, if the difference is negative, a tax credit is issued. Another possible treatment is partial exemption such as is used in Italy, France and Belgium, where 60 per cent, 90 per cent and 95 per cent of foreign source income is exempt from further domestic taxation.

With the exception of a number of countries which operate "enterprise zones" 100 per cent capital allowances are no longer available anywhere in Europe. Consequently European investments involve the allocation of initial investment costs over the life of the project in accordance with certain rules. Since the measurement of true economic depreciation is highly problematic (and would certainly be more costly than beneficial from the tax authorities' perspective) countries have had to choose more workable strategies for dealing with depreciation. Some countries such as France have elected to allow companies to use accounting depreciation, calculated according to the generally accepted rules of accounting, for tax depreciation purposes. Others, including the UK, have chosen the route of defining specified rates for specified classes of depreciable assets in statutory tax laws. With minor differences in detail, these two strategies represent the two basic approaches currently used in Europe.

Not only are different depreciation systems in operation but the definition of depreciable assets differs from country to country. Additionally, inflation erodes the present value of the depreciation tax shield which is fixed in nominal terms. The existence of differential rates of inflation adds yet another layer of complexity to trans-national tax calculations. With the exception of Denmark, no other European country permits the annual indexation of the remaining depreciable balance of assets.

Models which have been developed to calculate effective marginal tax rates have shown that some countries' tax systems actually subsidise investments made by companies in another country while other tax regimes discourage investment. For example, Devereux and Pearson (1989) showed that UK companies investing in a hypothetical 'average' project in Eire only needed to achieve a pre-tax return of 4.71 per cent to reach a post-tax rate of return of 5 per cent. In contrast, the same project would have to earn a return of 7.28 per cent in Denmark in order to provide the company's UK shareholders with an after-tax return of 5 per cent (based on 1989 tax rates and laws.) Such discrepancies obviously have important implications for financial strategists when considering competing location proposals and there are also issues linked to the concepts of economically efficient allocation of resources and European tax harmonization proposals.

Table 4.1 provides a summary of the major elements of different European countries' tax regimes. It covers the tax treatment of dividends receivable in the hands of a company's shareholders, the tax base used for calculating taxable income and a brief summary of other significant taxes levied on corporations operating in that country. Many of the items in this introductory table are treated in more detail in the tables which follow.

Before continuing to expand in detail on the components of Table 4.1, the following sections contain a brief summary of the headline rates of corporate tax in the countries under investigation, together with brief

Table 4.1
Major elements of European tax regimes

				Tax bases			
	Dividends	*Depreciation*	*Capital Gains*	*Losses*	*Stock*	*Interest*	*Foreign Source Income*
UK	Imputation	Statutory rules govern capital allowances	Taxed as income after indexation allowance	c/fd No limit c/bk 3 years	Lower of cost and N.R.V. Cost based on FIFO	Allowable charge on income	Taxable; credit given for withholding tax and underlying overseas taxes paid (subject to a min. 10% shareholding)
Bel	Mixed	In principle, based on anticipated useful lives	Taxed at income tax rates. There are certain exemption	c/fd No limit c/bk No	Lower of cost and N.R.V. FIFO, LIFO or AVCO are permissable	Allowable charge on income	Taxable subject to double tax treaties. 85-90% of dividends received on shares held for more than 1 year are exempt
Den	Imputation	Calculated mostly on a reducing balance basis (up to 30% p.a.). Advanced allowances are available on large capital investments	Taxed at corporate tax rate. Disposals of some assets which have been owned for longer periods of time may be exempt	c/fd 5 years c/bk No	Lower of cost or replacement value.Up to 26% of the stock balance may be written off of taxable profit	Allowable charge on income	Taxable, but 50% relief is available if it is received from a susidiary/branch with which the company is jointly taxed. Otherwise, a tax credit will be available

Eir	Imputation	Capital allowance system. Pre 1992 assets are eligible for enhanced initial allowances and 100% allowances are available in certain areas	Taxed as income. Taxation on gains may be deferred through re-investment	c/fd No limit c/bk 1 year	Lower of cost and market. Weighted average cost price but FIFO is also accepted	Allowable to the extent that interest is of a "reasonable" amount	Credit for underlying tax is available but this must not exceed the amount that would have been paid under Irish tax
Fra	Tax credit	Normally straight line over assets' useful life. Reducing balance method is allowable in some cases	Taxed at normal rates if short term. Normally a reduced rate (18%) if long term	c/fd 5 years c/bk 3 years	Lower of cost and market. Weighted average cost and FIFO bases are permitted	Allowable if charged at a commercial rate	Taxable when due to a resident corporation. Credit available via participation exemption (dividends) or tax credit (other income)
Ger	Imputation	Straight line or declining balance methods are allowed, based on officially established estimated useful lives	Taxed at normal corporate tax rates. Tax may be deferred through re-investment of proceeds	c/fd No limit c/bk 2 years	Generally acquisition or production cost. LIFO may be used under certain conditions	Allowable unless thin capitalization exists in which case debt is treated as equity	Tax credit available up to the amount of the German taxes payable on the foreign source income. Tax treaties often provide further exemptions.

Gre	Dividend deductions	Straight line rates for various types of asset are set out in law	Gains from disposals and voluntary revaluations are taxed as income. Exemptions exist for certain types of asset and where participating interests exist	c/fd 5 years c/bk No	Lower of cost and market. Any cost method is acceptable, provided it is applied consistently	Allowable	Tax credit available up to the amount of the Greek tax payable on the foreign source income
Ita	Tax credit	Depreciation rates are set by the Ministry of Finance. Only the straight line method is allowed	Taxed as income. Tax may be paid in instalments	c/fd 5 years c/bk No	Lower of cost and market value. Choice of methods (eg FIFO, AVCO) provided the valuation is not lower than if LIFO had been used	Allowable with restrictions	Tax credit of up to the amount which results from prorating total taxes by the proportion of foreign source income to total income
Lux	Classical	Straight line or declining balance methods may be used apart from buildings which must be depreciated straight line	Taxed at normal rates. Tax may be deferred through re-investment and certain exemptions exist	c/fd No limit c/bk No	Lower of cost and market. FIFO, AVCO or LIFO may be chosen	Allowable. Debt to equity rules apply very occasionally	Tax credit available for foreign source income which has been subject to a similar tax regime

Net	Classical	Straight line or declining balance over generally accepted useful life periods	Taxed at normal rates. Gains may be deferred and tax paid through lower, future allowances. The Participation Exemption may also apply	c/fd 8 years c/bk 3 years	Lower of cost and market. LIFO and base stock methods are acceptable. Replacement cost is not acceptable for tax purposes	Allowable	Where no tax treaties exist a unilateral decree provides relief for underlying tax on foreign source income
Por	Split rate	Maximum rates are set by law for specific industries and general purposes	Taxed as income. An adjustment may be claimed to account for currency devaluation	c/fd 5 years c/bk No	Various methods; acquisition or production cost, standard cost, sales price less normal margin (up to 20%) or special valuation methods	Allowable	Foreign source income, net of foreign tax, is taxable unless a tax treaty exists
Spa	Classical	Straight line or, for certain types of tangible assets, declining balance. Depreciation rates are fixed by law	Taxed as income. Exemptions exist where disposal proceeds are re-invested in qualifying assets	c/fd 5 years c/bk No	Acquisition or production cost on an average basis. FIFO is generally accepted but LIFO is not allowed	Allowable	If foreign tax is higher than would have been due under Spanish tax, relief is available up to the amount of the difference

Swe	Imputation	Straight line or declining balance. Assets with useful lives of less than 3 years may be expensed as purchased	Taxed as income	c/fd No limit c/bk No	Lower of cost and market value. Alternatively, stock may be valued at 97% of total purchase cost provided this method is applied to all stock	Allowable although equity must remain at a certain level to avoid compulsory liquidation	Unless a tax treaty exists relief is not usually available for foreign taxes paid
Swi	Classical	Standard rates are generally accepted. Some cantons have favourable first year provisions	Taxed as income. Some gains may be liable to a Real Property Tax. Shares are exempt in some cantons	c/fd 3 years c/bk No	Lower of cost and market value. Legislation allows this cost to be written down by one third for tax purposes	Allowable. Some cantons have legal debt to equity requirements	Income from permanent overseas establishments is not taxable

details of other significant local or municipal taxes and notable exceptions to the national base case.

Corporate tax rates

United Kingdom

Resident corporations are subject to tax on worldwide profits. Companies are resident if they are incorporated in the UK or central management and control is exercised from the UK. Non-resident corporations are subject to tax on UK source profits only.

Rates: resident and non-residents via UK branches are taxed at 33 per cent (for the year ended 31st March 1992.) Companies with profits of less than £250,000 are taxed at the small company rate of 25 per cent.

Belgium

Resident companies are taxed on their worldwide profits and non-residents are taxed on Belgian source profits. The rate for 1992 is 39 per cent.

Denmark

Resident companies are taxed on their worldwide income. A resident company is one which is incorporated in accordance with Danish company law: location of management control and trading activities are not relevant.

Non-resident companies are taxed on Danish source profits from permanent establishments, income from land, royalties, dividends and certain other sources.

The rate is 38 per cent plus a 30 per cent withholding tax on distributions from Danish companies.

Eire

Resident companies are taxed on worldwide profits (income and chargeable gains, excluding distributions received from other resident companies). Non-resident companies with branches or agencies in Eire pay tax on profits connected with those branches or agencies. Non-resident companies with no branches or agencies are liable to tax on Irish source income and capital gains tax on certain Irish assets.

Resident companies must account for advance corporation tax (ACT) on distributions unless payable to a foreign 75 per cent parent company which is resident in a country with which Eire has a tax treaty. ACT may be offset against income but not chargeable gains.

The standard rate of tax is 40 per cent. Capital gains tax is between 30 per cent and 50 per cent depending on the period during which the disposed assets were owned. Certain manufacturing, financial, shipping and service companies are subject to tax at a reduced rate of 10 per cent. Standard ACT is currently 1/3. On dividends paid out of profits taxed at 10 per cent the rate is 1/18.

France

Generally, resident and non-resident companies are liable to tax on profits earned in France. The corporation tax rate is 34 per cent.

Germany

Resident companies are taxed on worldwide profits and non-residents on German source income. Resident companies pay tax at 50 per cent on retained profits and 36 per cent on distributed profits.

All businesses are subject to an additional municipal trade tax (1992 average, 17 per cent) which is deductible for corporate tax purposes. Special reduced rates used to apply for West Berlin (22.5 per cent corporate tax and a reduction of approximately 50 per cent in trade tax.)

Greece

Resident companies are taxed on worldwide income. The definition of residency includes companies with permanent establishments in Greece such as offices, shops, agencies, warehouses and laboratories. Non-residents are taxed on Greek source income.

The corporate tax rate on retained profits is 46 per cent with a reduction to 40 per cent for manufacturing and mining companies and 35 per cent for companies registered on the Athens Stock Exchange.

Five per cent of net profits must be credited to a legal reserve each year and at least 35 per cent of net profits must be distributed as dividends, (or 6 per cent of paid in capital if this is more.)

There are a number of tax rates on dividends receivable:

Registered shares on the Athens stock exchange	42%
Bearer shares on the Athens stock exchange	45%
Unlisted registered shares	47%
Unlisted bearer shares	50%

Italy

There are both national and local corporate income taxes in Italy. Resident companies are taxed on worldwide profits for national tax purposes and non-residents are liable on Italian source profits. Local corporate taxes apply only to Italian source profits. The national tax rate is 36 per cent and the local tax rate is 16.2 per cent. Local taxes are 75 per cent deductible for national tax purposes which gives an overall combined tax rate of 47.826 per cent.

Upon distribution exempt profits become liable to a compensatory tax at the rate of 36 per cent. Exempt profits generally relate to "Mezzogiorno" investments in Southern Italy.

Luxembourg

Resident companies are taxed on worldwide income and non-residents on Luxembourg source income. The corporate tax rate is 33 per cent plus an additional 1 per cent surcharge for unemployment contributions. Municipal tax is levied at the rate of 9.09 per cent and is deductible for national tax purposes. Luxembourg also has a corporate net worth tax, charged at the rate of 0.5 per cent.

Netherlands

Resident companies are taxed on worldwide income and non-residents on Dutch source income. The rate is 40 per cent on profits of up to Dfl250,000 and 35 per cent thereafter. Certain elements of income may be excluded under the participation exemption.

Portugal

Resident companies are taxed on worldwide income at the rate of 36 per cent. Non-resident companies are taxed on Portuguese source income and non-residents without a permanent establishment are taxed at the reduced rate of 25 per cent. Municipal surcharges are levied at rates of up to 10 per cent of the national corporate tax rate, ie.3.6 per cent.

Spain

Residents are taxed on worldwide income and non-residents with Spanish branches are taxed on Spanish source profits at the rate of 35 per cent. Non-resident companies which do not have permanent establishments in Spain are subject to different rates of tax on different types of income:

General income, dividends, interest	25%
Fees for management support services	14%
Capital gains	35%
Income from re-insurance activities	4%

Sweden

Swedish corporate tax is charged at the rate of 30 per cent on the worldwide income of resident companies and the Swedish source profits of non-residents. Most companies can offset part of their profits against a tax equalisation reserve: either 30 per cent of the difference between assets and debts at the end of the fiscal year or 15 per cent of the salaries paid during the year. This can reduce the effective tax rate to a minimum of 23.7 per cent.

Switzerland

Resident companies are taxed on their worldwide income except that derived from real property or permanent establishments abroad. Non-residents are taxed on Swiss source income only. Federal and cantonal tax rates are graduated according to the return on equity ratio. A maximum Federal tax rate of 9.8 per cent occurs when earnings exceed 23.1478 per cent of equity. Canton and municipal tax rates vary widely between 10 per cent and 27 per cent of pre-tax income.

Table 4.2
The treatment of dividends

System	**Country**
Classical	Luxembourg
The corporation is regarded as an entity separate from its shareholders	Netherlands
	Spain
	Switzerland
Partial Integration	Greece
Dividend deductions	Portugal
Split rate system	
Imputational/tax credit system	Belgium
(Belgium is mixed with a shareholder choice between a low rate classical system or an imputation system.)	Denmark
	Eire
	France
	Germany
	Italy
	Sweden
	UK

The following section gives a brief summary of the most notable items of business expenditure which are not deductible for the purposes of corporate tax.

Non-deductible items

United Kingdom

Expenses not wholly and exclusively incurred for the purposes of trade are disallowed.
Entertainment: expenses are only allowable when entertaining overseas trading customers and clients and the amount involved are "reasonable".
Pre-commencement expenditure incurred more than three years before the start of trading is not allowable.
Dividends.
Corporation tax.

Belgium

Only 75 per cent automobile expenses are allowable.
Only 50 per cent of reception and restaurant expenses are allowable.
Provisions are only tax deductible if they relate to definite losses incurred during the operating year concerned and if they are accounted for.
Dividends.
Corporation tax.

Denmark

Formation and liquidation costs.
Penalties, fines and penalty interest paid to government bodies.
Dividends.
Corporation tax.
Certain stamp duties.
Entertainment costs, gifts etc. are only 25 per cent deductible.

Eire

Any expense not incurred wholly and exclusively for the purpose of earning income, with the exception of:

- superannuation / pension contributions
- capital expenditure on acquiring know-how and industrial information
- non-capital expenditure on scientific research (even if not incurred for the purposes of trade).

Certain premiums paid for the granting of a lease in respect of trading premises.

Entertainment expenses (food, drink and gifts). Food, drink and accommodation expenses for employees where incidental to entertaining customers are non-deductible.
Pre-trading start up expenses, with the exception of the acquisition of depreciable assets (depreciable as from the start date) and pre-commencement expenditure on recruitment and training of workers or staff for companies setting up a manufacturing trade (may be written off over three years.)
The deductibility of automobile expenses is restricted.
Interest deductions must be reasonable.

France

Dividends, corporation tax, personal expenses and goodwill.

Germany

Only 50 per cent of supervisory board fees and expenses incurred for non taxable income items are allowable.
Corporation tax.
Net assets tax.
Dividends.
Start up, formation and R & D expenses may not be capitalised for tax purposes.

Greece

Bad debts are only allowable if the debtor's insolvency is officially recognised.
Administration expenses allocated to branches by overseas foreign companies are only allowable up to an amount equal to 2 per cent of the gross revenues earned in Greece.
Corporation tax.

Italy

Restrictions on interest deductibility.
Not more than 50 per cent of organization and start up expenses may be amortised in any one year.
Maintenance, repair and transformation expenses are deductible as long as they are less than 5 per cent of the relevant total depreciable asset cost at the beginning of the fiscal year. Excesses may be carried forward for up to 5 years and written off at not more than 20 per cent p.a.
Dividends.
Corporation tax (however local income tax (ILOR) is deductible).

Luxembourg

Expenditure incurred in relation to exempt income is not allowable.
Corporation tax.
Dividends.

Netherlands

Business gifts exceeding Dfl. 50.
Meals, drinks, clothing and conference expenses are only partially deductible.
If expenses which are incurred for the benefit of shareholders exceed the normal (arm's length) level then the excess is considered non-deductible.
Corporation tax.
Dividends.

Portugal

Corporation tax.
Dividends.

Spain

Penalties and fines.
Corporation tax.
Gifts and donations to non-approved organisations.
Expenditure incurred for the enhancement or improvement of capital assets.
Depreciation charges that exceed the maximum statutory rates unless the excess can be proved to correspond to actual depreciation incurred.

Sweden

Certain payroll and inventory reserve allowances have now been discontinued. They have been replaced by a tax equalisation reserve provision. In general, a write off up to 30 per cent of the corporation's equity or 15 per cent of salaries paid during the year is available.

Switzerland

In general, any expense which is not directly related to the corporation's business is disallowed. In particular, hidden distributions to shareholders and excessive depreciation rates are not allowable.

Depreciation

Depreciation and capital allowance tax shields can have a major impact on the timing and magnitude of an investment project's cash flows. Table 4.3 summarises the type and scope of depreciation regimes currently operating in the countries covered in this chapter.

Capital gains

The treatment and taxation of capital gains throughout the countries of Europe is broadly similar in many respects. Most countries start by treating gains as part of ordinary income, liable to taxation at mainstream corporate tax rates. Also, most countries allow a number of exceptions and exemptions. Most of these are based on the type of assets disposed of, the period of ownership prior to disposal, the subsequent use of the disposal proceeds, or some combination of these criteria.

Similarly, most countries allow losses to be set against current and future income in order to mitigate tax liabilities. International differences occur relating to the allowable carry forward period and the types of income against which certain losses may be offset. Countries which still permit losses to be carried back against the income of preceding periods are now quite few. Details of the treatment of capital gains are provided in Table 4.4.

Interest deductibility

The theory and practuice of capital structure is discussed in detail in Chapter Six. There are two specific points to be made here.

Firstly, the extent to which companies are free to gear up their capital structures differs across Europe.

Secondly, in the situation where an overseas subsidiary make interest payment remittances to parent companies located in different countries, withholding tax on interest and the rates of tax on foreign source income have to be factored into the calculations. A problem of thin capitalization occurs because companies prefer to finance investments abroad through debt rather than equity because interest payments on loans are tax deductible. If a parent funds an overseas subsidiary through debt and pays the same tax rate there will be no net advantage. However, if the parent pays a lower rate there will be a gain - thin capitalization leads to a lower total tax burden.

Table 4.3
Depreciation regimes operating within the selected countries

	Buildings	Machinery & Equipment	Other Items	Further notes
UK	Capital expenditure on buildings and structures used for specified industrial and related purposes is allowed at 4% p.a. on a straight line basis. There is a temporary 20% initial allowance in the first year	Machinery and plant (including motor vehicles) can be written down at 25% of the new or second hand remaining cost, on a reducing balance basis. There is a temporary 40% initial allowance in the first year		Cars are subject to a maximum annual allowance of £2,000. Assets leased to a foreign lessee may, in some cases, qualify for only 10% relief (or no relief at all)
Bel	Readily accepted straight line rates: Office buildings 3% Industrial buildings 5% Chemical plants 8-12.5%	Readily accepted straight line rates: Machinery & plant 10-20% Office furniture & equipment 10-15% Small tools 33-100%	Rolling stock 20-25% Intangibles can be amortised over a period of not less than 5 years	In principle, depreciation rates are based on anticipated useful economic lives but these straight line rates are commonly accepted by the tax authorities. Declining balance and accelerated depreciation are allowed under certain circumstances. Intangible amortisation period exceptions exist for R & D expenses and Belgian audio-visual projects

Den	Commercial buildings (excluding offices): straight line based on cash equivalent cost price (ie cost price minus the excess of the nominal value of mortgage bonds, loans etc. over market value) Agricultural, industrial and retail buildings: straight line at 6% of cost up to 60%, 2% p.a. thereafter. Buildings for entertainment and hotel industry: straight line at 4% p.a. up to 40%, 1% p.a. thereafter	Machinery, equipment, cars and ships may be depreciated by 25% in the year of acquisition and by 30% (declining balance) thereafter. Depreciable assets with a unit price of less than DKK 4,500 (1988) or a useful life of less than 3 years may be expensed in the year of purchase. The limit is inflation adjusted annually	Installations in depreciable buildings may be depreciated at 8% p.a. up to 80%, 4% p.a. thereafter. Goodwill purchased prior to 01/07/82 may be amortised at 15% straight line. After this date amortisation is disallowed. Assets leased back to previous owners by Danish companies may not be depreciated if the lessee is not subject to Danish tax	Office buildings can only be depreciated if attached to a factory. Leasehold improvements may be amortised straight line over the agreed rental period subject to a minimum of 5 years. If there is no agreed period then over not less than 20 years. The depreciable balance of assets acquired after 01/01/82 may be adjusted in line with a price index. Advance depreciation using the straight line method may be claimed in certain circumstances
Eir	Industrial buildings, hotels, multi-storey car parks, farm buildings and mineral analysis laboratories are qualifying assets. Offices, shops and commercial premises (except in designated urban renewal areas) do not qualify. Qualifying buildings purchased after 31/03/92 may be written off at 4% p.a.	Assets purchased after 31/03/92 may be written off at 10%, 12.5% or 25% p.a. depending on the type and condition of the asset	Cars may be written off at up to 25% subject to a limit of IR£7,000. Capital allowances are also available on scientific research costs, patent rights, dredging, toll roads, bridges, viaducts and mining developments	Allowances of up to 100% on buildings, plant and equipment may be claimed by qualifying companies (mainly those in the Dublin Custom House Docks Area or the Shanon Airport Development Zone.) Prior to 1992 initial allowances (25% 1991-92, 50% 1990-91 and 100% pre 1990) were available with additional "free depreciation" claims available
Fra	Straight line method, based on cost @ 5% p.a. (industrial buildings), 2-5% p.a. (office & residential buildings)	Straight line method, based on cost @ 10% p.a. (machinery & equipment), 10-20% (office quipment)	Straight line method, based on cost @ 20-25% p.a.for motor vehicles	Some assets can be depreciated on the reducing balance method

Ger	Office and factory buildings constructed before 31/03/85 are usually depreciated over 50 years. Those constructed after this date may be depreciated straight line over 25 years or using accelerated depreciation at 10% for the first 4 years	Typically straight line method : Machinery & equipment @ 10% and office equipment @ 10-20% p.a.	Typically straight line method : Motor vehicles @ 20-33%, patents @ 12-20% p.a. and goodwill over 15 years.	Straight line or declining balance methods are allowed, the latter being limited to the lower of 30% and 3 times the straight line rate. Useful lives are published by the Ministry of Finance based on tax audit experience. Departures are allowed but require explanation
Gre	Industrial buildings @ 8%	Machinery and equipment @ 4-20%	Commercial vehicles and computers @ 20%	Straight line depreciation rates are set out in tax laws relating to specific assets. Rates for certain productive assets may go up to 150% depending on location and use
Ita	Straight line method @ 3-7% p.a.	Straight line method @ 6-17.5% for plant & machinery and 12% p.a. for office equipment	Vehicles depreciated @ 20-25% p.a. straight line. Purchased goodwill may be amortised at rates of up to 20% of cost. Patents, trademarks and know how may be amortised at up to one third of cost each year. Assets with a unit cost of less than L1,000,000 may be written off in full in the year of acquisition	Straight line rates are established by the Ministry of Finance. Higher rates may be used if assets are utilised at unusually high rates. In addition to normal depreciation, accelerated depreciation is allowed in the first 3 years at a rate equal to 1.5% of the ordinary rate. If actual depreciation is less than 50% of the official rate the difference cannot be carried forward unless utilisation is unusually low

Lux	Buildings used for commercial purposes generally have an estimated useful life of 25 years. Average straight line rates are between 1.5% and 4%	In general, machinery is depreciated over 10 years. Average rates are 20-25% (declining balance). Equipment may be depreciated over 5-10 years and cars over 3-5 years	Moveable assets may be depreciated using the declining balance method at up to 3 times the straight line rate or 30%, whichever is lower. Depreciable assets with useful lives less than 1 year and those with costs less than LF 35,000 may be written off in full in the year of purchase	
Net	Depreciation is generally charged over 33-50 years at a rate between 2.5% and 4%	Plant, machinery and equipment is charged over 5-10 years at between 10% and 20%. In 1991 the average rate was 20.33%.	Straight line typically - vehicles @ 20%, know-how/patents @ 25% p.a. and purchased goodwill is written off over 5 years	
Por	Industrial buildings 5% (Straight line) Commercial buildings 2% (Straight line)	Plant and machinery 5% to 25%	Vehicles 12.5 - 25% p.a. straight line	Maximum rates are established by law. Lower rates may be used but if the rate is below 50% of the official rate the balance may not be carried forward and total depreciation will not be achieved
Spa	Industrial buildings 3% (Maximum official rate)	Office furniture 10% Machinery 10% Vehicles 14% Computers 15% (Maximum official rates)	Intangible assets may be amortised if they can be shown to depreciate and have a limited useful life. All tangible assets with a useful life of at least 1 fiscal period may be depreciated	Depreciation rates are fixed by law. Higher rates may be used if companies can prove actual depreciation was higher. The declining balance method may be used only for certain assets, e.g. industrial and farming machinery, vehicles, information systems etc

Swe	General rates - Commercial buildings 1.5% to 5% Factory buildings 4% Office buildings 2% (Straight line rates)	Straight line up to 20% p.a. or 30% p.a. declining balance. (The same method must be used for both equipment and machinery in any year but changes can be made year to year)	The cost of land improvements may be written off at 5% p.a. Equipment with a useful life of less than 3 years or a cost of less than SEK1,000 may be written off in the year of purchase. Patents, trademarks and purchased goodwill may be written off on the same basis as machinery and equipment	
Swi	(Normally straight line) Commercial buildings 2% Industrial buildings 4%	(Normally straight line) Machinery 20%	Patents and goodwill 20% Small tools 22.5%	Standard rates are generally accepted. Some Cantons have favourable rates eg. Zurich allows up to 80% first year depreciation. If the declining balance method is used normal rates may be doubled

Table 4.4
Capital gains and capital and trading losses

	Treatment of Gains and Losses
UK	Indexation relief is available on capital gains which are then taxed at corporation tax rates. Gains on certain types of assets may be deferred if the proceeds are reinvested in specified types of assets 12 months before or 3 years after the disposal. Capital losses can be carried forward against capital gains without limit. They may not be carried back. Trading losses may be set against other income or chargeable gains during the year or carried back against the total profits of the previous three years. Losses may also be carried forward without time limit for relief against future income arising from the same trade. Losses from one company may be set against the income and capital gains for the same period of 75% owned subsidiaries.
Bel	Capital gains on disposals of tangible and intangible assets are generally taxed at corporate income tax rates. However, with the exception of shareholdings and other financial assets, if the asset has been owned for more than 5 years and the disposal proceeds are reinvested in qualifying assets within 3 years (5 years in certain cases) the taxation on the gain may be deferred for the depreciation period of the replacement asset. Gains on the disposal of shares and other financial assets which have been held for more than 5 years are exempt if the proceeds are reinvested in qualifying assets within 3 years. Otherwise gains are taxable at 50% of the corporate income tax rate. Capital and trading losses may be carried forward without time limit but may not be carried back. There are carryover limitations in the case of tax-free mergers between profitable companies and companies with carryover losses.
Den	Capital gains are usually taxed at corporate income tax rates. Gains realised on the sale of goodwill are exempt and gains on the disposal of certain bonds and debentures bought at discount, shares owned for more than 3 years and buildings owned for more than 7 years are also exempt unless sold as part of normal business activities. Trading losses may be carried forward for up to 5 years and may be set against income and chargeable gains. Limitations apply if more than 50% of a company's share capital changes hands. Losses arising from the disposal of shares in a subsidiary cannot be deducted.

Eir	Capital gains on the disposal of certain assets may be deferred if the proceeds are reinvested in replacement assets within 12 months prior to the disposal or up to 3 years after. Otherwise gains are taxed at the corporate income tax rate. Capital losses may be carried forward without limit but may not be carried back. Trading losses may be set against other income or chargeable gains in the year incurred or the preceding year, provided the same trade was carried on. Alternatively, losses may be carried forward indefinitely and set against future income arising from the same trade or may be transferred to profitable, 75% owned subsidiaries during the year they were incurred.
Fra	Gains on the disposal of assets owned for less than two years and recaptured depreciation must be included as part of the tax base in the year they occur and they are taxed as operating profits. Short term losses can be used to reduce ordinary income in the year they occur. Gains on the disposal of assets held for more than two years are taxed at 18%, with the exception of development land and certain types of securities, which are taxed at 25%. If the proceeds are distributed there is an additional complimentary tax. Long term losses can be carried forward for up to 10 years against long term gains. Trading losses may generally be carried forward for up to 5 years with the exception of losses due to depreciation which may be carried forward without limit. Companies subject to corporate tax may also carry back losses against undistributed profits in the previous 3 years. This results in a tax credit (limited in size to the amount of tax paid in the previous 3 years) which may be set against taxable income in the following 5 years. Any remaining balance is refunded at the end of the 5 years. These provisions are subject to the continuance of broadly similar trading activities during the carry forward period.
Ger	Capital gains are taxed at normal corporation tax rates. Gains on the sale of certain assets which are used to purchase similar replacement assets may be deferred. Noncompensated trading losses of up to DM10 million, incurred after 1985 must be carried back to the two prior years. Any remaining balance can be carried forward up to five years. This provision relates to corporate tax but not trade tax. Larger losses incurred after 1985 may be carried forward without limit.
Gre	Gains on the sale of fixed assets or those arising through voluntary revaluation are taxed as income. Gains on the disposal of real estate and ships are exempt. Gains on the disposal of intangible assets are subject to tax at 46% regardless of industry or exchange listing. Transfers of entire businesses or goodwill together with the transfer of a participating interest in a limited liability company are taxed at 20%. Losses may be carried forward for 5 years and may not be carried back.

Ita	Capital gains are treated as ordinary income, however, companies have the option of paying the tax on the gain in the year of realisation or in equal annual instalments over a period not exceeding 5 years. Losses may be carried forward for up to 5 years but may not be carried back. This applies only to national income taxes and does not extend to local taxes. Upon merger companies may carry forward unrelieved losses for the remainder of the unexpired carry forward period and these may be set against the merged company's profits. This provision is limited to the amount of each of the merged companies' net equity.
Lux	Capital gains are usually subject to tax at normal corporate tax rates. Gains on real estate and permanent investments held for longer than 5 years may be deferred if they are reinvested in business assets. Gains on shareholdings of 25% or with an acquisition cost of at least LF250 million are exempt provided that the share were owned continuously for a period of at least 12 months prior to the disposal. Losses incurred before the 1991 tax year may be carried forward for up to 5 years. Those incurred later may be carried forward without limit. In neither case may losses be carried back.
Net	Capital gains are usually taxed as income subject to a number of exceptions. Gains may be deferred by reinvesting the proceeds in similar assets provided certain conditions are met. The gain is credited to a replacement reserve and the replacement asset must be purchased before the end of the fourth year following the disposal. On purchase the gain is deducted from the cost of the new asset and the gain is effectively taxed through a lower depreciation allowance on the replacement asset. The Participation Exemption allows gains from investments in Dutch and foreign subsidiaries to be realized free of tax. To qualify for this exemption the Dutch company must own at least 5% of the paid in share capital of the subsidiary and the shares must not be held as inventory. Also, if the subsidiary is resident in a foreign country it must be subject to a tax regime similar to that in the Netherlands. Losses may be carried forward for 8 years and back for 3 years. Losses incurred during the first 6 years of a company's operations may be carried forward without limit. Where the Participation Exemption applies, losses on investments in subsidiaries may not be set against current or future taxable income, except in some defined, liquidation losses.
Por	Capital gains are in general taxed as income. The capital gain is the difference between the purchase value and the realized disposal value adjusted by depreciation and an officially set coefficient which accounts for devaluation of the currency. In certain circumstances the authorities may fix a different value for real estate disposals than was actual realized. Capital gains are exempt if disposal proceeds are reinvested in new fixed assets or participating interests during the following 2 years. Losses may be carried forward for up to 5 years but may not be carried back.

Spa	Capital gains are taxed as ordinary income unless the proceeds of a disposal are reinvested in other fixed assets used in the business, in which case, gains are exempt. Gains arising on the sale of movable property, including shares, are exempt provided the purchaser is resident in an EC country. This does not apply if shares are sold and the seller owns more than 25% of the company or the company's assets are predominately Spanish real estate.
Swe	Capital gains are generally aggregated with other income and taxed at normal corporate income tax rates, regardless of the timing of the disposal or receipt of the proceeds. Trading and capital losses can be set against all categories of income with the exception of capital losses on portfolios of shares and similar financial assets where losses may only be set against gains arising from similar assets. Losses may be carried forward without time limit but must be set against the first available income. Losses may not be carried back.
Swi	Capital gains are general treated as ordinary taxable income. In certain circumstances, gains on disposals of real property may be subject to a Real Property Tax and some cantons exempt gains arising from the sale of shares. Losses may be carried forward for up to 6 years for Federal tax purposes. Most cantons allow losses to be carried forwards for periods between 2 and 6 years. Losses may not be carried back at either level of taxation.

Two solutions have been proposed by the OECD :

1 A fixed debt/equity ratio for all projects within a country, and
2 the arms length principle: intervene only when abuses are obvious.

The practical difficulties of implementing and monitoring the first solution has meant that most European countries have chosen the second route. Table 4.5 summarizes the allowability of interest expenses and thin capitalization restrictions currently applicable throughout Europe. Reference should be made to Tables 4.6 and 4.7 for details of the treatment of foreign source income and the current rates of withholding tax charged on interest payments made to overseas lenders.

Foreign source income

As has been mentioned briefly before, companies with overseas subsidiaries potentially face three layers of taxation when they come to repatriate earnings generated in foreign countries. The preceding sections have outlined the taxation of earnings within the source country. This income is then subject to withholding taxes when remitted to overseas parent companies in the form of dividends, interest or royalty payments. These receipts may then be subject to further taxation in the parent company's hands, although this is often mitigated by tax treaties and domestic provisions which recognise that the underlying taxes paid fully or partially discharge the parent company's liability on that income.

As stated, most countries defer foreign source income taxation on subsidiaries until the income is repatriated and then provide a credit against domestic income tax for withholding taxes and underlying corporate taxes paid. However, France and Belgium exempt foreign source income fully; the Netherlands allow a partial exemption and exemption treaties exist in and between other states.

The Segre Report (1966) stated that tax considerations should not influence the choice of investment location or the choice between direct and branch investment. Free movement of capital is restricted by international double taxation of investment income and is distorted by various tax incentives and the differential treatment of non-resident and corporate investments.

A vital issue is the recognition of tax paid in other member states - the country where a company is resident should recognise the taxes paid on foreign income as satisfying the tax liability of shareholders. Without this, cross border investment will be frustrated and shareholders will continue to be drawn mainly from the same country as the company's country of residence.

Table 4.5
The allowability of interest expenses and thin capitalization restrictions

	Interest expense treatment
UK	The interest costs (and issue costs) of obtaining loan finance are treated as allowable expenditure for corporation tax purposes. Bank interest may be treated as a charge on income if not otherwise allowable as a trading expense
Bel	As in the UK
Den	Interest is allowable. Thin capitalization rules exist for consolidated groups
Eir	Certain forms of interest paid in an accounting period may be classified as a distribution and hence not treated as an allowable deduction (any part of interest that represents more than a reasonable return for the use of the money)
Fra	Interest is only deductible if the capital is fully paid up and if the interest rate exceeds the yearly average of gross interest paid on bonds issued by private corporations, then the excess interest payment is not deductible
Ger	Interest is allowable provided thin capitalization does not exist. Loan capital is, by law, treated as equity capital if the corporation's equity is considerably lower than the usual capitalization in the particular industry. The general limit is 10 per cent of assets although this is not applicable in industries with customarily lower rates of equity capitalization (*e.g.* banks and insurance companies
Gre	As in the UK
Ita	Interest expense is only deductible in the proportion that taxable income bears to total income, *i.e.*, taxable income plus exempt profits, including interest on government bonds or income which has been subject to final or definitive Italian withholding tax
Lux	As in the UK. (The tax authorities have stated that in some exceptional circumstances equity should not be less than 20 per cent of shareholders' capital and debt finance taken together)
Net	As in the UK: no thin capitalization rules
Por	As in the UK. For foreign investments, the Bank of Portugal normally requires 30 per cent of total assets to be funded by equity
Spa	As in the UK
Swe	As in the UK: no debt to equity rules although compulsory liquidation occurs when more than 50 per cent of a company's equity has been lost
Swi	A few cantons have legal requirements concerning capitalization

Table 4.6
Existing tax treaties

	UK	*Bel*	*Den*	*Eir*	*Fra*	*Ger*	*Gre*	*Ita*	*Lux*	*Net*	*Por*	*Spa*	*Swe*
Bel	Y												
Den	Y	Y											
Eir	Y	Y	Y										
Fra	Y	Y	Y	Y									
Ger	Y	Y	Y	Y	Y								
Gre	Y	Y	N	N	Y	Y							
Ita	Y	Y	Y	Y	Y	Y	Y						
Lux	Y	Y	Y	Y	Y	Y	N	Y					
Net	Y	Y	N	Y	Y	Y	Y	Y	Y				
Por	Y	Y	Y	N	Y	Y	N	Y	N	N			
Spa	Y	Y	Y	N	Y	Y	N	Y	Y	Y	Y		
Swe	Y	Y	Y	Y	Y	Y	Y	Y	Y	Y	Y	Y	
Swi	Y	Y	Y	Y	Y	Y	Y	Y	N	Y	Y	Y	Y

Table 4.7
The treatment of dividends receivable

	Treatment
UK	Dividends from resident companies are exempt
Bel	85-90 per cent of qualifying dividends (*i.e.*, those paid by a company subject to a tax regime similar to Belgian corporate tax) received on shares held for an entire taxable period are tax exempt
Den	Domestic dividends from 25 per cent owned companies (held for one complete period) are exempt
Eir	As for UK
Fra	Generally, dividends from home and foreign corporations are exempt tax. This is on condition that the investment is significant *i.e.*, company has owned at least 25 per cent of the share capital
Ger	As for UK. Also, dividends from foreign corporations in treaty countries are generally exempt
Gre	Taxable
Ita	Dividends are exempt from local income taxes. For national tax purposes a full imputation system applies when both distributing and receiving companies are resident in Italy
Lux	Dividends from 10 per cent owned domestic or foreign shareholdings, or where acquisition cost was greater than LF50,000,000 and those shares have been held for 12 months prior to receipt are exempt, provided the distributing company is subject to system similar to Luxembourg's
Net	Dividends are subject to tax unless the participation exemption applies. Withholding tax may be credited against corporate tax liabilities
Por	95 per cent of dividends from 25 per cent owned companies in which shares have been held for at least two years (or since incorporation) are exempt. Otherwise, companies are taxed on the gross dividend and given a credit of 20 per cent of underlying corporate tax and withholding tax on the dividend
Spa	Dividends from resident companies usually attract tax less credit relief of 50 per cent of that tax. If the distributing company is 25 per cent owned during the period of the payment and for one year prior to that period the dividend is 100 per cent tax free
Swe	Dividends from domestic companies are exempt if 25 per cent of the voting power is held by the recipient at the end of the fiscal year. Foreign source dividends are taxable in principle although treaties provide similar exemption
Swi	Dividends are subject to federal taxes but a reduction is granted where the recipient owns more than 20 per cent of the distributing company's equity or where the investment cost more than SFr2,000,000

Table 4.8
Indirect Taxation

	Standard rate	*Reduced rate & items*	*Zero rated, exempt*	*Luxury rate*
UK	17.5%	-	Insurance, education, finance, books transport, food	-
Bel	17% & 19%	Basic necessities 6%	-	25% Additional luxury tax of 8% on jewellery and expensive cars
Den	22%	-	-	-
Eir	21%	Clothing, footwear, theatre ,etc12.5%	Food, books and oral medicines	-
Fra	18.6%	Food, books and transport 5.5%	-	-
Ger	Generally 14%	Certain agricultural goods 7%	Export goods correctly documented	
Gre	18%	Basic necessities, certain food items, free professional services 8%	Export sales to ships and duty free sales	36%
Ita	19% (standard rates of 4% and 9% on certain goods also)	-	-	38%
Lux	12%	Certain meat, bakery dairy, pharmaceutical products 3%. Books, most fuels, most foods, public transport, prof. services, advertising 6%	-	-
Net	18.5	Basic necessities 6%	Exportation and related transactions	-
Por	17%	8%	-	30%
Spa	12%	6%	-	33%
Swe	19%	-	-	-
Swi	Wholesale 9.3% Retail 6.2%		Exports, foods, most services, newspapers, pharmaceuticals and books	

Table 4.6 shows the existing international tax treaties which are in force between European countries. "Y" indicates that a tax treaty exists and "N" indicates that no treaty has yet been agreed.

Many corporate structures are highly complex and situations where domestic holding companies have more than one overseas subsidiary in a particular foreign country are becoming more common. In such cases, the treatment of inter-company dividends within the foreign country becomes an important consideration in planning the flow of funds and remittance path within the group. Table 4.7 shows the tax treatment of dividends receivable in the European countries covered in this chapter.

Indirect taxes

Another issue which corporate planners must account for when developing cash flow forecasts for the purposes of project appraisal is the rates of indirect taxation in force in the country of operation. As the concluding section of this chapter mentions, there has been considerable progress towards indirect taxation harmonization within the European Community, but significant differences still exist. These are summarised in Table 4.8

VAT is a common method of indirect taxation in the EEC and was introduced in the UK with the 1972 Finance Act specifically in order to comply with European tax harmonization objectives. As with all indirect taxes the tax base is consumption rather than income or capital and although the tax is levied on value adding businesses, it is ultimately borne by the final consumer.

The Treaty of Rome (1957) Part II Titles I and III set the goals of free movement of goods, services, peoples and capital within Europe. The free movement of goods required steps towards the harmonization of indirect taxes and free movement of capital requires some level of harmonization of direct taxes. Harmonization of indirect taxes has, historically, been regarded as the most essential and integral step towards the creation of a common market.

The Commission aims to modify the 6th Directive (77/388), A Common System of VAT: Uniform Basis of Assessment (OJ L145/77) so as to treat sales and purchases across intra-community borders in the same way as those within member states. A working document of the Commission (Com(87)323) is concerned with the creation of a clearing house to ensure that VAT collected in exporting member states and deducted in the importing member states accrues to the revenue authorities of the latter.

The Community has proposed a standard rate band of between 14 per cent and 20 per cent and a reduced rate band between 4 per cent and 9 per cent for the following:

1 foodstuffs, excluding alcoholic beverages
2 energy products for heating and lighting
3 water supplies
4 pharmaceutical products
5 books, newspapers and periodicals and
6 passenger transport.

Conclusions

In this chapter comparisons have been made of the tax treatment in different European countries of dividends, depreciation, capital gains, losses, stocks, interest, foreign source income and VAT.

Details of corporate tax rates have been provided and examples of non-deductible items given. The implications of some of these issues for investment appraisal, capital structure and European tax harmonization are investigated in the following chapters.

References

King, M. and Fullerton, D. (eds, 1984), *"The taxation of income from capital : a comprehensive study of the United States, the United Kingdom, Sweden and West Germany"*, University of Chicago Press, Chicago

Devereux M. and Pearson M. (1989), "Corporate tax harmonization and economic efficiency", *Report Series No. 35*, Institute for Fiscal Studies, London.

5 Tax-induced investment incentives and leverage gains in the European Community

Suzanne Farrar and John Pointon

Introduction

In this chapter a model is derived to accommodate risk, personal and corporate tax rates, imputed credits and tax depreciation methods. Comparisons are made between:

1 the pre-tax equilibrium rates of return for different asset categories and risk levels under a post-tax model, and

2 the respective rates under a tax-free model.

Relative incentives and disincentives are evaluated across twelve European tax systems. Incentives are universal for plant and machinery projects of low and medium risk and disincentives are universal for building projects of medium and high risk. The relative incentives are ranked against countries and rank correlation coefficients computed. For high risk investments, the rankings under different asset categories are not normally strongly positively correlated. However, there is a strong positive correlation under different risk levels, but for the same type of buildings. There is a negative correlation in rankings between high and low risk investments in plant and machinery. Overall the strongest investment incentives are found in Ireland and Portugal and the weakest in Belgium and Greece. Using data from the design of the different tax systems, it is demonstrated that the gain to the geared firm can vary widely within the UK and between other European countries. In Greece, Italy, France and Germany the systems are approximately neutral, although there are very small losses to leverage in Greece and Italy and very small gains in France and Germany. Substantial leverage gains exist in Luxembourg, Spain, the Netherlands and Portugal, although dampened to some extent under an active debt management policy.

The effects of tax on project returns have been evaluated within the UK context, for example Devereux and Mayer (1984), Mole (1990) and Moon and Hodges (1989), particularly with an emphasis on changes in rates and allowances. Also, project interdependencies can be created due to the common tax base within a particular company, which can be investigated by mathematical programming models (Berry and Dyson, 1979). Corporate taxes can also distort beta risk as well as returns (Pointon, 1980). Personal tax can be accommodated by modifying the form of the capital asset pricing model (Ashton, 1989). Recommendations have been made to change the corporate tax system to a cash flow base (Meade, 1978), although the revenue-raising potential has been questioned (MacDonald, 1981).

From empirical studies it is clear that the full effects of tax on project appraisal are not always evaluated [(Hodgkinson, 1989) and (Morgan, 1987)]. This is also reflected in studies on tax and lease evaluation (Drury and Braund, 1990).

The need for harmonization of corporate tax systems in Europe has been stressed (Nobes, 1980). However, overall little progress has been made, although a number of countries have adopted imputation systems. Tax rates, tax depreciation systems and imputed credits still vary across Europe. There are some significant differences in accounting practices too (Emenyonu and Gray, 1992).

In attempting to understand the features of the different European tax systems the authors referred to publications by Price Waterhouse (1992a and 1992b), Grant Thornton (1992) and Bobbett and Kesti (1991). The views expressed here and indeed the interpretation of the tax systems are the authors!

The model

Adjusting the capital asset pricing model for tax essentially transforms a tax-free model, for example the one by Sharpe (1964):

$$\bar{r}_j = r_f + \left(\bar{r}_m - r_f\right)\beta_j^B \tag{1}$$

into:

$$z_j\bar{r}_j^* = r_f(1-m) + \left[z_m\bar{r}_m - r_f(1-m)\right]\beta_j^A \tag{2}$$

Although equation (2) is broadly consistent with Ashton (1989), tax depreciation systems will be reflected in the modelling process as well. Personal tax at the rate m is paid on income earned at the risk-free rate r_f.

The mean rate of return on the efficient market portfolio, $\bar{r}_m$, is subject to a tax reduction factor z_m. The pre-tax mean rate of return $\bar{r}_j^*$ is set at such a level that its post-tax rate $z_j\bar{r}_j^*$ is in equilibrium under a tax-adjusted model. The tax-reduction factor relating to investment j is z_j. The before tax beta is β_j^B and the after-tax beta is β_j^A. Under the tax-free model the equilibrium rate of return for investment j is $\bar{r}_j$. This is not necessarily the same as $\bar{r}_j^*$, the before-tax rate, which determines an equilibrium after-tax rate.

If there were no taxes, the required rate of return would be determined by the level of beta β_j^B. But tax can change the beta risk. At the new level of risk, β_j^A, there exists an equilibrium after-tax rate $z_j\bar{r}_j^*$. If the pre-tax rate $\bar{r}_j^*$, under the post-tax model, is less than $\bar{r}_j$, the tax-free rate under the tax-free model, then the investment needs to earn a pre-tax rate which is set at a level lower than the rate required to be earned in a tax-free world. This represents a tax incentive to invest. Alternatively, if the pre-tax rate $\bar{r}_j^*$, which results in a post-tax equilibrium rate, exceeds $\bar{r}_j$, the rate in a tax-free world, then the tax system produces a disincentive to invest.

Corporate tax reduction factors have been specified by Pointon (1980) as $(1-T)/(1-c_jT)$ where T is the corporate tax rate and c_j is the present value of capital allowances as a proportion of the cost. the inflows are taxed at the rate T, whilst the outlay has a net cost of $(1-c_jT)$ for every £1 of expenditure. Amending this for personal tax and assuming a full dividend payout, the tax reduction factor is:

$$z_j = \frac{(1-T)(1-m)}{(1-c_jT)(1-b)} \tag{3}$$

where b is the rate of dividend credit, as a proportion of the gross equivalent of the dividend. Similarly for the overall market portfolio:

$$z_m = \frac{(1-T)(1-m)}{(1-c_mT)(1-b)} \tag{4}$$

Since the overall market rate is reduced by tax to $z_m\bar{r}_m$ and the rate for investment j is reduced to $z_j\bar{r}_j$, then the after-tax beta for j is:

$$\beta_j^A = \frac{\operatorname{cov}(z_jr_j^*, z_mr_m)}{\operatorname{var}(z_mr_m)} = \frac{z_jz_m \operatorname{cov}(r_j^*, r_m)}{z_m^2 \operatorname{var}(r_m)}$$

i.e.

$$\beta_j^A = \frac{z_j}{z_m} \beta_j^B \tag{5}$$

Thus the after-tax beta is equal to the before-tax beta times the ratio of the z factors.

The pre-tax equilibrium rate, under the tax adjusted model, can now be re-expressed in terms of the tax rates, the capital allowance factors, the pre-tax market and the risk-free rates and the pre-tax beta:

$$\bar{r}_j^* = \frac{(1-c_j T)(1-b)r_f}{(1-T)} + \left[\bar{r}_m - \frac{(1-c_m T)(1-b)r_f}{(1-T)}\right]\beta_j^B \tag{6}$$

Direct comparisons will be made between the outputs of equations (6) and (1), respectively, for different asset categories, risk levels and tax systems across Europe.

There is an implicit assumption in the modelling that the markets are segmented, i.e. a UK firm investing in the UK is assumed to evaluate the systematic risk according to the risk relationship with the overall UK market, and similarly a French firm with the French market. Cross country investments are not under consideration. Instead, the emphasis is upon the effects of the overall structure of taxation in each country.

Tax depreciation factors

The tax allowances for capital expenditure vary between countries. Most, however, are based upon the straight-line method or the reducing balance method.

Discounting to the first tax payment date at the rate k, the capital allowance factor under the straight line method is given by:

$$c_j = \frac{s_r\left[1-\left(\frac{1}{1+k}\right)^n\right]}{1-\left(\frac{1}{1+k}\right)} + \frac{1-ns_r}{(1+k)^n} \tag{7}$$

where n is the number of allowances which may be obtained at the full s_r rate.

The declining balance method gives:

$$c_j = \frac{d_r}{1-\left(\dfrac{1-d_r}{1+k}\right)} = \frac{d_r(1+k)}{k+d_r} \tag{8}$$

The two methods are of equivalent value when the critical value of d_r is d_r^*. This occurs when:

$$\frac{d_r^*(1+k)}{k+d_r^*} = \frac{s_r\left[1-\left(\dfrac{1}{1+k}\right)^n\right]}{1-\left(\dfrac{1}{1+k}\right)} + \frac{1-ns_r}{(1+k)^n} \tag{9}$$

or simplifying and rearranging, where

$$d_r^* = \frac{s_r\left[1-\left(\dfrac{1}{1+k}\right)^n\right] + \left[\dfrac{k(1-ns_r)}{(1+k)^{n+1}}\right]}{1-\dfrac{s_r\left[1-\left(\dfrac{1}{1+k}\right)^n\right]}{k} - \dfrac{(1-ns_r)}{(1+k)^{n+1}}} \tag{10}$$

Where a choice of method exists, the declining balance method will be optimal if the depreciation rate available exceeds this d_r^* value, assuming a sufficiency of profits in each year. Critical values of the declining balance rate are shown in Table 5.1.

Table 5.1
Straight-line and equivalent declining-balance rates ($k = 10\%$)

Straight-line rate (s_r)	Critical declining balance rate (d_r)	Ratio (d_r^*/s_r)
0.40	0.5430	1.36
0.333	0.4846	1.45
0.30	0.4387	1.46
0.25	0.3819	1.53
0.20	0.3135	1.57

Table 5.2
Restrictions on the declining-balance rate

	$d_r = 1.5s_r$	$d_r = 2.0s_r$	$d_r = 2.5s_r$
France	3-4 years	5-6 years	> 6 years
Portugal	< 5 years	5-6 years	> 6 years
Spain	< 5 years	< 8 years	≥ 8 years

Several countries offer a choice of method, subject to some restriction. In Belgium, $d_r \leq 2s_r$ so, assuming a 10 per cent discount rate, there is an incentive to choose the declining balance method where available. In Germany and Luxembourg, $d_r = \min(3s_r, 0.30)$. Since 30 per cent declining balance depreciation is equivalent to just over 19 per cent on the straight-line basis, there is an incentive to use the declining balance method for assets with a life of five years or more. France, Portugal and Spain restrict d_r on the basis of asset life as shown in Table 5.2. Thus there is an incentive to choose the declining balance depreciation in all cases, except where an asset has a life of four years, that is, $s_r = 0.25$, since the equivalent declining balance rate is higher than that available. However, the Belgian system allows for a switch from the double-declining balance rate d_r to the straight-line rate s_r. Under this system the year of the switch is year y such that:

$$y - 1 \leq t^* < y \tag{11}$$

where

$$t^* = 1 + \left(\frac{\log\left(\frac{s_r}{d_r}\right)}{\log(1 - d_r)} \right) \tag{12}$$

If we take a 6 per cent double-declining balance rate and a 3 per cent straight-line rate then $t^* = 12.2$ and $y = 13.0$. The method changes in the thirteenth year.

Variations on the basic depreciation methods are used in some countries. For instance, the Danish system allows for an adjustment to take into account inflationary effects. For plant and machinery, the depreciable base is the balance of the depreciated collective book value at the start of the year less the proceeds of asset sales during the year, adjusted on the basis of the retail price index. Five-sixths of the cost price of assets acquired during the year is added without adjustment, with the remainder being added to the next year's depreciable base.

The sum of the allowances is:

$$c_j = 5/6d_r + \frac{\dfrac{5/6(1-d_r)(1+i)d_r}{(1+k)}}{1-\dfrac{(1-d_r)(1+i)}{(1+k)}} + \frac{\dfrac{1/6(1+i)d_r}{(1+k)}}{1-\dfrac{(1-d_r)(1+i)}{(1+k)}} \tag{13}$$

where i is the inflation rate, assumed to be constant. This simplifies to:

$$c_j = \frac{d_r}{6}\left[5+\frac{(1+i)(6-5d_r)}{d_r(1+i)+k-i}\right] \tag{14}$$

For buildings, the depreciable base is adjusted annually on the basis of the retail price index, with the depreciation allowance being based on this adjusted figure. Depreciation may be taken at any rate up to the maximum rate allowed, s, until the sum of the allowances reaches $10s$. In subsequent years the annual allowance is restricted to $s/3$. Taking the maximum depreciation in each year,

$$c_j = \frac{s\left[1-\left(\dfrac{1+i}{1+k}\right)^{10}\right] + s/3\dfrac{(1+i)^{10}}{(1+k)^{10}}\left[1-\left(\dfrac{1+i}{1+k}\right)^{3(1-10s)/s}\right]}{1-\left(\dfrac{1+i}{1+k}\right)} \tag{15}$$

i.e.

$$c_j = \frac{s(1+k)\left[1-\left(\dfrac{1+i}{1+k}\right)^{10}\right] + s/3\dfrac{(1+i)^{10}}{(1+k)^{9}}\left[1-\left(\dfrac{1+i}{1+k}\right)^{3(1-10s)/s}\right]}{k-i} \tag{16}$$

In Germany the depreciation rates for buildings are 10 per cent for the first four years, 5 per cent in the following three years and 2.5 per cent in the next eighteen years.

$$c_j = \frac{0.10\left[1-\left(\dfrac{1}{1+k}\right)^{4}\right] + \dfrac{0.05}{(1+k)^4}\left[1-\left(\dfrac{1}{1+k}\right)^{3}\right] + \dfrac{0.025}{(1+k)^7}\left[1-\left(\dfrac{1}{1+k}\right)^{18}\right]}{1-\left(\dfrac{1}{1+k}\right)} \tag{17}$$

As to the system in Italy, the first year's straight line depreciation allowance is reduced by half, so that

$$c_j = 0.5s_r + \frac{\frac{s_r}{(1+k)}\left[1-\left(\frac{1}{1+k}\right)^n\right]}{1-\left(\frac{1}{1+k}\right)} + \frac{(1-ns_r-0.5s_r)}{(1+k)^{n+1}} \tag{18}$$

i.e.

$$c_j = 0.5s_r + \frac{s_r\left[1-\left(\frac{1}{1+k}\right)^n\right]}{k} + \frac{[1-s_r(n+0.5)]}{(1+k)^{n+1}} \tag{19}$$

In Spain there is a tax credit of 5 per cent on new fixed assets in addition to the tax depreciation allowance. The tax credit is deducted from the tax payable. Financially this is equivalent to an additional tax depreciation expense in the first year of 5 per cent of the asset cost, divided by the corporate tax rate of 35 per cent. The effective tax depreciation factors for Spain are therefore increased by 0.143.

Table 5.3
Tax depreciation factors

Country	Plant and machinery	Industrial building	Commercial building	Overall
Belgium	0.7708	0.5837	0.4319	0.6995
Denmark	0.8973	0.6584	0.6584	0.8256
France	0.8250	0.3994	0.3994	0.6973
Germany	0.8427	0.5578	0.5578	0.7573
Greece	0.7751	0.6124	0.4682	0.7118
Ireland	0.7857	0.3994	0	0.6299
Italy	0.9010	0.4658	0.4658	0.7704
Luxembourg	1.0018	0.6206	0.4685	0.8722
Netherlands	0.7333	0.3162	0.3162	0.6082
Portugal	0.8340	0.4682	0.2181	0.6992
Spain	0.8762	0.4591	0.2806	0.7332
UK	0.8286	0.5746	0	0.6949

Luxembourg adopts a similar tax credit system. There is a 6 per cent credit on the first LF6,000,000 and a 2 per cent credit on the excess. In the simulation study the 6 per cent credit has been assumed to be representative. This increases the effective tax depreciation factors by 0.152. There are also other tax credits in Luxembourg that are pertinent for firms whose asset book values exceed the average of those over the previous five years. We have assumed a steady-state, rather than asset growth, and therefore ignored these other credits in the simulation exercise.

In Table 5.3 the tax depreciation factors have been calculated for different European countries, assuming a discount rate of 10 per cent per annum. For Denmark a 5 per cent inflation rate is assumed. The overall rate is a weighted average, assuming 70 per cent is invested in plant and machinery, 20 per cent in industrial buildings and 10 per cent in commercial buildings. This is broadly consistent with the National Institute UK model of the economy (Young, 1992).

Tax and beta effects

A simulation exercise was performed using the tax rates and imputed credits, where appropriate, as shown in Table 5.4. Although the highest marginal personal rates are given, their effects are self-cancelling. They do not appear in equation (6). For Ireland, where there is a different corporate tax rate for manufacturing companies, the lower rate was applied for investments in plant and machinery and industrial buildings and the higher rate for a non-manufacturing company's investment in commercial buildings. The Italian tax rate was adjusted for local income tax and the Portuguese rate for the municipal surcharge. For Greece the lower tax rate was chosen, being the one for quoted industrial companies. The tax rates relate to our own knowledge at 1 April 1993. For the UK this reflected the budget statement. For most countries they refer to the rates during 1992.

Table 5.4
Tax rates across Europe (%)

	Implied imputed credit (UK equivalent)	Corporate tax rate	Highest marginal personal rate
Belgium	25	39	55
Denmark	30	38	68
France	33.3	34	40
Germany	36	36	53
Greece	35	35	50
Ireland	25 or 0.05263	40 or 10	52
Italy	47.826	47.826	51
Luxembourg	0	39.39	50
Netherlands	0	35	50
Portugal	15	39.6	30
Spain	0	35	53
UK	20	33	40

In Table 5.5 we set out the values of $\bar{r}_j^*$, the required pre-tax rate of return to sustain a post-tax equilibrium rate of return. Higher, medium and low risk refer to pre-tax betas of 1.2, 1.0 and 0.8, respectively. The risk-free rate is assumed to be 8 per cent per annum and the overall market rate 14 per cent per annum.

Table 5.5
Equilibrium pre-tax rates of return in a post-tax model

	Investment category								
	Plant and machinery			Industrial buildings			Commercial buildings		
Risk level:	Low	Med.	High	Low	Med.	High	Low	Med.	High
Belgium	12.36	13.73	15.10	13.07	14.44	15.81	13.66	15.03	16.40
Denmark	12.19	13.75	15.31	13.01	14.57	16.13	13.01	14.57	16.13
France	12.08	13.65	15.22	13.25	14.82	16.39	13.25	14.82	16.39
Germany	12.12	13.76	15.39	12.94	14.57	16.21	12.94	14.57	16.21
Greece	12.22	13.82	15.42	12.68	14.28	15.88	13.08	14.68	16.28
Ireland	12.07	13.38	14.68	13.62	14.92	16.23	15.22	16.52	17.82
Italy	11.71	13.50	15.29	13.38	15.17	16.96	13.38	15.17	16.96
Luxembourg	12.26	13.33	14.39	14.24	15.31	16.38	15.03	16.10	17.17
Netherlands	12.60	13.46	14.32	14.40	15.26	16.12	14.40	15.26	16.12
Portugal	12.23	13.40	14.57	13.86	15.03	16.20	14.97	16.15	17.32
Spain	12.41	13.38	14.34	14.21	15.18	16.14	14.98	16.00	17.00
UK	12.25	13.58	14.91	13.05	14.38	15.71	14.86	16.19	17.52

In Table 5.6 the countries are ranked in order of the level of incentives. For example, from Table 5.5, for a low risk investment in plant and machinery, in Italy the pre-tax rate need only be 11.71 per cent to maintain a post-tax equilibrium rate of return. This is the lowest required rate and so in Table 5.6, Italy ranks first for this investment category. In a tax-free world the required rates for low, medium and high risk projects would be 12.8, 14 and 15.2 per cent, for the parameters chosen. With regard to plant and machinery, all countries provide incentives for low and medium risk investments, whereas for Denmark, Italy, Germany, France and Greece there are relative disincentives, for high risk investments. For every country except Greece, investments in industrial or commercial buildings have relative tax disincentives. The required pre-tax rate in a post-tax model exceeds the required rate in a tax-free world. The relative incentives in Greece relate only to low risk investments in buildings. For each country the mean rank order for each investment category was weighted 70 per cent for plant and machinery, 20 per cent for industrial buildings and 10 per cent for commercial buildings. This gave an overall rank order for the countries. Given the parameters of the model, Ireland then Portugal have the highest tax incentives, followed equally by Italy and Luxembourg. Greece and Belgium hold the lowest overall rankings.

Table 5.6
Ranking countries by the tax incentives

	Investment category									
	All	Plant and machinery			Industrial buildings			Commercial buildings		
Risk level:	All	Low	Med.	High	Low	Med.	High	Low	Med.	High
1st	Ire	Ita	Lux	Net	Gre	Gre	UK	Ger	Den	Net
2nd	Por	Ire	Ire	Spa	Ger	UK	Bel	Den	Ger	Den
3rd	Ita/Lux	Fra	Spa	Lux	Den	Bel	Gre	Gre	Gre	Ger
4th	-	Ger	Por	Por	UK	Den	Net	Fra	Fra	Gre
5th	Spa	Den	Net	Ire	Bel	Ger	Den	Ita	Bel	Fra
6th	UK	Gre	Ita	UK	Fra	Fra	Spa	Bel	Ita	Bel
7th	Fra	Por	UK	Bel	Ita	Ire	Por	Net	Net	Ita
8th	Net	UK	Fra	Fra	Ire	Por	Ger	UK	Spa	Spa
9th	Den/Ger	Lux	Bel	Ita	Por	Ita	Ire	Por	Lux	Lux
10th	-	Bel	Ger	Den	Spa	Spa	Lux	Spa	Por	Por
11th	Bel	Spa	Den	Ger	Lux	Net	Fra	Lux	UK	UK
12th	Gre	Net	Gre	Gre	Net	Lux	Ita	Ire	Ire	Ire

Table 5.7
Rank correlation coefficients of investment and risk

Category 1		Category 2		Correlation
Investment	Risk	Investment	Risk	
Plant	Low	Plant	Med.	-0.21
Plant	Low	Plant	High	-0.62
Plant	Med.	Plant	High	+0.84
Indust.	Low	Indust.	Med.	+0.91
Indust.	Med.	Indust.	High	+0.57
Comm.	Low	Comm.	Med.	+0.92
Comm	Med.	Comm.	High	+0.85
Plant	Low	Indust.	Low	+0.43
Plant	Med.	Indust.	Med.	-0.80
Plant	High	Indust.	High	+0.01
Indust.	Low	Comm.	Low	+0.75
Indust.	Med.	Comm.	Med.	+0.38
Indust.	High	Comm.	High	+0.15

However, for particular asset and risk categories the situation can be much different. Rank correlation coefficients are computed in Table 5.7.

The rankings of a country for high risk investments, under different asset categories, are not normally strongly positively related. But rankings of low risk investments are positively related. Yet the country rankings of plant and machinery and industrial buildings of medium risk are strongly negatively correlated. There is a strong positive correlation under different risk levels, but for the same type of asset, whether buildings or plant. The exception is that the country ranking of plant and machinery projects of low risk is negatively correlated with the ranking of plant and machinery projects of medium or high risk.

Leverage gains

Let us now turn our attention to potential gains from gearing under alternative European tax systems. The choice of capital structure has been, and still is, an important theme in corporate finance, following the propositions by Modigliani and Miller (1958) and the correction for corporate taxation (Modigliani and Miller, 1963). The marginal gain from gearing can be specified to recognize both personal and corporate taxes, although general equilibrium would eliminate any gain completely (Miller, 1977). Insights into the tax requirements of neutrality in debt and dividend policies have been made by a number of authors, including Stapleton and Burke (1977) and Ashton (1991). Any net tax advantage to the levered firm can also be adjusted for a firm pursuing an active debt management policy, by adjusting the debt each period by a fixed leverage ratio, according to the changing value of the firm. (Miles and Ezzell, 1980), (Appleyard and Strong, 1989), and (Clubb and Doran, 1991).

It has been suggested by a number of authors, including Dempsey(1991), that the marginal gain should reflect differences between borrowing and lending rates. The view taken here is that these may very well reflect different levels of risk and that the observed lending rate is likely to be of lower risk than the observed borrowing rate, neither being risk-free. Having borrowed, industrial firms can increase their financial risk further by investing in assets of higher risk or by increasing their dividend payout rates, and thereby retaining less. To an extent this can be monitored with consequential agency costs (Jensen and Meckling, 1976). However, major clearing banks that increase their lending would almost always be directly supported, or indirectly controlled, by the appropriate central bank if real difficulties followed.

An empirical study by Rutterford (1986), testing the Miller (1977) model, found that tax was not a significant factor for several countries. One possible factor is a signalling effect. For example, for UK unlisted firms, debt can be considered to be part of the package of signals from manager-insiders to investor-outsiders' (Buckland, Davis and Yeomans, 1989). For the United States, Norton (1991), found that applying factor analysis to questionnaire responses, taxation considerations *inter alia* do affect capital structure decisions. Patterson (1985) has also observed that gearing is indeed relevant to corporate valuation.

The focus of this section is first on the specification of the marginal gain and second on the magnitude of the gain using data from the design of different European tax systems. It is proposed that the marginal gain from gearing reflects the tax rules for investment.

The model

The post-personal tax price of risk is given by λ, such that:

$$\lambda = \frac{\left[z_m \bar{r}_m - r_f\left(1 - aT_{PSF}\right)\right]}{\operatorname{var}\left(z_m r_m\right)} \tag{20}$$

where

$\bar{r}_m$ = the mean pre-tax rate of return on the efficient market portfolio,
z_m = the tax factor which changes the mean pre-tax market rate of return, $\bar{r}_m$ to $z_m\bar{r}_m$ after corporate and personal tax,
r_f = the pre-tax risk-free rate,
a = a zero-one variable, and
T_{PSF} = the tax rate of the investor who invests in a risk-free asset or borrows at a risk-free rate in addition to investing in shares.

If interest received or paid is taxable, or allowable for tax, then $a=1$ and if non-taxable or disallowable, then $a=0$.

Following the capital asset pricing model (Sharpe, 1964) the value of the unlevered firm V_u, is related to the mean net operating cash flow $\bar{x}$, the effective corporate tax rate T_E, the effective personal tax rate T_{PS}, the systematic risk and the tax savings on capital expenditure, by the equation:

$$V_u = \frac{\left[\bar{x}\left(1 - T_E\right)\left(1 - T_{PS}\right) - \lambda \operatorname{cov}\left(x, z_m r_m\right)\left(1 - T_e\right)\left(1 - T_{PS}\right)\right]}{\left[1 + r_f\left(1 - aT_{PSF}\right)\right]} + cT_E V_u \tag{21}$$

where c = the present value of capital allowances, or other tax depreciation allowance, for every unit of value.

For 100 per cent instantaneous tax relief on all expenditure, $c=1$.

It follows that:

$$V_u\left[1+r_f(1-aT_{PSF})\right](1-cT_E)=\bar{x}(1-T_E)(1-T_{PS})$$
$$-\lambda\operatorname{cov}(x,z_m r_m)(1-T_E)(1-T_{PS}) \tag{22}$$

Allowing for the deductibility of interest R_d, the value of the shares in the equivalent geared firm is S_G, such that:

$$S_G\left[1+r_f(1-aT_{PSF})\right]\left(1-\frac{cT_E V_G}{S_G}\right)=\bar{x}(1-T_E)(1-T_{PS})-\lambda\operatorname{cov}(x,z_m r_m)(1-T_E)(1-T_{PS})$$
$$-\bar{R}_d(1-T_E)(1-T_{PS})+\lambda\operatorname{cov}(R_d,z_m r_m)(1-T_E)(1-T_{PS}) \tag{23}$$

The capital allowance shield is based on the total firm value and accrues to the shareholders. The value of the debt D, reflects personal tax at the rate T_{PD} :

$$D\left[1+r_f(1-T_{PD})\right]=\bar{R}_d(1-T_{PD})-\lambda\operatorname{cov}(R_d,z_m r_m)(1-T_{PD}) \tag{24}$$

It follows that the value of the geared firm is V_{GO} , such that:

$$V_{GO}=V_u+\frac{D}{(1-cT_E)}\left[1-\frac{(1-T_E)(1-T_{PS})\left[1+r_f(1-T_{PD})\right]}{(1-T_{PD})\left[1+r_f(1-aT_{PSF})\right]}\right] \tag{25}$$

But an end period value of $\dfrac{(1-T_E)(1-T_{PS})\left[1+r_f(1-T_{PD})\right]}{(1-T_{PD})}$ can be interpreted within the context of a multi-period model as $\dfrac{(1-T_E)(1-T_{PS})r_f(1-T_{PD})}{(1-T_{PD})}$ for each period. By capitalizing at the rate $r_f(1-aT_{PSF})$, the value of the geared firm is now V_{G1P} such that:

$$V_{G1P}=V_u+\frac{D}{(1-cT_E)}\left[1-\frac{(1-T_E)(1-T_{PS})}{(1-aT_{PSF})}\right] \tag{26}$$

The model developed so far is appropriate for a geared firm pursuing a passive debt management policy, where a fixed gearing ratio determines a constant level of debt for the forseeable future. By contrast under an active debt management policy, following Miles and Ezzell (1980), the fixed gearing ratio and the variable value of the firm at the beginning of each period together determine a variable level of debt for each period. Adapting the valuation equations accordingly, the value of the geared firm pursuing an active debt management policy is V_{G1A}, such that:

$$V_{G1A} = V_u + \frac{\left[(1-T_{PD})-(1-T_E)(1-T_{PS})\right]r_f D}{(1-cT_E)\left[1+r_f(1-aT_{PSF})\right]} + \frac{\left[(1-T_{PD})-(1-T_E)(1-T_{PS})\right]r_f D/\left[1+r_f(1-aT_{PSF})\right]}{(1-cT_E)r_u(1-T_{PS})} \qquad (27)$$

where r_u is the rate of return before personal tax for the equivalent ungeared firm.

A European dimension of non-linear leverage gains

Before applying the model, adjustments have been made for the effect of local income taxes on the firm in Italy and for a municipal surcharge in Portugal. The personal tax rates chosen assume that the investor is in the highest tax bracket. For Denmark this has been adjusted for the local income tax. The German church tax has been excluded, since investors in other countries may be inclined to make similar voluntary contributions. In Greece the corporate tax rate reflects the type of corporation and in Ireland there is a lower rate for manufacturing companies. In Portugal the tax credits depend upon the type of company.

Tax payment dates vary too. In some countries the dates are after the year-end, for example in Denmark, the UK, Italy, Ireland and Greece. In others, payments are made during the year, for example, in Belgium, Germany, Luxembourg, Portugal and Spain. The corporate tax rates have been discounted or compounded to the year-end date assuming a rate of 8 per cent for the time value of money.

The systems of tax depreciation are not uniform. A weighted average of the present value of such allowances as a proportion of cost has been calculated on the assumption that 70 per cent of investment relates to plant and equipment with an 8 year life and a zero scrap value, 20 per cent represents new industrial buildings and 10 per cent commercial buildings. The tax benefits depend upon a profit sufficiency and so a slightly higher discount rate of 10 per cent has been chosen. In the case of Denmark, tax depreciation is index-linked to inflation. We have assumed a 5 per cent annual rate. Despite differences in systems the weighted averages fall into groupings. Firstly, Ireland and the Netherlands have tax depreciation c factors of between 60 and 63 per cent. Secondly, Belgium, France, Greece, Spain, Portugal and the United Kingdom have factors estimated between 69 and 74 per cent. Germany and Italy have factors between 75 and 78 per cent, whilst Denmark and Luxembourg have factors between 82 and 88 per cent. As far as the UK is concerned the tax depreciation factor is broadly consistent with the National Institute model of the UK economy (Young, 1992).

In Table 5.8, the tax parameters and gains as a proportion of debt are identified for a firm pursuing a passive debt management policy. V_u represents the value of the ungeared firm and D the value of the debt in the geared firm. Where there are tax-induced gains to leverage, the gain as a percentage of debt increases with the proportion of debt, *i.e.* there is a non-linear relationship. Conversely, in the case of Greece and Italy, where there is a small loss attached to leverage, the loss as a percentage of debt decreases as debt increases. In France and Germany the gains are small, but positive. In the UK and Denmark the gains exceed 10 per cent. The gains in Ireland are approximately 5 per cent in manufacturing and 26 per cent in non-manufacturing. There is a gain of around 30 per cent in Belgium and the gains in the remaining countries are very substantial, namely in Portugal, the Netherlands, Spain and Luxembourg, in ascending order.

The gains are recomputed for a firm adopting an active debt management policy, as set out in Table 5.9. The rate of return before tax for the ungeared firm is denoted by r_u. The gains now are smaller than those found under a passive policy and reduce further as the unlevered rate of return increases. The tax systems are approximately neutral for France, Greece, Italy and Germany, yet the gains to leverage are still high for Luxembourg, Spain, the Netherlands and Portugal. The relative rankings between countries are, however, the same for a passive debt management policy.

Substantially different levels of tax distortions can, however, occur even within the jurisdiction of one particular tax system. For example, let us take the UK and make the following assumptions:

1 The firm pursues a passive debt management policy.
2 The rates of corporation tax of 33, 35 or 25 per cent are adjusted for advance corporation tax payments and tax lags to give effective rates of 31.9677419, 25 and 33.7096774 per cent respectively.
3 The effective tax rates on dividend income are either zero, for a basic rate taxpayer, or 18 per cent, allowing for a personal tax lag associated with the excess of the higher rate over the basic rate. This computation was made before the March 1993 budget.
4 The effective personal tax rates on interest are 25 or 38.5 per cent, allowing for a tax lag.
5 The capital allowance factor is 0.72.
6 The debt value is 50 per cent of the value of the equivalent ungeared firm.

By applying this data to the model we see, from Table 5.10 that for the UK the gain from gearing can vary from zero to 86 per cent.

Table 5.8
Leverage gains under a passive debt management policy

	Personal tax rate (%)	Effective personal tax rate (%)	Corporate tax rate (%)	Effective corporate tax rate (%)	Tax depreciation factor	Gain as a percentage of debt $(V_u = 100)$ D=20 (%)	D=50 (%)	D=80 (%)
Belgium	55	40.0	39	40.1	0.6995	29.6	32.5	36.1
Denmark	68	54.2857	38	36.8	0.8256	14.4	15.1	15.8
France	40	10.0	34	34.0	0.6973	1.3	1.3	1.3
Germany	53	26.5625	36	37.4	0.7573	3.1	3.1	3.1
Greece (a)	50	23.0769	35	34.1	0.7118	(1.8)	(1.8)	(1.8)
Greece (b)	50	16.6667	40	39.1	0.7118	(2.1)	(2.1)	(2.1)
Greece (c)	50	7.4074	46	44.8	0.7118	(3.2)	(3.2)	(3.2)
Ireland (a)	52	36.0	40	38.2	0.6299	24.3	26.2	28.5
Ireland (b)	52	49.3333	10	9.6	0.6299	4.9	5.0	5.1
Italy	51	6.0835	47.826	46.2	0.7704	(4.8)	(4.7)	(4.7)
Luxembourg	50	50.0	39.39	40.9	0.8722	72.8	93.2	129.4
Netherlands	50	50.0	35	35.0	0.6082	48.8	57.1	69.0
Portugal (a)	30	17.6471	39.6	40.2	0.6992	44.9	52.0	61.5
Portugal (b)	30	12.5	39.6	40.2	0.6992	37.8	42.6	48.8
Portugal (c)	30	6.6667	39.6	40.2	0.6992	29.9	32.8	36.4
Spain	53	53.0	35	35.3	0.7332	52.6	62.5	76.9
UK (a)	40	20.0	33	31.1	0.6949	10.6	10.9	11.3
UK (b)	40	25.0	33	31.1	0.6949	18.4	19.4	20.6

Notes:
Greece (a) quoted industrial societes anonymes,(b) industrial societes anonymes,(c) societes anonymes.
Ireland (a) companies,(b) manufacturing companies.
UK (a) pre-April 1993,(b) post March 1993.

Table 5.9
Leverage gains under an active debt management policy

	Gains as a percentage of debt r_u=10%	r_u=12%	r_u=14%
Belgium	17.2	14.5	12.5
Denmark	8.0	6.7	5.8
France	0.7	0.6	0.5
Germany	1.6	1.4	1.2
Greece (a)	(1.0)	(0.8)	(0.7)
Ireland (a)	14.2	12.0	10.4
Italy	(2.1)	(1.8)	(1.6)
Luxembourg	51.4	43.2	37.4
Netherlands	35.9	30.2	26.1
Portugal (a)	28.7	24.3	21.2
Spain	38.4	32.3	28.0
UK (a)	6.4	5.4	4.7

Table 5.10
Ranking leverage gains in the UK

Gain (% of debt)	Parameters
0	Small co. rate, lending
12	Full co. rate, lending
15	Higher marginal co. rate, lending
30	Small co. rate, borrowing, basic rate taxpayer
41	Full co. rate, borrowing, basic rate taxpayer
44	Higher marginal co. rate, borrowing, basic rate taxpayer
47	Small co. rate, borrowing, higher rate taxpayer
57	Full co. rate, borrowing, higher rate taxpayer
60	Higher marginal co. rate, borrowing, higher rate taxpayer

Conclusion

A model of the effects of personal and corporate tax, reflecting alternative tax depreciation methods and imputed credits was presented. Variations in tax depreciation factors and tax rates were noted across Europe. A simulation exercise was perfored in which equilibrium pre-tax rates of return in a post-tax model were computed for different investment categories and different levels of systematic risk. However, despite these differences, within the parameters of the model the different European tax systems can each create tax incentives to invest in plant and machinery projects of low and medium risk, and disincentives to invest in building projects of medium and high risk. For high risk investments, there are significant variations in the ranking of relative incentives between countries under different asset categories. Low risk investment rankings are positively related. Also for the same type of buildings under different risk categories there is normally a strong positive correlation. Finally, there is a negative correlation in country rankings between low and high risk investments in plant and machinery. Overall, the strongest investment incentives were found in Ireland and Portugal and the weakest in Belgium and Greece.

Tax depreciation rules were shown to affect the relationship between the value of the levered and unlevered firm, and different European tax systems were used to evaluate the leverage gains under both active and passive debt management policies. Wide variations were found. In some countries, for example Greece and Italy, the gains are negative, although very small. The French and German systems are also approximately neutral, although the gains are positive, but small. By contrast in Portugal,

Luxembourg, the Netherlands and Spain the gains are large. The gains, though still significant for these four countries, are smaller under an active debt management policy and reduce further as the unlevered rate increases.

The UK system was examined in more detail, demonstrating that the gains can range from zero to very substantial values, depending upon the personal and corporate tax rates and whether the investor borrows or lends at the margin.

References

Appleyard, A.R. and Strong, N.C. (1989), 'Beta Geared and Ungeared: The Case of Active Debt Management',*Accounting and Business Research*, Spring, pp170-4.

Ashton, D.J. (1989), 'The Cost of Capital and the Imputation Tax System', *Journal of Business Finance and Accounting*, Spring, pp75-88.

Ashton, D.J. (1991), 'Corporate Financial Policy: American Analytics and UK Taxation', *Journal of Business Finance and Accounting*, June 1991, pp465-82.

Berry, R.H. and Dyson, R.G. (1979), 'A Mathematical Programming Approach to Taxation-Induced Interdependencies in Investment Appraisal', *Journal of Business Finance and Accounting*, Winter, pp425-441.

Bobbett, C.S. and Kesti, J. (eds. 1991), *European Tax Handbook*, Amsterdam, International Bureau of Fiscal Documentation.

Buckland, R.,Davis, E.W. and Yeomans, K.A. (1989), 'Debt Management by Companies Entering the Unlisted Securities Market', *Accounting and Business Research*, Spring, pp99-111.

Clubb, C.D.B. and Doran, P. (1991), 'Beta Geared and Ungeared: Further Analysis of the Case of the Active Debt Management', *Accounting and Business Research*, Summer, pp215-9.

Dempsey, M.J. (1991), 'Modigliani and Miller Again Revisited: The Cost of Capital Under the Assumption of Unequal Borrowing and Lending Rates', *Accounting and Business Research*, Summer, pp221-6.

Devereux, M.P. and Mayer, C.P. (1984), *Corporation Tax : The Impact of the 1984 Budget,* Institute for Fiscal Studies Report Series, No.11, June.

Drury, C. and Braund, S. (1990), 'The Leasing Decision: A Comparison of Theory and Practice', *Accounting and Business Research*, Summer, pp179-191.

Emenyonu, E.N. and Gray, S.J. (1992), 'EC Accounting Harmonization: An Empirical Study of Measurement Practices in France, Germany and the UK', *Accounting and Business Research*, Winter, pp49-58.

Grant Thornton International (1992), *Corporate Taxation in Europe*, Grant Thornton International, London.

Hodgkinson, L. (1989), *Taxation and Corporate Investment,* London, Chartered Institute of Management Accountants.

Jensen, M.C. and Meckling, W.H. (1976), 'Theory of the Firm: Managerial Behaviour, Agency Costs and Ownership Structure', *Journal of Financial Economics,* Vol. 3 (1976) pp305-60.

MacDonald, G. (1980), 'Can a Corporation Tax Under an Expenditure Tax Regime be Non-Distortionary?', *Accounting and Business Research,* Winter, pp66-70.

Meade, J.E. (1978), *The Structure and Reform of Direct Taxation,* London, Institute for Fiscal Studies.

Miles, J.A. and Ezzell, J.R. (1980), 'The Weighted Average Cost of Capital, Perfect Capital Markets and Project Life - A Clarification', *Journal of Financial and Quantitative Analysis,* September, pp719-30.

Miller, M.H. (1977),'Debt and Taxes', *Journal of Finance,* May, pp261-75.

Modigliani, F. and Miller, M.H. (1958), 'The Cost of Capital, Corporation Finance and the Theory of Investment', *American Economic Review,* June, pp261-290.

Modigliani, F. and Miller, M.H. (1963), 'Corporate Income Taxes and the Cost of Capital: A Correction', *American Economic Review,* June, pp433-43.

Mole, R. (1990), 'Post-Tax Capital Investment Appraisal: Plant and Machinery', *Accounting and Business Research,* Spring, pp123-34.

Moon, P. and Hodges, S. (1989), 'Implications of the Recent Tax Changes for Corporate Capital Investment', *Journal of Business Finance and Accounting,* Spring, pp25-39.

Morgan, E.J. (1987), *Corporate Taxation and Investment: The Implications of the 1984 Tax Reform,* Aldershot, Gower.

Nobes, C.W. (1980), 'Imputations Systems of Corporation Tax within the EEC', *Accounting and Business Research,* Spring, pp221-31.

Norton, E. (1991), 'Factors Affecting Capital Structure Decisions', *Financial Review,* August, pp431-46.

Patterson, C.S. (1985), 'Debt and Taxes: Empirical Evidence', *Journal of Business Finance and Accounting,* Summer, pp187-206.

Pointon, J. (1980), 'Investment and Risk: The Effect of Capital Allowances', *Accounting and Business Research,* Autumn, pp432-9.

Price Waterhouse (1992a), *Corporate Taxes: A Worldwide Summary,* London.

Price Waterhouse (1992b), *Individual Taxes: A Worldwide Summary,* London.

Rutterford, J. (1986), 'An Empirical Investigation into the Effects of Corporate and Personal Taxation on Company Capital Structure', *PhD Thesis,* London School of Economics.

Sharpe, W.F. (1964), 'Capital Asset Prices: A Theory of Market Equilibrium Under Conditions of Risk', *Journal of Finance,* September, pp425-42.

Stapleton, R.C. and Burke, C.M. (1977), 'European Tax Systems and the Neutrality of Corporate Financing Policy', *Journal of Banking and Finance,* Vol.1, pp55-70.
Young, G. (1992), 'A New Approach to Modelling Corporation Tax', *National Institute Economic Review,* May, pp98-105.

6 Capital structure: An econometric perspective on Europe

Jon Tucker

Introduction

One of the most controversial, and as yet unresolved questions in financial economics is, 'Does corporate capital structure actually matter?' Although, prima facie, this might appear a somewhat philosophical question, its answer lies in the realms of theoretical models and empirical research. The capital structure of the firm is basically the balance of debt and equity it employs to finance investments. A firm's debt-equity ratio, is often used as a measure of a firm's capital structure mix.

If the capital structure decision is relevant to the firm, then the firm should strive towards some optimal funding mix, to reduce its cost of capital, as well as striving towards maximising the returns on its investment projects. If such a decision is irrelevant to the firm, then the firm should simply concentrate on maximising its value through the maximisation of its investment project returns.

Corporate and personal taxation introduce further complexity to the question of capital structure relevance, demanding a more intricate consideration of firm/investor interactions. Depending on the complexity of such tax-framed theories, capital structure irrelevancy may be either supported or refuted.

Theories have concentrated on developing realistic tax frameworks, but other factors, ignored by some authors, are pertinent to a comprehensive consideration of capital structure theory. Corporate tax exhaustion, bankruptcy costs and agency costs all need to be included in any examination of capital structure, as do firm-specific strategic and operational factors.

Some financial economists have even pointed to the link between country capital structure differentials and economic success. Although the direction of causation is difficult to ascertain, some authors link Japanese industrial strength, for example, with the country's high average debt-equity ratio.

This chapter will attempt to reconsider the question of the relevance of capital structure to the firm in a logical, and generally, a chronological manner. The review of theoretical literature places modern finance theory in a historical perspective, by reviewing the development of the theoretical framework within which the capital structure question is placed. The review of empirical literature reviews the evidence available to support the theories reviewed, allowing greater validity to be attached to those theories which have some 'real world' application. The next section describes, in summary, new research undertaken with the purpose of examining European capital structure patterns and differentials, and the scientific search for the factors which appear to determine firm-level capital structures across Europe. The final section summarises the important features of each section, to generate a view of the relevance of capital structure to the firm, with particular reference to the European firm.

Review of theoretical literature

The question of capital structure relevancy is one which has caused much controversy and debate in the twentieth century, and probably before that. This section of the chapter attempts to summarise some of the main theoretical developments in the area in a very succinct manner, and may unfortunately omit some work which other authors feel to be important or omit detail which some may feel they would need to fully appreciate a particular concept or idea. However, this section is merely a summary to enable the construction of a view of basic modern finance theory, as an exhaustive review of the literature would require at least a book to itself.

The first part of this section describes some of the early, conventional theories, which were based more on pragmatic conservatism than mathematical derivation. The second part summarises the theories of Modigliani and Miller (1958,1963) and Miller (1977), which are central to the debate, and on which most of the theoretical developments and critique are based. Thirdly, various imperfections such as bankruptcy and agency costs, and signalling theories are then described, with reference to their effect on the relevance of capital structure. Fourthly, the more recent developments in capital structure theory are explained, many of which are not based on the Modigliani and Miller (hereafter known as MM) and Miller models. Finally, the theories are drawn together to attempt to establish a more coherent view of modern capital structure theory.

Conventional theories of capital structure

The three conventional theories of capital structure are: the Net Income Approach, the Net Operating Income Approach and the Traditional Approach.

Durand's (1952) Net Income Approach simply stated that the overall cost of a firm's capital may be reduced by increasing its leverage, and thus the firm can increase its total market value. Neither the cost of debt capital nor the cost of equity capital are affected by an increase in leverage, as the market does not perceive any increase in financial risk. His theory appears to suggest that total debt financing would maximise the value of the firm by minimising the overall cost of capital.

The Net Operating Income Approach argues that there are indeed implicit costs associated with debt, such that equity holders *do* require a higher return as debt increases. Thus:

> The market will increase the discount rate just sufficiently to keep the market value of the firm constant with increasing debt. [1]

There can be no advantage to debt financing, then, and capital structure irrelevance would seem to hold.

The Traditional Approach is based on a pragmatic view of the ideal operation of the 'healthy firm'. At low levels of debt, interest rates are the only cost of debt, as in the Net Income Approach. At some higher debt level, equity holders begin to require increasing compensation for the risks inherent in high debt funding, such as bankruptcy risk. At some higher level of debt there will be a net disadvantage to debt as the compensation to equity holders increases, and debt holders' monitoring costs become significant. Thus, the weighted average cost of capital can be minimised at a specific level of debt, above which the cost rises with incremental debt. This theory supports the concept of the optimal firm-level capital structure, and thus supports capital structure relevancy.

Thus, the earlier, conventional theories vary in their conclusions on capital structure relevancy, proposing 100 per cent debt; capital structure irrelevancy; and firm-level optimal capital structures, respectively.

The Modigliani and Miller (1958,1963) and Miller (1977) models

The MM (1958) model introduced a coherent partial equilibrium framework to the capital structure debate, reinstating the idea of capital structure irrelevance, and was based on mathematical derivation and empirical evidence which apparently gave it support. The 1963 model extended the earlier model to correctly incorporate taxation, and produced the proposition of a distinct tax advantage to debt funding. However, with the introduction of personal as well as corporate taxation by Miller in 1977, capital structure irrelevance was reinstated. Each of these models shall be briefly summarised.

The MM (1958) model extended the Net Operating Income framework, arguing basically that a firm cannot increase its value by repackaging its cash flows, and thus proposed the idea of capital structure irrelevance. The weighted average cost of capital does not change as debt is increased, as the return on equity is equal to the expected return on an ungeared firm plus a premium, which is a linear function of the amount of debt. However, MM employed assumptions, many of which have led successive authors to strongly question their conclusions. Their assumption of efficient capital markets is somewhat supported by the evidence. [2] The assumption of equal interest rates for lenders and borrowers is questioned by casual observation of real capital markets. The lack of brokerage costs in their model cannot be reconciled with the real world where individual investors find such costs prohibitive in some circumstances. The lack of consideration of bankruptcy costs in the model may be unrealistic, as such costs or the risk of incurring such costs may contribute significantly to the equilibrium funding decision. The existence of two firms, identical except the first is geared and the second is not, may be unrealistic as gearing might increase price competitiveness, through economies of scale, for example. However, Stiglitz (1969) showed in his general equilibrium state preference model that the existence of such risk classes is not vital to the theorem. Finally, the model attempted to incorporate corporation taxes, but did so erroneously, to be corrected by the later 1963 model. The model, overall, represented a landmark in finance theory, regardless of its questionable assumptions, due to its basis in mathematical proof and its apparent support by empirical evidence.

The MM (1963) model correctly introduced corporate tax into its framework, and this resulted in the proposition that there was a distinct advantage to debt which arises from the corporate tax deductibility of the interest payment expense. The firm value thus becomes the value of an identical ungeared firm plus the value of the tax shield, the latter being simply the corporate tax rate multiplied by the market value of the debt issued. Thus, the weighted average cost of capital decreases as the proportion of funding represented by debt increases. The higher returns demanded by equity holders as debt increases are then outweighed by the much cheaper post-tax debt. Such a limitless advantage to debt should be embodied in 100 per cent debt-financed firms in the real world, but few such firms exist. One criticism of the model is that debt holders should logically demand increased returns at extreme debt levels, as bankruptcy risk should logically be perceived by all parties with interests in the firm, making the cost of debt curve steeper. This would mean that the rate of increase of the cost of equity would have to decrease, to maintain the decreasing overall cost of capital, creating a paradox. Bailey and Fung (1978) noted this weakness, arguing that the yield on equity cannot decline at extreme debt levels. The existence of uncertainty creates another problem for the model, as the tax savings associated with debt are not certain, and, in times of tax exhaustion the tax advantage to debt may be entirely negated. The MM (1963) paper, despite its criticisms, did correctly introduce corporate taxes into capital structure theory to propose a distinct tax advantage to debt, meaning that capital structure relevance was reinstated.

The Miller (1977) model once again established capital structure irrelevance at the level of the firm, as personal taxes can reduce or even eliminate the corporate tax advantage to debt of the 1963 model. [3] With personal taxes introduced the present value of the tax shield becomes:

$$\text{TAX SHIELD VALUE} = \left[1 - \frac{(1-T_c)(1-T_{ps})}{(1-T_{pd})}\right]B$$

where:

T_c = the corporate tax rate
T_{ps} = the personal tax rate on equity income
T_{pd} = the personal tax rate on debt income
B = the value of debt

Thus, the value of the tax shield depends on the relative size of corporate and personal taxes. Miller proposed the existence of an 'investor clientele' effect, whereby a tax-exempt investor would invest in debt whereas a highly-taxed investor would invest in equity. Firms adjust their funding to take advantage of these clienteles until an equilibrium position is revealed, at which point the individual firm can no longer increase its value by further adjustment. Thus, capital structure is irrelevant to the individual firm in equilibrium, but an optimal capital structure results, in aggregate.

The Modigliani and Miller (1958,1963) and Miller (1977) models set the framework within which modern finance theory was developed, proposing capital structure relevance, irrelevance, and relevance, respectively. The strength of the models lay in their mathematical base of testable relationships, their apparent support by accompanying empirical evidence, and the appeal of irrelevance propositions in finance generally. Much of the later work in the area developed in the style of the Modigliani and Miller work, and critique of their work alone enabled careful consideration of other factors which they assumed insignificant.

Imperfections such as bankruptcy costs, agency costs and the signalling nature of the finance decision, are capable of overturning the Modigliani and Miller models, if such imperfections are indeed significant. Each imperfection thus demands brief discussion to examine the theory which has arisen from critiques of the MM models.

The imperfection of bankruptcy costs is capable of changing the conclusions of the MM models. Holders of equity bear ex-ante bankruptcy costs, which lower the valuation of the firm, whereas holders of debt bear the ex-post costs of bankruptcy, passing on the ex-ante costs of bankruptcy to equity holders in the form of higher interest rates. Thus bankruptcy costs have a negative effect on firm value, trading-off against any tax advantage to debt. Kraus and Litzenberger (1973) argued that such a trade-off was capable of producing some optimal level of debt at firm level. Warner (1977) found, however, that expected direct bankruptcy costs were likely to be much less than 1 per cent of the market value of the firm seven years before bankruptcy. In contrast, Baxter (1967) found that bankruptcy costs were as large as 20 per cent of the value of the firm, but concentrated on personal rather than corporate bankruptcies. Haugen and Senbet (1978) criticised many authors for examining liquidation costs rather than bankruptcy costs, thus overstating their magnitude. Indeed, Jensen and Meckling (1976) argued that bankruptcy does not necessarily lead to liquidation, but may merely lead to reorganisation, which is not nearly as costly and allows continuation of the business. Thus, the direct costs of bankruptcy are likely to be small; the indirect costs may be large but are by definition difficult to measure; but both, when considered together, may enable a trade-off, to some extent, against any tax advantage associated with debt.

The imperfection of agency costs is perhaps best explained by firstly defining the concept of agency. Jensen and Meckling (1976) defined the agency relationship as:

> a contract under which one or more persons (the principal (s)) engage another person (the agent) to perform some service on their behalf which involves delegating some decision-making authority to the agent. [4]

This agency relationship is complicated by conflicts of interest, especially between managers and debt holders, whereby managers may attempt to transfer wealth from the debt holders to the shareholders. Thus, to protect themselves, debt holders monitor the firm (monitoring costs) and impose debt covenants (covenant costs), both of which can be described as agency costs. Jensen and Meckling argued that if the extent of debt funding is extreme, managers have an incentive to undertake investments which promise very high pay-offs if successful, even if they have a low probability of success. It is as if the manager is 'gambling' with predominantly debt holders' funds and only a token amount of equity holders' funds. The debt allows the manager (on behalf of the shareholders) to realise high rewards if the risky projects are successful, but in the event of failure the token amount of equity funds is lost but bankruptcy means that the debt holders will also see their claims reduced. This transformation of business risk is an important agency cost. Myers (1977) argued that firms have both 'assets-in-place' and future growth opportunities. The former will support more debt than the latter, meaning that the manager of a highly geared firm may miss out on valuable investment opportunities, reducing the value of his firm. There is essentially, then, a trade-off between the tax advantage to debt and the costs of sub optimal future investment strategy. Overall, agency costs will demand some optimal capital structure which minimises the agency costs of both debt and equity.

The signalling nature of a firm's capital structure is explained by Ross (1977) and Leland and Pyle (1977). Ross argued that low value firms will not have high debt-equity ratios due to the risk of insolvency, and thus high value firms will generally display high debt-equity ratios and low value firms will display low debt-equity ratios. Thus the capital structure of the firm is a signal to investors of firm value, a theory which Ross supported with empirical evidence.

Leland and Pyle (1977) also argued that higher debt-equity ratios were associated with higher value firms. They observed that managers will often invest a large part of the required equity themselves, signalling business confidence to investors, who will in turn lend more, increasing the debt-equity ratio of the firm. Thus, the signalling nature of the firm's capital structure alters the market's perception of the value of the firm. The theory suggests a positive relationship between the extent of debt funding and the value of the firm, which would appear to support the MM (1963) model of firm-level optimal capital structures.

All three imperfections appear to support a theory of an optimal firm-level capital structure. Bankruptcy costs, both direct and indirect, when considered together may trade-off to some extent against any tax advantage to debt. Agency costs may be minimised at a certain capital structure mix, which must then be considered optimal. The signalling nature of a firm's capital structure reveals a positive relationship between the extent of debt and firm value, supporting the MM (1963) model of capital structure relevancy.

More recent developments in capital structure theory

Developments in capital structure theory since the Miller (1977) general equilibrium theory have been many and diverse. Some of the more interesting developments may be grouped into the following areas: corporate tax exhaustion; incomplete markets; the Pecking Order Theory; the adaptation of Modigliani and Miller models for differing tax systems; the existence of unequal interest rates for the lenders and borrowers of debt; and product and input market imperfection models. Such theories will be briefly discussed, as they represent alternative frameworks, extensions of imperfection theories or simply further evolution of the relevancy/irrelevancy debate.

Corporate tax exhaustion occurs where a firm has a surplus of capital allowances or losses carried forward over taxable profits. The existence of such allowances may mean that the marginal value of one pound of debt will not be the full corporate tax rate, but will decrease as the probability of tax exhaustion increases. DeAngelo and Masulis (1980) argued that such tax exhaustion may overturn the relevancy theorem, because allowances are firm-specific, leading to firm-level optimal capital structure solutions. Indeed, they go as far as to argue that as long as non-debt tax shields are positive, Miller irrelevancy will no longer hold. The Government Green Paper on Corporation Tax stated that only 40 per cent of UK companies paid mainstream corporation tax in any year, and there is a wealth of evidence to support such significant tax exhaustion in other countries (reviewed in the next section). Mayer (1984) developed a model in which the level of gearing is ultimately determined by 'expectations of future earnings in relation to taxable allowances'. [5] Thus, corporate tax exhaustion is certainly capable of producing a firm specific optimal capital structure solution of its own accord, an optimum which may occur well before bankruptcy or agency costs come into play.

Auerbach and King's (1983) theory of incomplete markets shows that Miller equilibrium can hold only if investors are constrained from engaging in infinite tax arbitrage by constraints on borrowing and short sales. If there are no such constraints then investors will 'undo' corporate leverage by purchasing a proportion of the firm's debt which is in the same proportion to his equity holding in the firm as total debt issued is to the firm's total equity.

The Pecking Order theory was created by Myers (1984), and further discussed by Myers and Majluf (1984). Myers (1984) argued that firms face the dilemma, when funding new projects, of either issuing equity at a price which they think is too low or missing out on positive NPV projects. To avoid this dilemma they will prefer funding from retained earnings to debt funding to equity funding, thus creating a capital structure preference rather than a strict optimum. Myers and Majluf (1984) argued that the signal to investors coming from positive NPV projects funded by the issue of equity is mixed, as the projects are advantageous and the new issue disadvantageous to current investors. To avoid this problem, firms would much rather issue debt than equity, so that they can fund all new positive NPV projects. [6] Again, this supports the relevance of capital structure to the firm. However, Brennan and Kraus (1987) and Constantinides and Grundy (1989) criticised this theory. Brennan and Kraus argued that, if there existed two firms, the first with high value current assets and the second with low value current assets, the former can issue new equity to fund new projects *and* retire outstanding debt, whereas the latter can only fund new projects. The former can issue equity at a high price and repurchase debt at a good price, whereas if the latter issues equity at a high price its repurchase of debt at face value far outweighs the new funds from equity sales. Thus, there will be an aversion to the issue of debt, and equity issuing will predominate. Constantinides and Grundy (1989) argued that, in equilibrium, all firms undertaking positive NPV projects financed the issue of securities which are neither straight debt nor equity. This new security enables firms to finance new projects and to repurchase some of their existing equity, making it costly for firms to overstate or understate their value. Neither debt nor internal funding would thus be required, and the Pecking Order theory would no longer apply. Thus, the Pecking Order theory remains a contentious theory, with little consensus of opinion as to the order, or even existence, of firm preferences for different financial instruments. This research area thus adds little to the capital structure relevancy debate.

Most of the capital structure theory was developed within the US tax framework. However, Ashton (1989) reworked the MM formulae for the UK imputation tax system and found that the tax advantage to debt was far less than the 35 per cent to 50 per cent often quoted for the US, being as little as 13 per cent of the debt's market value in the UK. Thus, the type of tax system will considerably change the perspective within which the relevancy debate is placed.

If the imperfection of unequal interest rate for the lenders and borrowers of debt is introduced, Dempsey (1991) argued, this gap constitutes a cost of borrowing, and:

> This 'cost' of borrowing is sufficient to nullify entirely the formerly perceived financial tax benefits of corporate borrowing. [7]

He shows that such an imperfection is capable of reducing the tax advantage to debt under the UK imputation system to a *net disadvantage* of 6 per cent or 7 per cent of the debt's market value. Thus, the real world spread of debt interest rates between lenders and borrowers may even result in a disadvantage to debt for the UK. This contrasts strongly with the widely perceived and agreed tax advantage to debt.

Finally, product and input market imperfection models have been developed to attempt to explain the interaction of the capital structure decision with industrial organisation factors. Brander and Lewis (1986) argued, using a Cournot equilibrium model, that oligopolists increase risk by pursuing a more aggressive output policy. Their model shows that the firm must choose its output before its marginal profit is known. The holders of levered equity receive payoffs only in good states of nature, as equity returns payments are not mandatory, and thus they ignore the possibility that the marginal profit of output may be low. Leverage thus creates an incentive to increase output, if the marginal profit of output is large. Therefore, the level of debt is related both explicitly and implicitly to the product market strategies of firms to the extent that the relationship may cause firms to actually produce too much.

Maksimovic (1988) argued that debt capacity is positively correlated with the elasticity of demand for a firm's products and negatively correlated with the discount rate. Titman (1984) argued that firms which produce goods, such as durables, which require some guarantee of after-sales service, will employ less debt to ensure against liquidation, to maintain product prices. Maksimovic and Titman (1991) stated that the incentive to produce high quality goods decreases as debt funding increases, as the reputation of quality would be lost after bankruptcy anyway.

Finally, Sarig (1988) postulated that holders of debt bear most of the costs of bargaining failure when negotiating with the suppliers of inputs, but equity holders receive most of the gains if such bargaining is successful. Thus, all of these theories expand upon relationships between product and input market factors and firm capital structures, with varying or unresolved directions of causality. These theories certainly contribute, whether marginally or significantly, to the establishment of firm-level optimal capital structures.

To summarise, the more recent developments in capital structure theory have tended to move away from detailed refinement of the Modigliani and Miller models, towards models which explain the interaction of capital structure with a single factor or group of factors. There is a realisation that a general equilibrium framework can rely on a particular tax system or that the institutional factors of a country may simply disable such equilibrium positions. The weight of theory examining significant imperfections in the real world is probably capable of preventing the equilibrium of the Miller (1977) model, and the factors and theories discussed appear to gravitate towards a firm-level optimal capital structure mix.

Summary and conclusions

Some of the more important theories of capital structure have been discussed in this section, albeit in a concise and somewhat simplistic manner.

There is a progression from the pragmatic conservatism of early finance writings towards an increasingly scientific and derivation-based approach, which probably commenced with the MM 1958 paper. Although crude and with restrictive assumptions, the irrelevancy proposition of this paper was as appealing to finance managers of the day as 'laissez-faire' economics is to lethargic politicians of today, and was further legitimised by apparent empirical evidence in its support. The 1963 MM model corrected the model to take a more accurate account of corporation taxes, producing the greatly contrasting relevance conclusion and restating a definite advantage to debt finance due to the interest-deductibility of interest payments. The Miller 1977 model introduced personal taxes into the model, and proposed a general equilibrium solution, with the aid of his investor clientele theory, whereby capital structure is irrelevant to the individual firm but the aggregate amount of debt-to-equity in the market is said to be optimal.

The various market imperfections, which Modigliani and Miller assumed not to exist, are probably capable of distorting the models discussed, and may create optimal firm level capital structures of their own accord, particularly in the case of bankruptcy and agency costs.

The more recent developments of capital structure theory have sought to determine factors of a less direct relationship to capital structure, and have explored the effect of the institutional and behavioural constraints on firm finance.

To summarise, the theories examined suggest the existence of optimal firm-level capital structures. Capital structures must be optimal at firm-level due to the multitude of firm-specific factors, many of which are institutional in nature. The theories stress the importance of firm-level factors, and thus capital structure *must* be relevant to the individual firm.

Review of empirical literature

For theory to be accepted by society, it must be validated, or at least not refuted, by data from the real world. Collection of useful data, empirical testing on that data, and the correct interpretation of results are of vital importance to the acceptance of any theory.

Empirical evidence on the subject of capital structure is surprisingly scarce, partly owing to the difficulties of constructing viable tests of the sometimes extremely complex theories. Often, indirect testing of theories must suffice, concentrating on the testable implications or probable effects of such theories, if they indeed stand.

The availability of data appears to be a difficulty with earlier empirical work, as well as the computer technology with which to analyse such data. The expression of required variables in each book or market values is a debate in itself. However, some useful results are drawn from such tests, which may be used to support or refute some of the central theories.

Firstly, tests of the Modigliani and Miller (1958,1963) and Miller (1977) models will be reviewed. Secondly, evidence available on the significance of bankruptcy and agency costs to the capital structure decision will be discussed. Thirdly, there will be a summary of the tests of the more recent developments in capital structure theory. Fourthly, tests for the existence of target debt-equity ratios will be summarised, as such target debt-equity ratios provide prima facie evidence in support of the existence of firm-level optimal debt-equity ratios. Finally, this section of the chapter discussing the empirical evidence available will be summarised, and conclusions drawn as to those theories which appear to hold in the real world.

Tests of the Modigliani and Miller (1958,1963) and Miller (1977) models

Modigliani and Miller attempted to support their 1958 theory with data from large electric utilities and oil companies, each being considered of an homogeneous risk class. They found that the ex-post cost of capital was not significantly correlated with the degree of leverage, supporting their irrelevancy proposition. They found also that the expected yield on equity of a given class was positively correlated with gearing, again supporting their theory. Thus, they provided preliminary evidence to support their model. However, Barges (1963) and Weston (1963) strongly questioned MM's results, owing to the nature of their data and the methodology used. Barges (1963) argued, as did Weston, that oil companies were far too diverse to be considered in the same risk class. Barges also argued that: MM did not test enough observations on certain parts of the capital structure range; current earnings could not be used as a proxy for future earnings in the oil industry; and that the model was flawed with bias with respect to factors such as business risk, firm size, and the degree of market imperfection. [8] The latter criticism of bias was serious enough, he argued, to strongly question MM's results. Barges corrected for these flaws and tested three US. 'homogeneous' industries, but did not find evidence to support the MM (1958) model.

Weston (1963) argued that the MM model did not allow for growth, assuming, unrealistically, constant earnings. Thus, the critique of the MM testing negates the support it gives to the 1958 model. Sametz (1964), however, stated that:

> The major secular constant in corporate financial decision-making is the debt-equity ratio. [9]

He basically argued that, as the ratio was left unchanged in the long term, it appeared not to matter and that:

> Any debt-equity ratio is optimum and no matter how chosen originally, it might just as well be left unchanged. [10]

He did, however, concede that his study was only a rough sub-optimising model as it did not explain how the debt-equity ratio is determined. Thus, the evidence supporting the MM (1958) model is mixed, and more evidence is required to come to a firm conclusion concerning the basic irrelevancy model.

Modigliani and Miller (1966) tested their 1963 capital structure relevance model using US electric utilities data. This time they allowed for growth, avoided testing the diverse oil industry, and used total assets to normalise for firm size. The results of the test were that the tax subsidy advantage of debt contributed significantly to the value of the firm, giving support to optimal firm-level capital structures. However, there are some problems with the data and methodology as discussed by Boness and Frankfurter (1977) and Freear (1980). Boness and Frankfurter (1977) argued that even utilities could not be considered an homogeneous risk class. Freear (1980) criticised the narrowness of the leverage range with which MM modelled the whole leverage range. Sametz (1964) made the general point that if there was a distinct tax advantage to debt, then the leverage ratio should have increased steadily with the rise in corporate tax rates in the US over time. His research showed the aggregate debt-equity ratio to be stable over the long-term. Rutterford (1985) tested the relationship between the tax advantage to debt and firm debt-equity ratios for a sample of UK FT 30 Share Index firms for the period 1930 to 1980. She found no evidence of a relationship between corporate gearing levels and the tax advantage to debt over the period, which might suggest that firms do not perceive such a tax advantage to debt, otherwise they would adjust their capital structures to utilise it, thus maximising their value. Thus, the work of Boness and Frankfurter, Freear, Sametz, and Rutterford appears to question the validity of the MM (1963) model, but there is some strong evidence to support it.

Hamada (1972) and Masulis (1980,1983) carried out research which gave support to the model. Hamada showed, amongst other results, that unlevered betas were far less spread than levered betas, supporting the MM model. Masulis (1980) studied the impact of capital structure change announcements on security prices, looking at exchange offers, and found a strong relationship between the market value of a firm and its capital structure. Masulis (1983) studied exchange offers again and found again that changes in firm debt level and leverage are positively related to stock prices and firm value. Thus, Hamada and Masulis' research supports the MM (1963) capital structure relevance models. Although there are some methodological problems with the MM (1966) empirical evidence, the available evidence generally supports the MM (1963) capital structure relevance model where there is a distinct tax advantage to debt.

Miller's 1977 general equilibrium model, with its irrelevance proposition, was tested mainly by Kim, Lewellen and McConnell (1979), who concentrated on three 'empirically testable implications' of the Miller model. Firstly, they argued that one would not expect to observe similar leverage ratios in firms that are similar (in same risk classes) if the value of the firm is independent of its capital structure. This argument was tested by Schwartz and Aronson (1967), Scott (1972), Scott and Martin (1975), and Ferri and Jones (1979). The first three pieces of research found significant differences in leverage ratios between different industries but not within industries. The latter research paper found a wide dispersion of leverage ratios within an industry. The evidence on the first implication is thus mixed, but on balance would appear to give some support to the Miller model. Secondly, Kim, Lewellen and McConnell argued that the Miller model demands a negative relationship between corporate leverage ratios and investor tax rates, but found no such relationship in their empirical tests. Thirdly, they argued that they would expect a bimodal distribution of firm's leverage ratios to exist if Miller's 'bondholder' concept holds. The surplus here may be earned by the low tax bracket investor, who invests in the stocks of highly levered firms, at the expense of the tax authority, as he can unlever corporate borrowing by holding the firm's bonds. The condition of the bondholder surplus is that:

> Investors whose marginal tax rates exceed the corporate rate will demand firms with zero (or negative) leverage, while investors whose marginal tax rates are less than the corporate rate will demand firms with highly levered capital structures. [11]

Firms thus specialise their capital structures in one of the extremes. They argued that such a bimodal distribution of corporate leverage ratios should result, with one mode at zero and the other at some higher level, if the bondholder surplus concept, and thus Miller equilibrium holds. They did find evidence of such a bimodal distribution for US firms, but the higher mode did not reflect the 'all or nothing' implication of the financial leverage clientele hypothesis. However, Rutterford (1985) found evidence to support a one-to-one relationship between the total debt-equity ratio and the percentage of the investor population in value terms preferring debt for tax reasons, thus arguing that the Miller clientele hypothesis could not be rejected. On the balance of the evidence available, however, the Miller 1977 capital structure irrelevance model appears not to be supported by the evidence.

To summarise, of the three Modigliani and Miller (1958,1963) and Miller (1977) models, the 1958 and 1977 models are strongly challenged by the available evidence. However, MM's 1963 capital structure relevance model, which proposes a distinct tax advantage to debt, appears to be supported by the evidence.

Evidence on bankruptcy and agency costs

Bankruptcy and agency costs, if found to be important, may significantly affect the relevance of the firm's capital structure choice.

Evidence on the magnitude of bankruptcy costs has already been discussed in the last section, where it was found that such costs were probably of little significance. However, if bankruptcy costs, or some proxy to them, are modelled in a multivariate regression analysis, they might be a significant determinant of the capital structure decision, regardless of their magnitude. Marsh (1982) tested various measures of bankruptcy risk, such as a firm's equity beta and the standard deviation of returns of a company's shares, and found that firms with greater bankruptcy risk are likely to issue equity than debt, revealing bankruptcy risk to be a significant independent variable. Thus, bankruptcy costs may be a significant factor in the determination of firm-level capital structures.

Evidence on the significance of agency costs is generally of an indirect nature, as agency costs are somewhat intangible and difficult to test. However, a study by Smith and Warner (1979) researched debt contracts, which are contracts set in place by bondholders to protect their interests, as a measure of the importance of agency costs. Their qualitative study of public issues of debt showed that most bondholders employ very complex and restrictive bond covenants, which must mean that agency costs are very significant, otherwise such intricate covenants would not exist. Rutterford (1988), in her study of the capital structures, inferred from institutional factors, corporate cultures and consideration of country-specific agency relationships, that agency costs appeared to explain differences in debt-equity ratios between Japanese, French and German corporations. Thus, qualitative evidence from Smith and Warner, the observations of Rutterford, as well as evidence from many other more complex and abstract studies, show agency costs to be a significant determinant of the firm's capital structure decision.

Although evidence on bankruptcy and agency costs is limited, and somewhat tangential at times, the evidence available, as well as the rational nature of investors, would suggest that such costs must be significant. The question of the magnitude of such costs is likely to be specific to the individual firm, as financial risks and agency relationships vary, demanding a firm-level optimal capital structure solution.

Tests of the more recent developments of capital structure theory

Empirical evidence supporting the more recent developments of capital structure theory will be examined next, and includes evidence on factors which have not yet been expressly discussed within any theoretical framework. The determinants of capital structure discussed in this section are corporate tax exhaustion, the corporate tax rate, company size and profitability.

Corporate tax exhaustion reduces the tax advantage to debt, and comes about due to the use of non-debt tax allowances, such as those used to encourage investment, and/or insufficient profits. Evidence from Cordes and Sheffrin (1981,1983), Mayer and Morris (1982) and the Government Green Paper on Corporation Tax (1982) indicate the significance of corporate tax exhaustion. Cordes and Sheffrin (1981) conducted research which revealed that the tax liability of US non-financial corporations was reduced by only 32 cents for each dollar of interest deductions at a time when the corporate tax rate was 46 cents in the dollar. They repeated this research for all US corporations in 1983 and found a similar value for tax deductions, finding also that marginal tax rates were reasonably constant over time. Thus, tax exhaustion is, and has been in the long-term, a significant determinant of capital structure, reducing the tax advantage to debt. For the UK, Mayer and Morris (1982) conducted similar research which supported the significance of corporate tax exhaustion. Indeed, the UK Government's Green Paper on Corporation Tax (1982) revealed that a third of companies have an effective tax rate of zero, with approximately another third paying *any* corporation tax only on an occasional basis. Thus corporate tax exhaustion definitely appears to detrimentally affect any tax advantage to debt in the real world, reducing taxable income towards zero. As the degree of corporate tax exhaustion, caused by insufficient profits and investment and other non-debt allowances, is firm-specific, this implies firm-level optimal capital structures, which appears to support the MM (1963) relevancy model.

Corporation tax is assimilated into many of the capital structure models, but is rarely explicitly considered on its own as a determinant of corporate capital structure. DeAngelo and Masulis (1980) argued that changes in the rate of corporation tax should directly affect the debt-equity ratio, such that an increase in the corporate tax rate should increase aggregate debt-equity-ratios. Indeed, Holland and Myers (1977), studying US non-financial organisations, found that the aggregate debt-equity ratio increased dramatically between 1940 and 1942. [12] There is strong evidence to support a strong positive long-term relationship between the debt-equity ratio and the corporate tax rate.

Inflation appears to be an important determinant in a firm's choice of capital structure mix. DeAngelo and Masulis (1980) hypothesised that:

> Ceteris paribus, decreases in allowable investment-related tax shields ....due to changes in inflation which reduce the value of tax shields will increase the amount of debt that firms employ. [13]

Indeed, Corcoran (1977), Zwick (1977) and Holland and Myers (1977) all found the inflation rate to be positively related to firms' leverage ratios. For example, Corcoran (1977) argued that higher inflation produced higher nominal interest rates, which produced higher tax deductions, which in turn would produce increases in debt funding. Corcoran showed, by empirical testing, that significant increases in the leverage of non-financial corporations in the US were paralleled by the acceleration of inflation. Thus, there is strong evidence to support a positive relation between the rate of inflation and the extent of debt in a firm's capital structure.

Size is a possible determinant of the firm's capital structure. Marsh (1982) and Scott and Martin (1975) found the debt-equity ratio of the firm to be positively related to its size. Marsh explained this relationship as being due to the economies of scale associated with flotation costs. However, Gupta (1969) and Remmers et al (1974) found no such relationship. Gupta found the ratio of total debt to total assets to be negatively related to firm size, but that the type of debt employed by smaller firms was predominantly short-term in nature. Remmers et al tested a wide range of countries for a relationship between capital structure and firm size, but found no evidence of a significant relationship. Although the evidence is mixed, there appears to be some evidence, then, that the debt-equity ratio increases as the size of the firm increases.

There may be a relationship between the profitability of a firm and its capital structure, some authors have postulated. Gupta (1969) tested such a relationship in his study of US manufacturing firms but found no such relationship to exist, questioning the theory that more profitable firms have more internally generated funds and thus require less debt funding. [14]

To summarise this section, tests of some of the more recent developments in capital structure theory have been discussed, and inferences drawn from the results. The debt-equity ratio of the firm does appear to be significantly related to the degree of corporate tax exhaustion, the nominal tax rate, the rate of inflation and firm size, but does not appear to be related to the profitability of the individual firm. The degree of corporate tax exhaustion and firm size are firm-specific factors, which give further support to the existence of firm-level optimal capital structures. The theory of capital structure relevancy to the individual firm appears to be reinforced by empirical testing of the individual determinants of capital structure.

Tests for the existence of target debt-equity ratios

Owing to the difficulties inherent in testing for the existence of an optimal leverage ratio for the firm, some authors chose instead to determine empirically whether there exists a 'target' leverage ratio for individual firms. Indeed, Ang (1976) argued that:

> The existence of an optimum leverage ratio implies the existence of a target ratio, but not necessarily vice versa. [15]

The evidence supporting such target debt-equity ratios, based on industry average debt-equity ratios, is, however, quite considerable, and includes research conducted by: Ang (1976), Briscoe and Hawke (1976), Schwartz and Aronson (1967), Scott (1972), Lev (1969), Remmers et al (1974), Scott and Martin (1975) and Donaldson (1961). Evidence questioning the existence of such target debt-equity ratios is presented by Stonehill et al (1975) and Stonehill and Stitzel (1969).

There is thus much support for the existence of industry-average target debt-equity ratios. Ang (1976) postulated many different models of debt policy and tested them all for performance on real world data. He found that a 'partial-adjustment towards a target debt-equity ratio' model performed best of all the models, suggesting that firms do indeed have a target debt-equity ratio, but adjustment towards this ratio is only partial in any one period, implying that a time-series lag structure might be present. Briscoe and Hawke (1976), Schwartz and Aronson (1967), Scott (1972), Lev (1969), and Scott and Martin (1975) all conducted empirical tests on capital structure data, and found that firms appeared to adjust their financial ratios to industry-wide averages. They generally found that differences in gearing between industries is greater than differences in gearing between firms in the same industry. Remmers et al (1974) found that industry class was an important determinant of a firm's capital structure in France and Japan, but not in the US, the Netherlands and Norway. The existence of target ratios may therefore be more prevalent in certain countries. Donaldson (1961), conducted research into firms' behaviour with respect to financial ratios and found that, with respect to debt, there was:

> Considerable evidence of conformity in industry thinking and practice and a sensitivity to the reactions of those competitors who were considered to be near rivals. [16]

Thus, Donaldson's questionnaire and interviews gave further support, from a behavioural viewpoint, to firms basing their target debt-equity ratios on industry averages. The evidence in support of the existence of industry average target debt-equity ratios appears to be substantial.

Evidence questioning the existence of industry average debt-equity ratios is much weaker. Stonehill et al (1975) conducted a survey of firms from a number of different countries and found that firms did not consider their industry's norm as a target debt-equity ratio to be an important factor. Stonehill and Stitzel (1969) found that debt ratios clustered more by country than by industry, but this is contrary to the large body of research reported earlier in this section. There thus appears to be little evidence refuting the existence of firms setting their target debt-equity ratios as industry average ratio levels.

The evidence in support of the existence of firm-level target debt-equity ratio based on an industry average is therefore substantial. The evidence thus *suggests* that firms do have an optimal debt-equity ratio (capital structure), but the theory arrives at a 'relevancy' conclusion by different means than the MM (1963) tax-based model. The evidence supports an optimal solution on a behavioural, pragmatic approach by firms, rather than a complex solution based on tax factors.

Summary and conclusions

The main conclusion from the review of theory in the second section of this chapter was that many of the theories gravitated towards firm-level optimal capital structure solutions. The empirical evidence, somewhat interestingly, also points towards such a firm level optimal solution. Tests of the Modigliani and Miller (1958,1963) models reveal that only MM (1963) is supported by the evidence, the model which reinstates firm-level capital structure relevancy based on a distinct tax advantage to debt funding. Bankruptcy and agency costs appear to be significant determinants in a firm's capital structure choice, and both costs trade-off against the tax advantages to debt to produce an optimal capital structure. Financial risk and the agency relationship are specific to the individual firm, also suggesting the likelihood of solutions at firm level. The degree of corporate tax exhaustion, the nominal corporate tax rate, the rate of inflation, and firm size all appear to be significant determinants of corporate capital structure, when tested empirically. Again such factors support a firm level optimal capital structure mix. Finally, there is strong evidence of firm level target debt-equity ratios based on an industry average, a theory which arrives at a 'relevancy' conclusion by different means than the MM (1963) tax-based model. Thus, the theories of capital structure and the empirical evidence appear to suggest the existence of optimal firm-level capital structures, which are determined by a large number of factors, some firm-specific, some environment specific, and some of which are certainly influenced greatly by specific tax frameworks. The capital structure decision should thus be of great *relevance* to any individual firm, which should choose a capital structure which minimises the costs and maximises the benefits associated with the funding instruments available to it.

Testing for the significance of taxation and other factors that affect capital structure in Europe

Introduction and Methodology

The purpose of this section is to test some of the theories examined, and to extend the work of some of the empirical tests reviewed, particularly as many of the tests concentrate on the US and the UK alone. Using the Datastream 'on-line' financial information database, data were drawn for the following 11 European countries: Belgium, Denmark, France, United Germany, Eire, Italy, the Netherlands, Spain, Sweden, Switzerland, and the UK. Data on Greece, Luxembourg and Portugal were not available. Utilising this accurate and extensive dataset, then, summary statistics, regression analysis, and other techniques may be used to test the main theories of finance. The work is only preliminary, and perhaps naive in parts, but some important and at times surprising results are produced.

Firstly, the distributions of debt-equity ratios across Europe are described, producing some interesting results which appear to question the Miller 1977 general equilibrium model. This section also takes a prima facie look at the variation of the mean debt-equity ratio with a country's tax system and nominal corporate tax rate.

Secondly, econometric regression analysis is used to examine the relationship between a firm's capital structure (its debt-equity ratio) and some basic tax measures, firm size and various financial ratios.

Finally, the main results are drawn from the empirical research undertaken, along with a consideration of whether the theories examined earlier in the chapter do in fact apply across Europe, rather than solely for the US.

Preliminary observations and non-regression descriptive analysis

A wealth of information may be derived from casual observation of European capital structure data, as well as simple statistical summary measures of the data. The variables required to construct the capital structure measure, the debt to debt plus equity ratio, were not available for all firms, reducing the sample size in each country. For most of the countries this was not a problem, but for countries such as Eire, the effect of this was to reduce the sample size to only 14 companies, greatly reducing the viability of statistical and econometric analysis. The debt constituent of the ratio is the total loan capital of the firm, and the equity constituent is the market value of the firm's total equity. [17] Rutterford (1988) argued that inter-country comparisons were plagued by differences between countries such as: different cost conventions, the degree of consolidation of accounts, the predominance of short-term or long-term debt, and differences in the treatment of provisions and pensions in the accounts. However, as this study is merely a preliminary observation of European capital structures, any adjustments to take account of such differences will feature in future studies to develop this work.

Table 6.1 presents some useful summary statistics for each of the countries in the study. Table 6.2 ranks the countries by their debt-equity ratio. Switzerland has the highest long-term debt, as a proportion of total funding, in Europe, and the UK has the lowest. Most countries have ratios in the debt range of 20 per cent to 40 per cent. One might expect companies in Switzerland to have the highest debt in Europe, due to the highly developed banking and debt institutions and banking culture in Switzerland. The relatively high proportion of equity funding in the UK is probably a result of the UK's highly developed stock markets.

Table 6.1
Summary statistics of the debt to debt plus equity ratios of European countries

Country	Mean	Standard Deviation	Minimum	Maximum	Number of Observations
Belgium	0.51	0.35	0.00	0.99	63
Denmark	0.34	0.29	0.00	0.92	46
Eire	0.40	0.22	0.00	0.74	14
France	0.34	0.28	0.00	1.00	346
Germany	0.30	0.29	0.00	0.98	201
Italy	0.45	0.34	0.00	1.00	92
Netherlands	0.26	0.26	0.00	0.99	59
Spain	0.25	0.26	0.00	0.80	47
Sweden	0.27	0.28	0.00	0.98	119
Switzerland	0.55	0.28	0.00	1.00	142
UK	0.20	0.24	0.00	1.00	1497

Table 6.2
The ranking of European countries by the debt to debt plus equity ratios of their firms

Rank	Country	Debt to debt plus equity ratio	Rank	Country	Standard deviation of the ratio
1	Switzerland	0.55	1	Belgium	0.35
2	Belgium	0.51	2	Italy	0.34
3	Italy	0.45	3	Denmark	0.29
4	Eire	0.40	3	Germany	0.29
5	Denmark	0.34	5	France	0.28
5	France	0.34	5	Sweden	0.28
7	Germany	0.30	5	Switzerland	0.28
8	Sweden	0.27	8	Netherlands	0.26
9	Netherlands	0.26	8	Spain	0.26
10	Spain	0.25	10	UK	0.24
11	UK	0.20	11	Eire	0.22

Table 6.2 also shows that the standard deviations of capital structure distributions are mainly found within the range of 0.26 to 0.29, and that such standard deviations increase with the size of the debt-equity ratio. [18] A preliminary interpretation of these results must be that there are a wide range of capital structure mixes across European firms, and differentials between countries appear to be significant. The degree of development of financial institutions, the degree of specialism in particular funding instruments, and the 'financial culture' of a country might be important factors in corporate finance within a country.

Table 6.3 again shows countries ranked by the mean of their firms' debt-equity ratios, but also shows the type of tax system which each country employs. Apart from the two extremes, Switzerland and the UK, the countries with the highest mean debt-equity ratios employ imputation/tax credit tax systems and the countries with the lowest ratios employ classical tax systems. This result is fascinating as it is clearly counterintuitive.

The classical tax system effectively taxes the returns on equity twice, first at the corporate level and then at the personal level, thus discriminating against equity returns. One thus might expect countries with classical tax systems to use more debt in their capital structures than countries of non-classical tax systems. This counterintuitive result appears to be supported by evidence from Rutterford (1988).

Table 6.3
The ranking of European countries by their debt to debt plus equity ratios and taxation system types

Rank	Country	Debt to debt plus equity ratio	Tax system	Corporate tax rate %
1	Switzerland	0.55	Classical	10 to 27
2	Belgium	0.51	Imputation/Tax Credit	39
3	Italy	0.45	Imputation/Tax Credit	36
4	Eire	0.40	Imputation/Tax Credit	40
=5	Denmark	0.34	Imputation/Tax Credit	38
=5	France	0.34	Imputation/Tax Credit	34
7	Germany	0.30	Imputation/Tax Credit	50
8	Sweden	0.27	Imputation/Tax Credit	30
9	Netherlands	0.26	Classical	35
10	Spain	0.25	Classical	35
11	UK	0.20	Imputation/Tax Credit	33

Rutterford found in a study of the capital structures of various countries that:

> Despite the reductions in the tax advantage of debt as Japan, France, Germany, and the UK moved towards an imputation tax system during the 1960's and 1970's ... leverage ratios appear in most cases to have increased over time. [19]

She also explained why there was a distinct preference for equity funding in the UK and that the UK had a well developed equity market:

> With efficient information dissemination, stringent auditing and monitoring procedures and low issue costs, which keep the agency costs of equity to a minimum. [20]

Figure 6.1 Belgium: The distribution of corporate capital structures

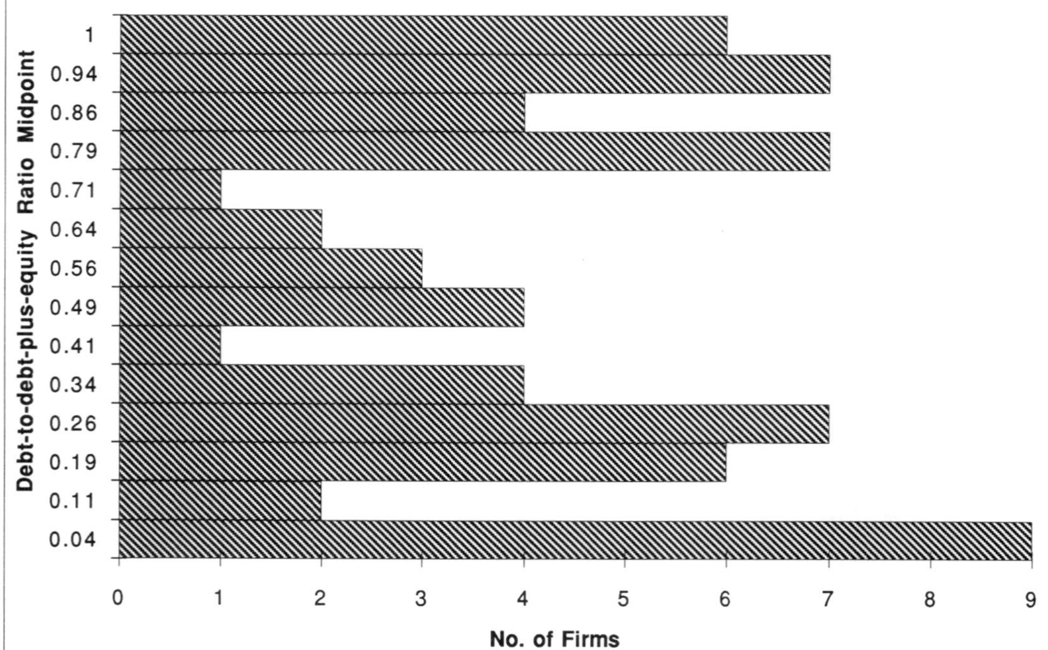

Thus, such institutional factors, especially agency and issue costs, may explain the extreme capital structure seen in the UK, and may explain the extreme debt preference seen in Swiss firms.

Table 6.3 also shows the corporate tax rate of each country, but there appears to be no obvious relationship between the mean debt-equity ratio of a country and its nominal corporate tax rate. This result questions the theory of DeAngelo and Masulis (1980), who argued that the rate of corporation tax was an important determinant of the debt-equity ratio, and the result also contrasts the evidence of Holland and Myers (1977), which supported their theory. Thus, the counterintuitivity of the relationship between a country's mean debt-equity ratio and its tax system may suggest that factors other than taxation are more important determinants of a firm's capital structure mix across Europe. This statement is further tested in the univariate analysis of simple tax ratios, described later in this section.

Figures 6.1 and 6.2 depict the two main types of debt-equity ratio distribution observed across Europe. Figure 6.1 shows the distribution for Belgian firms, which represents, approximately, a bimodal shape. Figure 6.2 shows the distribution for UK firms, which clearly represents an exponential decay shape. Debt-equity ratio distribution histograms are plotted for each European country studied, but because most conform to one of the distribution types already described, that is, either bimodal or exponential decay, the other histograms are described rather than depicted later in this section. Kim, Lewellen and McConnell (1979) argued that, if Miller's 1977 capital structure irrelevance theory held, then the distribution of capital structures within a country should be bimodal. They argued that investors would specialise their stock holdings in those firms whose capital structures satisfy their personal tax requirements. Thus, they would gain higher returns, after tax, for a given amount of leverage and a given amount of investment, by specialising in such a manner. Low tax bracket investors would buy shares in highly geared firms, whereas high tax bracket investors would buy shares of firms with low gearing or no gearing at all, thus obtaining the gearing they require through personal borrowing. They inferred from this that low tax bracket investors demand firms with low gearing policies and high tax bracket investors demand firms with high gearing policies. Thus firms accommodate investors by employing no debt or high debt relative to overall funding. A bimodal capital structure distribution will thus arise, whereby low (high) tax bracket investors will hold stocks of firms in the higher (lower) mode.

Table 6.4 summarises the shapes of the various distributions. The table shows that such bimodal distributions can only be said to exist in Belgium, Italy and Spain, and that most distributions are of an exponential decay shape. Thus, Kim, Lewellen and McConnell's indirect test of Miller's financial leverage theory, which tests for the presence of

Figure 6.2 U.K.: The distribution of corporate capital structures

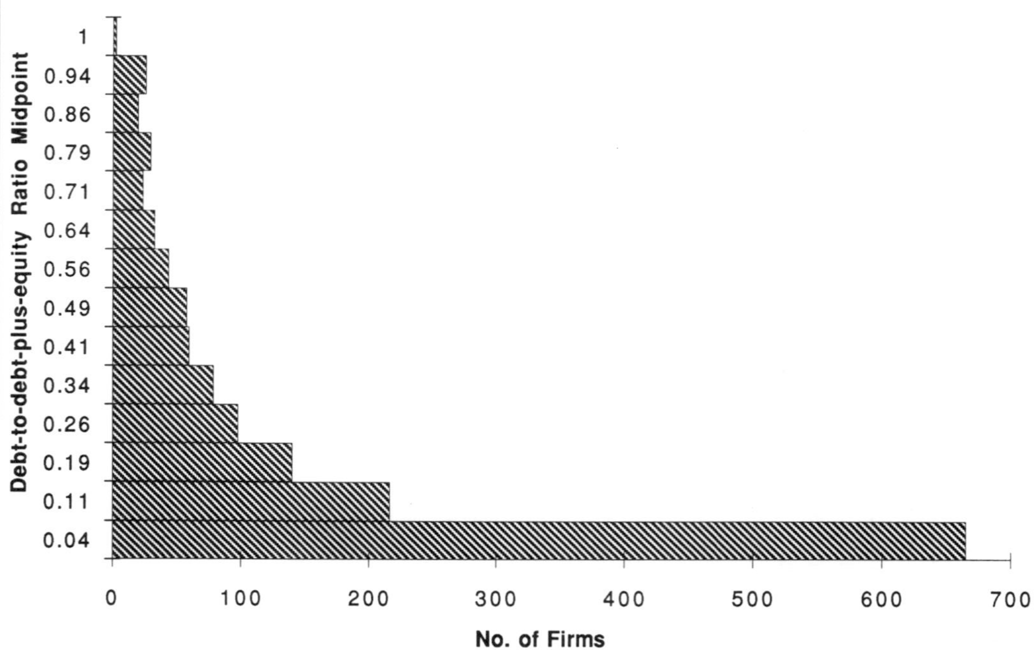

bimodal corporate capital structures, generally reveals a lack of such bimodal distributions across Europe. Such results, albeit as part of a somewhat indirect test of the Miller 1977 model, may severely weaken the model, as it would appear to have only limited application across Europe. Firm-level capital structure irrelevance is thus questioned, a proposition that is supported by both the theoretical and empirical sections of this chapter.

Table 6.4
Summary of European firm debt to debt plus equity ratio distribution types

Country	Debt to debt plus equity distribution shape	Bimodal Distribution (Yes/No)
Belgium	bimodal	Yes
Denmark	exponential decay	No
Eire	flat	No
France	exponential decay	No
Germany	exponential decay	No
Italy	bimodal	Yes
Netherlands	exponential decay	No
Spain	bimodal	Yes
Sweden	exponential decay	No
Switzerland	flat/unimodal	No
UK	exponential decay	No

To summarise, perusal and simple analysis of European capital structure data reveals that: there are significant differentials in the mean debt-equity ratios (the capital structure mix) across European countries; that institutional factors may be an important factor determining capital structures; that apart from the extreme cases, the countries with higher debt-equity ratio firms employ imputation/tax credit systems, a result which is both fascinating and counterintuitive; that the degree of debt funding appears unrelated to the nominal corporate tax rate of a country; and, finally, that the general lack of bimodality of capital structure distributions questions the usefulness of the Miller (1977) general equilibrium model in explaining European capital structures.

A univariate regression analysis of the factors affecting capital structure

Introduction

Least squares regression analysis is a method used for fitting linear, and non-linear via data transformations, mathematical functions to observed data. This process reveals the linear relationship between two variables, so that a model can be developed which predicts the movement of one of the variables as the other is varied.

The data to be examined are cross-section data for 11 European countries, drawn from the Datastream on-line database computer system. The data are tidied and imported into SPSS, a versatile statistical and data manipulation package. The regression analysis is performed within the SPSS package, which is also used to produce some useful descriptive statistics.

Methodology

Univariate regression analysis is used to examine the relationship between capital structure (the debt to debt plus equity ratio) and a number of variables, which are either absolute variables or ratios. The variables tested using regression analysis are either drawn directly from Datastream or calculated, as in the case of some of the ratios, after drawing such data. Table 6.5 shows the results of all the univariate tests across the European firms, detailing the direction of any significant relationship between the debt-equity ratio and each measure. The t-test is used to test for the significance of independent slope coefficients, and are tested using a 1-tail test at the 5 per cent level. The purpose of the tests is to discover the important determinants of European firms' capital structures, as well as to test some of the theories discussed earlier in this chapter. Where tests are similar to previous empirical research, the results shall be compared and discussed. The general observations, results and interpretation are described in turn, and are summarised.

i) Size measures

The debt to debt plus equity ratio was regressed on firm size, which was measured by the value of total assets. Such an analysis was undertaken to extend the research of authors, such as Marsh (1982) and Scott and Martin (1975) who found a positive relationship and Gupta (1969) who found a negative relationship, for Europe rather than the US alone. A significant positive relationship was found to exist for firms in Belgium, Germany and Spain, but no such relationship was apparent for the rest of Europe. This therefore supports the findings of Marsh and Scott and Martin, but only for these countries. Remmers et al (1974) found that no significant relationship existed between the debt-equity ratio and firm size in Japan, the Netherlands, Norway and the United States, but found a significant positive relationship for France, thus questioning the wider application of any relationship. Thus, generally, no significant relationship exists for European firms, between the debt-equity ratio and the size of the firm, refuting theories of such a relationship being positive due to the reduced risk, reduced debt and flotation costs and so on, of larger firms.

Table 6.5

Summary results of the univariate regression analyses

(The table shows those slope coefficients which are significant at the 5% level using a 1-tail t-test)

Variable	Country Code (refer to key)										
	BG	DK	IR	FR	BD	IT	NL	ES	SD	SW	UK
Total assets employed (size)	P				P			P			
Tax ratio							N				
Tax ratio (dep'n adjusted)						N	N				N
Quick assets ratio		N			N	N		N			N
Current assets ratio		N			N	N				N	N
Payout ratio							N				
Dividend yield		P		P		P	P				P
Current dividend cover	N	N		N	N	N	N		N	N	
Earnings per share		N		N	N		N	N	N	N	N
Price/earnings ratio					N		N			P	
Return on capital employed	N	N		N	N	N	N	N		N	N
Net profit margin		N		N	N	N	N	N			
Interest cover	N	N	N	N	N	N	N	N		N	N
Beta				P			P				P

KEY:
P = significant positive relationship at the 5 per cent level (1 tail)
N = significant negative relationship at the 5 per cent level (1 tail)

Country codes: BG=Belgium ;DK=Denmark ; IR=Eire; FR=France; BD=Germany; IT=Italy; NL=Netherlands; ES=Spain; SD=Sweden; SW=Switzerland; UK=United Kingdom

ii) Tax measures

The two tax ratios used were: tax to pre-tax profit, and tax to (pre-tax profit plus depreciation), where tax is the corporation tax charged on profit for the current period, and depreciation is depreciation charged per the profit and loss account for the period. The tax ratios are expressed as a ratio of profit to enable testing of *relative* measures of taxation. Development of the Modigliani and Miller (1958,1963) and Miller (1977) models centred on the importance of taxation at the level of the firm and in aggregate. The results reveal that the simple tax ratio is significantly negatively related to the debt-equity ratio only for the Netherlands, and when the ratio is adjusted for depreciation, the Netherlands, Italy and the UK display a significant negative correlation. Depreciation is added back in to pre-tax profit to allow for a better comparison of firms, as some firm may employ more fixed assets than others. The direction of the relationship appears to support the theory, because as the extent of debt in the capital structure is increased, the tax charged is proportionately reduced, due to the tax-deductibility of debt interest payments. However, the general insignificance of the simple and depreciation-adjusted tax ratios does suggest that these ratios are greatly over-simplified. The actual tax charged in a particular year is the product of a number of years of tax computations, and is based on the profits/losses, investment and funding decisions, general corporate strategies of the individual firm, as well as changes in tax laws, tax rates and the economic environment generally. [21]

Thus, although a significant relationship does not generally appear to exist, a negative relationship does exist in some of the countries between the debt-equity ratio and simple tax ratios, but such ratios are generally over-simplifications of reality. However, Rutterford (1988) supported the apparently weak relationship between debt-equity ratios and tax factors in her comprehensive empirical study of various countries and concluded that:

> Tax factors, whether assuming a Modigliani and Miller model or an investor clientele model such as that proposed by Miller, do not appear to be able to explain cross-sectional differences (in debt-equity ratios). [22]

There is certainly impetus here for further work to discover a relative firm-level measure of corporate taxation which determines the capital structure of European firms, but due to the diversity of tax systems, a common measure would appear to be difficult to find.

iii) Liquidity measures

The liquidity ratios tested are the current assets ratio and the quick assets ratio. The current assets ratio is the total current assets of the firm divided by total current liabilities, whereas the quick assets ratio is the ratio of total current assets less total stock and work in progress to total current liabilities. The results show that both are significantly negatively related to the debt-equity ratio. Such relationships occur for Denmark, Germany, Italy and the UK, with the relationship for the current assets ratio also occurring in Switzerland, and the relationship for the quick assets ratio also occurring in Spain. The relationship is most interesting, as a relationship must then exist between a firm's long-term capital structure and its short-term liquidity position. Thus, both measures suggest that higher long-term debt is generally associated with higher short-term, as a proportion of funding. A questionnaire researched by Stonehill et al (1975) to discover the important determinants of debt ratios in a number of countries, found that liquidity was generally not an important determinant, as it only ranked highly in Norway. The results of the research detailed in this section of the chapter appear to refute the results of Stonehill et al (1975), then, as measures of liquidity appear to be very important determinants of (or indeed a consequence of) capital structure mix.

iv) Dividend measures

The dividend measures tested separately in a univariate regression analysis, to discover their significance in the determination of firms' capital structures, were the payout ratio, dividend yield and current dividend cover. The payout ratio is simply the dividend per share expressed as a proportion of earnings per share. The dividend yield is the dividend per share divided by the share price. Current dividend cover expresses the number of times earnings cover the payment of a dividend. The results show that there is little evidence of a relationship between the debt-equity ratio and the payout ratio across Europe, as such a relationship is significant only for the Netherlands. Martin and Scott (1975) found the payout ratio to be an important variable in their discriminant function of the debt-equity decision, and suggested that an increase in the payout ratio might logically lead to an increase in leverage usage. [23] However, for the exceptional case of the Netherlands, although data on incremental funding decisions was not analysed, a negative relationship resulted from the regression analysis, which is of the opposite direction to that which might be expected. There is evidence, however, of a significant positive relationship between firm debt-equity ratios and dividend yield in Denmark, France, Italy, the Netherlands and the UK. This may be due to the higher rate of return demanded by shareholders as debt is increased, thus increasing the relative size of the dividend payment. Finally, there is generally a significant negative relationship between the debt-equity ratio and current dividend cover across Europe, with the exception of Eire, Spain and the UK. This suggests that as the level of debt funding increases as a proportion of total funding, so does the likelihood of firms not being able to afford to pay dividends to equity holders. Thus, an increase in debt funding increases the riskiness of the firm, although non-payment of dividends does not result in bankruptcy as non-payment of debt-commitments does. To summarise, univariate regression analysis of various dividend measures against the debt-equity ratio of firms suggests that: the payout ratio is not an important determinant, contrary to expectations; that higher debt funding is associated with higher dividend payments as a proportion of earnings; and that higher debt funding increases the risk of non-payment of dividends.

v) Earnings measures

The earnings measures which were regressed against the debt-equity ratio were: earnings per share and the price/earnings ratio. Earnings per share is the total earnings in the last 12 months, expressed as a percentage of the price of a share. The price/earnings ratio is the price of a share divided by the earnings per share. Earnings per share are found to be negatively related to debt-equity ratios across Europe, except in Belgium, Eire and Italy. Thus, earnings per share decrease with an increase in the proportion of debt funding. However, Tamari (1978) argued that such a ratio is of limited use because:

> As there is little significance in the number of shares issued by economically similar companies, inter-firm comparisons are made devoid of any real meaning. [24]

The price/earnings ratio is a far better measure of relative earnings. The price/earnings ratio, however, is only significantly related (negatively) to the debt-equity ratio in Germany and the Netherlands, and significantly related (positively) to the debt-equity ratio in Switzerland. The price/earnings ratio for a share, Tamari argued, should reflect investor expectations regarding the earnings of the firm. Thus, investor expectations of earnings generally have no statistically significant influence on the debt-equity mix of European firms, and equity earnings appear to be reduced as long-term debt funding is increased, the latter probably due to the increased commitments associated with debt repayment.

vi) Profitability measures

Toy et al. (1974) hypothesised that:

> A firm with a high earnings rate (profitability), ceteris paribus, would maintain a relatively lower debt ratio because of its ability to finance itself from internally generated funds. [25]

They found evidence of a significant negative relationship in the US, Holland, Japan and Norway. However, Gupta (1969), in his study of US manufacturing firms, found that there was no significant relationship between profitability (as measured by the productivity of assets or the rate of return on net worth) and the ratio of total debt to total assets (a debt-equity measure).

The two profitability ratios tested, using univariate regression analysis, were the return on capital employed, the ratio of profit before interest and taxes to capital employed, and the net profit margin, the ratio of net profit before interest and taxation to turnover. Of these measures, the return on capital employed is probably the better measure of profitability as it indicates how successful a firm is at utilising its assets. The results show that a significant negative relationship exists between the debt-equity ratio and the return on capital employed in all countries with the exception of Eire and Sweden. A significant negative relationship also exists between the debt-equity ratio and the net profit margin, but only for Denmark, France, Germany, Italy, the Netherlands and Spain. The latter ratio may suggest that the higher debt firms in the above countries are associated with lower selling prices, or higher costs.

Overall, it must be concluded that Gupta's (1969) results for the US do not hold for Europe, and that the research of Toy et al (1975) appears to be supported by evidence from European firms. Therefore, the more profitable firms in Europe appear to employ less debt as a proportion of funding, funding themselves more from the funds generated by past and current profits.

vii) Bankruptcy measures

The two bankruptcy measures tested were: the firm's equity beta and interest cover. Beta relates movements in the price of a stock to movements in the market as a whole. Thus, the higher beta is, the more erratic is the movement of a stock's price and thus this could be a proxy for bankruptcy risk. Interest cover is simply adjusted operating profit, plus total non-operating income, expressed as a percentage of total interest charges. It is thus a measure of how safely a firm can cover its interest charges on debt, and can thus be used as a good proxy for bankruptcy risk.

The results show that there is a significant positive relationship between the debt-equity ratio and beta for France, the Netherlands and the UK. However, although most countries show no such relationship, the beta factor is not widely available across Europe. Thus, there does appear to be a significant positive relationship between the debt-equity ratio of a firm and its beta, showing that as the proportion of debt funding increases, so does risk generally, and bankruptcy risk in particular. Apart from Sweden alone, there is a very significant negative relationship between interest cover and debt-equity ratios across Europe. This provides very strong evidence in support of bankruptcy risk/costs being a significant determinant of firm-level corporate capital structure. The results confirm the work of Marsh (1982), who found bankruptcy risk to be a significant determinant of firm capital structures in the UK. The risk of bankruptcy is therefore probably one of the most important limiting factors to the extent of debt employed in the capital structures of European firms.

Summary of univariate regression analyses

The salient results from the univariate regression analyses of shall be summarised, to identify the most important determinants of European firm capital structures.

There is limited evidence of a positive linear relationship between the debt-equity ratio and firm size, but such a relationship is certainly not found right across Europe, supporting the results of authors such as Remmers et al (1974). The simple and depreciation-adjusted tax ratios did not appear to be related to firms' debt-equity ratios across Europe, probably due to the naiveté of such ratios. Contrary to the evidence of Stonehill et al (1975), the liquidity ratios appeared to be significant determinants of the debt-equity mix. The payout ratio did not appear to be an important determinant of capital structure in Europe. However, higher debt firms were associated with higher dividend payments as a proportion of earnings, and the risk of default on dividend payments appears to increase as debt funding increases across Europe. Equity earnings are reduced as debt funding is increased, because of the increased mandatory payments associated with debt as opposed to equity. Testing of the significance of the earnings measures suggests that the more profitable European firms employ less debt in their capital structure, funding themselves instead from retained earnings. The bankruptcy risk measures appear to be extremely important determinants of European firms' capital structures, as the increased risk of bankruptcy limits the extent of funding by long-term debt.

The direction of causation remains unresolved in many of these univariate models. For example, more profitable firms may use less debt, or alternatively, firms with greater debt may be less profitable. Univariate regression analysis merely produces a model with a significant relationship between the debt-equity ratio and profitability measures. It is therefore difficult to ascertain the direction of causation, and thus the univariate models must be interpreted within a wider perspective, utilising the knowledge of the real-world mechanisms by which variables are linked to make assumptions about causation.

Therefore, univariate regression analysis has enabled identification of the more important, or at least statistically significant, determinants of European firm-level capital structures. It is interesting to note the cases where theory and tests of US firms do not hold or produce similar results across Europe. Future development of this research will attempt to combine the more important determinants of corporate capital structure into a model of capital structure, across Europe and for each individual country, so that the relative importance of determinants may be ascertained for each country, and so that differentials may be further interpreted.

Summary and conclusions deriving from the European capital structure research

The purpose of this section of the chapter was to test some of the theories discussed, and to expand upon some of the empirical work reviewed earlier in this chapter, with particular attention to extending tests across Europe where such tests appear to have concentrated on the US and UK economies alone.

Preliminary investigation of the data yielded many interesting observations. Significant differentials in the mean debt-equity ratios of firms exist across European countries, which may partly be explained by institutional factors. Apart from extreme cases, the countries with higher debt-equity ratios firms employ imputation/tax credit systems, which is counterintuitive. The general lack of bimodality of European capital structure distributions questions the usefulness of the Miller (1977) general equilibrium model in explaining European capital structures.

This section of the chapter also summarised the results of an extensive test of the possible determinants of European corporate capital structure. There appeared to be only limited evidence of a relationship between firm size and capital structure. The naive tax models tested generally revealed no relationship with capital structures. Higher debt European firms appeared to be associated with higher dividend payments as a proportion of earnings. As debt funding increases, the risk of default on dividend payments increases across Europe. Equity earnings are generally reduced as debt funding is increased. The more profitable European firms employ less debt, and prefer to fund from retained earnings. Measures of bankruptcy risk appear to be very important determinants of corporate capital structure in Europe.

Therefore, the general points arising from the empirical research of European capital structure are that there are significant differences between corporate capital structures in Europe, which is partly explained by tax and institutional framework differentials. Intra-country capital structure differences appear to be explained by differences in dividend policy, profitability and earnings, and bankruptcy and dividend risk. The theory of firm-level optimal capital structures within a country would appear to be supported by the importance of firm-level, firm-specific capital structure determinants.

Conclusion

The chapter set out with the objective of readdressing the question, 'does capital structure actually matter?', in the light of modern theory and empirical research. Evidence from European firms would suggest that it certainly does matter, and suggests possible determinants of capital structure.

The review of theoretical literature revealed a progression away from the pragmatic conservatism of conventional finance theory towards a more scientific approach, based on mathematical derivation and empirical proof. Although Modigliani and Miller proposed capital structure irrelevance in 1958, to be reinstated by Miller in his 1977 general equilibrium model, the less appealing capital structure theory of MM (1963), and the other theories supporting optimal firm-level capital structures, appear to have greater validity. Imperfections present in the models, such as bankruptcy and agency costs, appear to militate towards an optimal firm-level solution, as do most of the institutional and behavioural constraints on firms, discussed in the more recent theories of capital structure. The multitude of firm-specific factors suggest that capital structures must be optimal to the *individual* firm.

The review of empirical literature promotes Modigliani and Miller's 1963 tax advantage to debt model as being supported by the evidence, and the irrelevance models appear to be greatly weakened. A distinct tax advantage arising from debt funding thus seems plausible. Bankruptcy and agency costs, although difficult to test for significance, are probably capable of producing a non-tax optimal solution. Indeed, corporate tax exhaustion may produce an optimal capital structure before even bankruptcy and agency cost become significant. The scale of operations of the firm appears to point towards a particular capital structure mix, as does the external imposition of the corporate tax rate and inflation. There is also strong evidence of firm-level target debt-equity ratios, based on industry average ratios, evidence which arrives at a capital structure 'relevancy' proposition by different means than taxation. The evidence thus supports the existence of firm-level optimal capital structures, both within and without a tax framework, to arrive at a capital structure 'relevancy' conclusion which is supported by theoretical reasoning.

Research conducted on capital structure data reveals significant differences between corporate capital structures of different European countries. There is evidence, derived from capital structure distribution patterns, refuting the existence of investor clienteles, a concept central to the Miller (1977) general equilibrium model. There is evidence also that tax and institutional factors may have an important influence on differentials. The determinants of capital structure across Europe appear to be factors such as: dividend policy, earnings and profitability, and bankruptcy and dividend risk. The testing of such determinants across

Europe allows evidence from US oriented research to be extended, rather than assuming US results to have universal application. The highly developed taxation, economic and communications framework in place in the US is not present to such an extent across Europe, and many determinants of capital structure are thus shown to be specific to some individual countries and not others.

To summarise, the review of theoretical and empirical literature suggests optimal firm-level capital structures. The research conducted on European capital structure data supports this proposition, and highlights the importance of institutional, taxation and firm-specific determinants in producing optimal capital structure solutions, reinforcing the theory of capital structure 'relevance'. Capital structure does appear to matter.

Notes

1. Franks, J.R. and Broyles, J.E., "Modern Managerial Finance", John Wiley and Sons Ltd., 1979, page 292.
2. Brealey (1970) produced empirical evidence in support of weak-form efficiency, as did Firth (1967) for semi-strong-form efficiency.
3. For derivation refer to Miller (1977).
4. Jensen and Meckling (1976), page 308.
5. Mayer (1983), page 32.
6. However, Rutterford (1986) notes that equity will be issued if there are insufficient retained earnings and there is bankruptcy risk attached to too high a level of debt, thus questioning the validity of the Myers and Majluf funding preference model.
7. Dempsey (1991), page 221.
8. The fact that MM did not test enough observations on certain parts of the capital structure range may of itself suggest that firm capital structures were in fact bunched and that firms might be adjusting their debt-equity ratios towards some target ratio based on the average for their industry. The bunching may provide support for the theory of target debt-equity ratios, and thus optimal firm-level capital structures.
9. Sametz (1964), page 451.
10. Sametz (1964), page 468.
11. Kim, Lewellen and McConnell (1979), page 91.
12. Although this cannot really be considered a standard period, it does appear to suggest a relationship.
13. DeAngelo and Masulis (1980), page 21.
14. A general problem with respect to the direction of causation is highlighted here as in many of the empirical tests. For example, it could be postulated that more profitable firms will employ less debt,

preferring instead to fund investments using retained earnings. Alternatively, higher debt firms may be less profitable due to the mandatory commitments associated with debt repayment.

15. Ang (1976), page 555.
16. Donaldson (1961), page 81.
17. The debt-to-debt-plus-equity ratio describes only the long term funding of the firm. Long term funding is studied because of its relative stability when compared with short term funding, and also because long term funding is an important strategic decision of the firm, rather than the simple operational nature of short term funding decisions.
18. The standard deviation increases with increases in the debt-equity ratio, as the ratio is bounded between 0 and 1 by definition.
19. Rutterford (1988), page 202.
20. Rutterford (1988), page 206.
21. It could be argued that it would be better to study the variation in the use of debt with changing tax rates, as there may be little direct relationship between the tax actually paid and the relative use of debt.
22. Rutterford (1988), page 206.
23. Alternatively, this might represent an increase in the payout ratio as leverage is increased, for the purpose of compensating equity holders.
24. Tamari (1978), page 27.
25. Toy et al. (1974), page 877.

References

Ang, J.S. (1976), 'The Intertemporal Behaviour of Corporate Debt Policy', *Journal of Financial and Quantitative Analysis*, Vol. 11, Nov. 1976, pp. 555-66.

Ashton, D.J. (1989), 'Textbook Formulae and UK Taxation: Modigliani and Miller Revisited', *Accounting and Business Research*, Vol. 19, No. 75, pp. 207-12.

Auerbach, A.J. and King, M.A. (1983), 'Taxation, Portfolio Choice, and Debt-Equity Ratios: A General Equilibrium Model', *Quarterly Journal of Economics*, Nov. 1983, pp. 587-609.

Bailey, F.A. and Fung, W.K.H. (1978), 'A Note on Extreme Leverage MM and Ezra Solomon', *Journal of Business and Accounting*, Vol. 5, No. 2, pp. 253-59.

Barges, A. (1963), '*The Effect of Capital Structure on the Cost of Capital*', Prentice-Hall, Englewood Cliffs, New Jersey.

Baxter, N. (1967), 'Leverage, Risk of Ruin and the Cost of Capital', *Journal of Finance*, Vol. 22, pp. 395-403.

Boness, A.J. and Frankfurter, G.M. (1977), 'Evidence of Non-Homogeneity of Capital Costs Within Risk-Classes', *Journal of Finance*, Vol. 32, June 1977, pp. 775-87.
Brander, J.A. and Lewis, T.R. (1986), 'Oligopoly and Financial Structure: The Limited Liability Effect', *American Economic Review*, Vol. 76, pp. 956-70.
Brealey, R.A. (1970), 'The Distribution and Independence of Successive Rates of Return from the British Equity Market', *Journal of Business Finance*, Vol. 2, Summer, pp. 29-40.
Brennan, M. and Kraus, A. (1987), 'Efficient Financing under Asymmetric Information', *Journal of Finance*, Vol. 42, pp. 1225-43.
Briscoe, G. and Hawke, G. (1976), 'Long Term Debt and Realisable Gains in Shareholder Wealth: An Empirical Study', *Journal of Business Finance and Accounting*, Vol. 3, Spring 1976, pp. 125-35.
Constantinides, G.M. and Grundy, B.D. (1989), 'Optimal Investment with Stock Repurchase and Financing as Signals', *The Review of Financial Studies*, Vol. 2, pp. 445-66.
Corcoran, P. (1977), 'Inflation, Taxes, and Corporate Investment Incentives', *Federal Reserve Bank of New York Quarterly Review*, Vol. 2, pp. 1-9.
Cordes, J.J. and Sheffrin, S.M. (1981), 'Taxation and the Sectoral Allocation of Capital in the US', *National Tax Journal*, Dec. 1981, pp. 419-32.
Cordes, J.J. and Sheffrin, S.M. (1983), 'Estimating the Tax Advantage of Corporate Debt', *Journal of Finance*, Vol. 32, March 1983, pp. 95-105.
DeAngelo, H. and Masulis, R.W. (1980), 'Optimal Capital Structure Under Corporate and Personal Taxation', *Journal of Financial Economics*, Vol. 18, pp. 3-29.
Dempsey, M.J. (1991), 'Modigliani and Miller Again Revisited: The Cost of Capital with Unequal Borrowing and Lending Rates', *Accounting and Business Research*, Vol. 21, No. 83, pp. 221-26.
Donaldson, G. (1961), '*Corporate Debt Capacity: A Study of Corporate Debt Policy and the Determination of Corporate Debt Capacity*', Harvard Business School, Division of Research.
Durand, D. (1952), '*Cost of Debt and Equity Funds for Business: Trends and Problems of Measurement*', paper presented at a conference on Research in Business Finance, National Bureau of Economic Research, New York, reprinted by Archer and D'Ambrosio (1967).
Ferri, M.G. and Jones, W.H. (1979), 'Determinants of Financial Structure: A New Methodological Approach', *Journal of Finance*, Vol. 34, June 1979, pp. 631-44.
Franks, J.R. and Broyles, J.E. (1979), '*Modern Managerial Finance*', Chichester: John Wiley and Sons.
Freear, J. (1980), '*The Management of Business Finance*', Pitman Publishing Limited, London.

Gupta, M.C. (1969), 'The Effect of Size, Growth, and Industry on the Financial Structure of Manufacturing Companies', *Journal of Finance*, Vol. 24, June 1969, pp. 517-29.

Hamada, R.R. (1972), 'The Effect of the Firm's Capital Structure on the Systematic Risk of Common Stock', *Journal of Finance*, Vol. 27, pp. 435-52.

Haugen, R.A. and Senbet, L.W. (1978), 'The Insignificance of Bankruptcy Costs to the Theory of Optimal Capital Structure', *Journal of Finance*, Vol. 33, June 1978, pp. 383-93.

HMSO, '*Corporation Tax*', CMND. 8456, January 1982, Government Green Paper, London.

Holland, D. and Myers, S. (1977), '*Trends in Corporate Profitability and Capital Cost*', Working Paper (MIT, Cambridge, MA).

Jensen, M.C. and Meckling, W.H. (1976), 'Theory of the Firm: Managerial Behaviour, Agency Costs and Ownership Structure', *Journal of Financial Economics*, Vol. 3, pp. 78-133.

Kim, H., Lewellen, W. and McConnell, J. (1978), 'Financial Leverage Clienteles: Theory and Evidence', *Journal of Financial Economics*, Vol. 7, pp. 83-109.

Kraus, A. and Litzenberger, R. (1973), 'A State Preference Model of Optimal Financial Leverage', *Journal of Finance*, Vol. 28, pp. 911-22.

Leland, H. and Pyle, D. (1977), 'Informational Asymmetry, Financial Structure and Financial Intermediation', *Journal of Finance*, Vol. 32, May 1977, pp. 371-87.

Lev, B. (1969), 'Industry Averages as Targets for Financial Ratios', *Journal of Accounting Research*, Vol. 7, Autumn 1969, pp. 290-99.

Maksimovic, V. (1988), 'Capital Structure in Repeated Oligopolies', *Rand Journal of Economics*, Vol. 19, pp. 389-407.

Maksimovic, V. and Titman, S. (1991), 'Financial Policy and a firm's Reputation for Product Quality', *Review of Financial Studies*.

Marsh, P. (1982), 'The Choice Between Equity and Debt: An Empirical Study', *Journal of Finance*, March 1982, pp. 121-44.

Martin, J.D. and Scott, D.F. (1975), 'A Discriminant Analysis of the Corporate Debt-Equity Decision', *Financial Management*, Winter 1974, pp. 71-79.

Masulis, R.W. (1980), 'The Effects of Capital Structure Change on Security Prices', *Journal of Financial Economics*, Vol. 8, pp. 139-78.

Masulis, R.W. (1983), 'The Impact of Capital Structure Change on Firm Value', *Journal of Finance*, Vol. 38, March 1983, pp. 107-26.

Mayer, C. (1984), '*Corporation Tax, Finance and the Cost of Capital*', Working Paper 81, The Institute for Fiscal Studies, October 1984, London.

Mayer, C.P. and Morris, N. (1982), 'Marginal Rates of Corporation Tax - A Disaggregated Analysis', *Fiscal Studies*, Vol. 3, July 1982, pp. 142-60.

Miller, M. (1977), 'Debt and Taxes', *Journal of Finance*, Vol. 32, No. 2, pp. 261-75.
Miller, M. and Modigliani, F., 'Some Estimates of the Cost of Capital to the Electric Utility Industry, 1954-57', *American Economic Review*, Vol. 56, pp. 333-91.
Modigliani, F. and Miller, M. (1958), 'The Cost of Capital, Corporation Finance and the Theory of Investment', *American Economic Review*, Vol. 48, No. 3, pp. 261-97.
Modigliani, F. and Miller, M. (1963), 'Corporation Income Taxes and the Cost of Capital: A Correction', *American Economic Review*, Vol. 53, pp. 433-43.
Myers, S.C. (1977), 'Determinants of Corporate Borrowing', *Journal of Financial Economics*, Vol. 5, pp. 147-75.
Myers, S.C. (1984), 'The Capital Structure Puzzle', *Journal of Finance*, Vol. 39, July 1984, pp. 575-92.
Myers, S.C. and Majluf, N.S. (1984), 'Stock Issues and Investment Policy when Firms have Information that Investors do not have', *Journal of Financial Economics*, Vol. 12, pp. 187-221.
Remmers, L., Stonehill, A., Wright, R., and Beekhuisen, T. (1974), 'Industry and Size as Debt Ratio Determinants in Manufacturing Internationally', *Financial Management*, Vol. 3, pp. 24-32.
Ross, S.A. (1977), 'The Determination of Financial Structure: The Incentive Signalling Approach', *Bell Journal of Economics*, Vol. 8, No. 1, pp. 23-40.
Rutterford, J. (1986), '*An Empirical Investigation into the Effects of Corporate and Personal Taxation on Company Capital Structure*', Unpublished PhD, London School of Economics.
Rutterford, J. (1988), 'An International Perspective on the Capital Structure Puzzle', in J.M. Stern and D.H. Chew, eds., *New Developments in Corporate Finance*, Basil Blackwell, pp. 194-207.
Sarig, O.H. (1988), '*Bargaining with a Corporation and the Capital Structure of the Bargaining Firm*', Tel Aviv University.
Sametz, A.W. (1964), 'Trends in the Volume and Composition of Equity Finance', *Journal of Finance*, Vol. 19, pp. 450-69.
Schwartz, E. and Aronson, J.R. (1967), 'Some Surrogate Evidence in Support of the Concept of Optimal Capital Structure', *Journal of Finance*, Vol. 22, March 1967, pp. 10-19.
Scott, D.F. (1972), 'Evidence on the Importance of Financial Structure', *Financial Management*, Summer 1972, pp. 45-50.
Scott, D.F. and Martin, J.D. (1975), 'Industry Influence on Financial Structure', *Financial Management*, Vol. 4, Spring, pp. 67-73.
Smith, C. and Warner, J.B. (1979), 'On Financial Contracting: An Analysis of Bond Covenants', *Journal of Financial Economics*, Vol. 7, pp. 117-61.

Stiglitz, J.E. (1969), 'A Re-Examination of the Modigliani-Miller Theorem', *American Economic Review*, Vol. 59, December, pp. 784-793.

Stonehill, A., Beekhuisen, T., Wright, R., Remmers, L., Toy, N. Pares, A., Shapiro, A., Egan, D. and Bates, T. (1975), 'Financial Goals and Debt Ratio Determinants: A Survey of Practice in Five Countries', *Financial Management*, Autumn, pp. 27-41.

Stonehill, A. and Stitzel, T. (1969), 'Financial Structure and Multinational Corporations', *California Management Review*, Fall, pp. 91-96.

Tamari, M. (1978), '*Financial Ratios: Analysis and Prediction*', Paul Elek, London.

Titman, S. (1984), 'The Effect of Capital Structure on a Firm's Liquidation Decision', *Journal of Financial Economics*, Vol. 13, pp. 137-51.

Toy, N., Stonehill, A., Remmers, L., Wright, R. and Beekhuisen, T. (1974), 'A Comparative International Study of Growth, Profitability, and Risk as Determinants of Corporate Debt Ratios in the Manufacturing Sector', *Journal of Financial and Quantitative Analysis*, November, pp. 875-86.

Warner, J. (1977), 'Bankruptcy Costs: Some Evidence', *Journal of Finance*, Vol. 32, pp. 337-47.

Weston, J.F. (1963), 'A Test of Cost of Capital Propositions', *Southern Economic Journal*, Vol. 30, No. 2, reprinted in Archer and D'Ambrosio (1967), pp. 105-12.

Zwick, B. (1977), 'The Market for Corporate Bonds', *Federal Reserve Bank of New York Quarterly Review*, Vol. 2, pp. 27-36.

7 The harmonization of corporate taxation within the European Community

Peter Pierpoint

Introduction

The aims of this chapter are:

1 to outline the concepts of fiscal harmonization and fiscal neutrality with particular reference to the systems of corporate taxation that currently operate within the European Community (EC), and more generally within the Organisation of Economic Cooperation and Development (OECD);

2 to set out a putative case for a harmonised system of corporate taxation, within the EC, the major components of which are the elimination of welfare reducing production distortions and the reduction of related administration and compliance costs;

3 to consider the nature of the route that might be taken to achieve harmonization. The merits of a decentralized market -led route are contrasted with a rational centralised solution.

The current position within the EC and OECD

A recent study performed by the Institute for Fiscal Studies for the OECD (Institute for Fiscal Studies, 1991) concluded that a variety of non-neutralities continue to exist within the demesne of corporate taxation. As a result of the way in which tax régimes within the OECD operate, debt finance is made preferable to non-debt sources of finance, investment in machinery is favoured over investment in buildings, transnational investments are subject to less favourable tax treatment than domestic investments. These non-neutral differentials in tax treatment arise in a number of ways, not only national tax rates and national systems of depreciation allowance but also, for example, through the impact of such as withholding taxes on repatriated profit.

Figure 7.1, reproduced from the IFS Newsletter (IFS, 1992) summarises the position with respect to the differential tax treatment of various forms of capital investment within, into and out of a number of the major industrialised countries. The figure shows the various pre-tax rates of return that are required on various forms of investment to generate a post-tax rate of return of 5 per cent. Quite clearly there is a widespread lack of fiscal uniformity with respect to the international corporate tax régime. Domestically invested resources quite evidently do not have to be as productive pre-tax to leave the enterprise with 5 per cent post-tax.

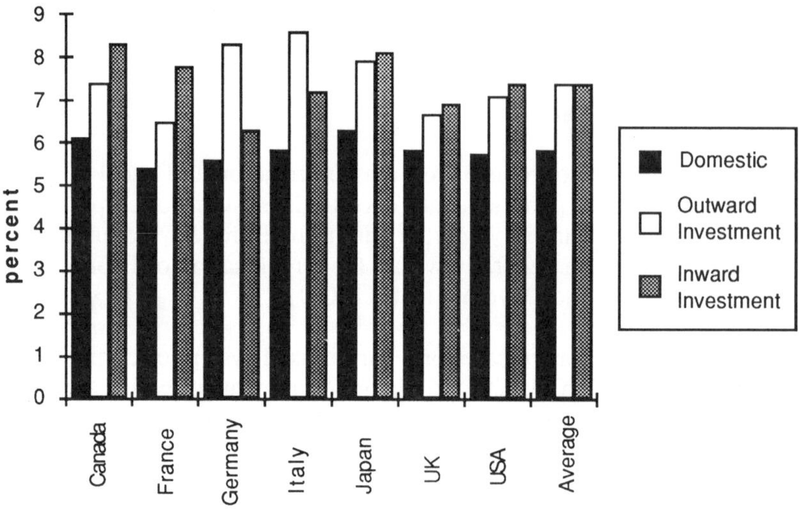

Figure 7.1
Relative taxation of domestic and foreign investment

Note: Inward investment figures are the average of required returns when companies from all other non-OECD countries invest in the country. Outward figures are the average required return when a multinational from the named country invests abroad.

Source: IFS Newsletter, Spring 1992

Furthermore the results of a survey of business opinion, conducted by the Ruding Committee (Report of the Committee of Independent Experts on Company Taxation, 1992), indicate that the differentials highlighted Figure 7.1 above do impact on the real world of decision making.

The following question is posed:

> The decision as to the location of an operation may be more or less influenced by the tax systems of the countries concerned. In deciding in which country to locate the following types of operation, how often are taxes faced by your firm in alternative locations a relevant consideration and major factor in your decision?

The results reported in Table 7.1 were generated. Clearly the decision concerning the financial centre is more tax differential dependent than the production plant decision. In both cases though actual real world decisions are affected, that is distorted, by the variability of corporate tax systems within the EC.

Table 7.1
Survey of business opinion
on influence of corporate tax differentials

Nature of Investment	Always	Usually	Sometimes	Never
Production Plant	22	26	34	19
Financial Service Centre	53	26	13	9

Source: Ruding Committee (1992) 'Report of the Committee of Independent Experts on Company Taxation'. Commission of the European Communities: Brussels.

If all the required rates of return within a country were equal then the tax system would be deemed to be neutral with respect to the tax treatment of corporate investment.To the extent that these required rates differ there exist non-neutralities. If all countries' pre-tax required rates of return were equal then the global/regional system of tax treatment of corporate investment would be harmonious. The process whereby the harmonious outcome is achieved is often referred to as the process of harmonization or, more simply, harmonization.

Approximation is a term used to describe a staging post en route for the ultimate objective of harmonization. Such a term has been used in respect of the recent developments, towards harmonisation, in the field of indirect taxation- value added tax and various excise duties within the EC.

The existence then of the aforementionned non-neutralities and disharmony are likely to have an impact on the investment decisions of enterprises. Investment may be diverted from the first preference location and use to a less desirable location and use. A wedge exists that keeps investible funds from its most efficient location and most efficient use.

Taxation may not be the only source of non-neutralities and disharmony. Taxes are but one factor in the investment decision. Enterprises come into contact with government in a wide variety of situations. They are subject to explicit and implicit taxation (Prest, 1985) as well as being the recipients of explicit and implicit subsidies. The distinction between the explicit and the implicit dimensions of taxation and subsidization are not widely understood. Health and safety legislation require that enterprises make specified expenditures. In effect these costs are taxes but of an implicit variety. The imposition of a pricing formula on newly privatized industries constitutes an implicit tax on those organizations. The grant of a licence to an enterprise may subsequently yield a rent or profit. In effect the enterprise is subsidised but implicitly. Explicit taxes are such as corporation tax and explicit subsidies are such as grants to various types of 'inward' investors and depreciation allowances.

The award of investment grants to foreign direct investment within the EC may have an influence on the resting place of that foreign direct investment. Such 'tax expenditures' are made to stimulate regional development and increase local employment. Different member states of the EC do operate systems that are, in some respects, significantly divergent and hence of potential relevance to the investor. In the case of Eire rather "generous rates of grant" are available but these are "counterbalanced by a system of grant administration involving considerable discretion and rigorous eligibility and repayment conditions" (Bachtler, 1990). Grants and associated regulations in the UK relating to, for example, the circumstances in which grants become repayable, are "broadly in line with other European countries" (Bachtler, 1990).

The use of a wide variety of government driven instruments can then cause business to take investment decisions on the basis of narrow 'tax' implications rather than wider economic implications. The enterprise has to take account of the net impact of the whole basket of implicit and explicit factors. Internationally mobile capital has to consider the relative desirability of a multitude of such baskets. Ultimately not only the 'wrong' level of investment might be made but also that investment actually made might take place in the 'wrong' place.

Why corporate tax harmonisation?

The EC came into existence in order to, amongst other reasons, get rid of the multitude of barriers and hurdles that diminish and distort the efficient working of the economies of the member states of the EC allowing people, workers, capital, goods and services to flow unimpeded and the overall welfare of the 340 million inhabitants of the EC to be enhanced. The Single Market programme constituted a substantial step forward towards the goal of a true and level playing field unencumbered by obstacles and traps for the frustrated wary and the unwary. The goal of corporate taxation harmonization is but one element of a continuing programme. The vision is of pro-marketeers of the playing field populated by efficient appropriately developed enterprises operating on a communitywide basis. This vision could well be characterised by the presence of a harmonized Community-based corporate tax régime.

A case for the harmonisation of corporate taxation within the EC would contain a number of elements. Consider one possible case as set out in Devereux and Pearson (1990):

1 Unharmonized corporate tax systems result in an unfair distribution of tax revenues.

2 Unharmonised corporate tax systems create administrative difficulties for both governments and business which may lead to the cross-border economic activity being discouraged.

3 Unharmonized corporate tax systems distort competition and thence reduces the level of economic activity.

The nature of fairness and unfairness is not dealt with in any detail by Devereux and Pearson. The way in which the corporate tax burden and tax revenue is currently shared out within the EC is a complex matter. For an enterprise with roots in one country but with branches in others, a number of revenue authorities may wish to have a slice of the tax action. The country in which value was added, the source country, may demand a slice. Monies may then get transferred to an intermediate country/final country, the residence country-,for possible distribution to equity holders. This country will also demand a slice.

If we define fairness in terms of the absence of envy then we require that all participating countries would not wish to exchange their tax revenue for the tax revenue of any other participating country. To expect any outcome to be fair is thence a matter of wishing for milk and the milk that made the butter. Devereux and Pearson are correct to conclude that "no principle of fairness can be invoked to justify this distribution of revenue". Fairness, in this context is but a chimera.

If the twelve member states of the EC have twelve distinct corporate tax régimes and there exist enterprises within the EC that are involved in cross-border activities it will be the case that these enterprises will incur additional tax compliance costs. They well need to employ resources to ensure that they satisfy the fiscal requirements of all of the fiscal authorities with which the enterprise comes into contact. Of course some other resources will be devoted to ensuring that the enterprise operates in a tax efficient mode. In this respect issues of transfer pricing and thin capitalisation are particularly relevant.

In addition to the costs of compliance incurred by the enterprise there will be additional costs of administration incurred by the appropriate tax authorities as they attempt to net tax from increasingly sophisticated taxpayers. Adam Smith's fourth maxim of taxation is not being satisfied by the current situation- more is being taken out of the pocket of the tax payer than is yielded up to the Exchequer. It is an empirical matter as to how much of a problem these two sets of extra costs constitute.

With a harmonized communitywide corporate tax and cooperating tax authorities, such compliance and administrative costs will be reduced. There will be a net welfare gain. Costs will be reduced and tax burdens might be reduced. Of course, although the intra-EC regional problem would be resolved the rest of the world continues to exist and the same games will stilled be played out, but on a global scale.

The third element of the putative case presented by Devereux and Pearson concerns the relationship between a non-harmonized EC tax régime and so-called allocative inefficiency. Non-harmonized tax systems may cause distortion induced allocative inefficencies. Firm A may decide that it is preferable to invest in Country X, even though costs of production are higher there than in Country Y, simply because of the low company taxation that exists in Country X. In effect, an inefficient location decision has been induced. Resources will be used inefficiently. Resources are being wasted. The resources would be more productively employed in Country Y. The capacity of the total economy, say the EC, has been diminished. The principle of 'capital export neutrality' (CEN) has been breeched. With regard to Figure 7.1 a firm in Germany might wish to locate in Canada but the tax treatment of the said firm in Canada is such that it might actually locate in France.

If the UK were the cheapest place to produce dog biscuits, within the EC, but the tax system in Spain caused the dog biscuit investment to be made in Spain then we have a Capital Export Non-Neutrality (CENN) and resources are being used inefficiently. More resources are being used to produce the biscuit than are strictly necessary. Resources are thereby being invested inefficiently.

Capital Import Neutrality (CIN) is a second element in the allocative inefficiency argument. The Musgravian variant (Musgrave, 1987) requires that the taxes faced by companies investing in a host country should be the same. The example used by Devereux and Pearson to illustrate CIN is a bridge project in the UK. The French are assumed to be the most efficient when it comes to such projects. If, however, the Dutch built the bridge the tax treatment of the Dutch would be such that they could tender at a lower price and hence win the contract. The EC would, as a result of this mal-investment, be a poorer place than if the French had won the contract. Resources would be unnecessarily diverted from other uses to the bridge project.

In general terms if Company D, located in Country X in spite of being **the** efficient firm in cost terms, finds that its market in Country Y is captured by Company E located in another country, then the principle of CIN is breached.

An alternative definition of CIN is proposed by Devereux and Pearson. This definition requires that companies selling in the same market should face the same tax régime. The argument used to support this innovation is based on the presumption that most goods are not bridge-type products. They are pen-type products. Pens can be produced wherever and then exported to the UK. To the extent that pen-type products are more common, in the marketplace, than bridge-type products the Musgravian variant is a less appropriate basis for analysis than this latter variant. A bridge in the UK could actually be a pen-type product after all. The bridge, located in the UK, could have been designed in France and built from imported prefabricated components.In principle virtually all of the bridge could have been produced 'hors de UK'.

If however we accept the distinction of Devereux and Pearson, we require that all who sell pens in the UK should face the same tax régime. If pen makers do not face the same, that is harmonised, tax régime then it is quite conceivable that a less efficient pen maker could win out in the market for pens in the UK.

Consider this more general example. In a no tax situation Company X can produce dog biscuits, regardless of location, cheaper than Company Y. The impact of tax is that Company X, whereever it produces, becomes the more expensive producer and Company Y cleans up the dog biscuit market. We are in the world of Capital Import Non-Neutrality (CINN). CIN á la DP, requires that X should win out.

Problems arise when the inefficient firm beats the efficient firm in the marketplace. Achieve CEN and CIN and the EC will be able to produce more goods and services with the same quantum of inputs. Answers to the questions such as how much more is producible and where will the production take place are, at present, unanswered.In general we have reason to believe that efficient firms will thrive and the inefficient firms will either change their ways or suffer the consequences.

Achieving harmonisation: by which route?

Let us assume that the non-neutralities associated with CINN and CENN are such that it becomes accepted that something needs to be done. The economic costs of the non-neutralities are considered to be substantial and excessive. What should be done? CEN is achievable by taxing all enterprise profits on the basis of their home base domicile- in effect the destination of the profits. CIN is achievable by taxing all enterprises on the basis of the country of origin of the enterprise profits.

If corporate tax harmonization were to take place then simultaneously CEN and CIN might be achieved. In a non-harmonized system one might then have to choose between destination and origin as the principle to be adopted. Which system would minimize welfare losses? Should we go for CEN and suffer the slings and arrows of CINN? Why not go for CIN and suffer the outrageous fortune of CENN?

Clearly some kind of case appears to exist for the reform, of a tax harmonizing nature, of corporate taxation within the EC. The size of the welfare gain is unknown. Business has a predilection for the business environment to be of a competitive, stable and not subject to governmental caprice. A harmonized system would tend to serve up these desiderata. Does, though, a case for a non-harmonized system exist?

Chown (1991), in consideration of the issue of corporate tax harmonization, identifies three problems for companies, involved in cross-national activities within and without, the EC:

1 How can we ensure that corporate decisions, notably on plant location, are not unintentionally distorted by differences in tax rates, base and systems?

2 How can we reduce the administrative burden, on small as well as large enterprises, of the jurisdictional battles between different revenue authorities?

3 Why are true trans-national mergers impossible?

The appropriate solution, argues Chown, is to consider reform at the level of the system and structure, whilst leaving tax rates and the tax base to be taken care of by market forces. Chown claims that differences in corporate tax rates are compatible with the existence of a single market and, by implication, an absence of the kinds of distortions discussed by Devereux and Pearson. So, for example, the Swiss federal tax rate is quoted as standing at 9.8 per cent. The additional impact of cantonal taxation causes this burden to rise to 45 per cent in Zurich and Geneva whereas in other cantons no further taxes are raised. The impact of federal-plus-state burdens in the USA result in relatively high burdens in New York (45 per cent) but relatively low burdens in Arizona (34 per cent).

> "These differentials do not distort competition, and if they were removed might cause even greater concentration of activity in the more obviously popular locations".

Such a particular conclusion is not warranted. The fact that tax differences exist does mean that distortion cannot exist. Of course we could argue that these tax differentials reflect the extent of differential location dependent productivity. So New York is a more productive, and hence popular, location than Arizona. Tax authorities are then gaining revenue in a perfectly reasonable and acceptable way. They do have to be careful not to tax the milk cow to death. As long as they are careful to milk the rent of location, they will not distort the location decision. As long as we assume that governments are omnicompetent, then we might not be in fear of distorted location decisions. What though if we recognise that governments inhabit the real world and are not omnicompetent? Do governments really understand what the implications of their tax policies are? We might then wish to avoid allowing individual governments the kind of discretion that could then be used to generate inefficiencies and welfare losses.

Chown (1991) continues. "Serious differences in tax rates and tax base between countries, within a free market area, are unlikely to persist for very long except for valid economic reasons. Provided there is freedom of movement of people and capital as well as goods, no member state can afford to impose taxes drive away capital, create unemployment and erode the tax base. Equally no country is going to unnecessarily forgo revenue by reducing taxes any lower than is needed to retain and encourage the required level of activity".

Such a particular conclusion is warranted but only partially so. This applies even if we disregard the problems that arise in the actual definition of "serious differences" and "very long". Are we to accept that quite serious differences could persist for quite a long time? Might not such a possibility generate quite serious distortions?

If capital is infinitely mobile and knows no home then it can settle and nestle whereever it will. Profit will be earned but what then? The profit will get repatriated to somewhere and will, to an extent, be distributed. If the company equity is held by UK residents then the repatriated profit will have to face UK tax authorities. If the cost of repatriation has a differential, compared to the domestic UK tax treatment, then the capital might have been advised to stay at home in the first place.

Rather than being concerned with driving capital away, domestic tax authorities might be more concerned with encouraging the capital to stay at 'home' .The tax authority might actually prefer the lower tax yield that stay-home sweeteners might incur in exchange for higher levels of domestic investment. A problem with Chown's analysis is that it is rooted in a presumption that the mobile capital does not ultimately have a home base. It is as if the capital turned up from outer space looking for a home. In reality two kinds of capital exist within the UK. Some is UK based and some is non-UK based.

It is probably the case that it is widely accepted that a company, operating within the borders of a number of states, should be liable to corporate taxation, in one form or another, in all of those states. Companies will have a continuing incentive to arrange for profit to be declared in the most 'fiscally friendly' state. The physical capital can be located where it is most efficiently located, whereas the profits on that capital can be so arranged as to be produced, *deus ex machina*, where it is most profitable with respect to its tax treatment. A degree of transfer pricing will be undertaken to achieve this objective. As long as transfer pricing possibilities exist then the allocative inefficiencies referred to earlier can be avoided and tax differentials will not matter.

Chown raises the issue of the so-called 'prejudice against foreign earnings'. This prejudice operated, at the time of writing, in such a way as required that, in order to service a dividend payment made in the UK, the level of gross profit would have been considerably higher if the were to be paid out of non-UK sourced profits. Chown argues that a 'prejudice point' at which, for a UK-based company, the growth of non-UK sourced profits relative to UK sourced profits requires that the non-UK sourced profits should be higher in gross terms in order to pay out the same dividend. In the example set out by Chown required profits, when non-UK sourced, might have to be a third higher than in the situation where profits arise within the UK.

Given this disincentive to grow at home rather than away, one would expect, to some extent, that UK-based companies would tend neither to expand to the efficient size nor locate themselves in the efficient location. These distortions will create welfare losses. The marketplace, it could be argued, appears to be tolerating a serious distortion. In the longer run, it might be argued, the impact will be that the UK will become a less productive economy. This could then be reflected in a weakening exchange rate. Foreign earnings, when repatriated, will become worth more and the 'prejudice' could wither away.

The process of tax reform

This complex environment which an enterprise inhabits is thus characterised by a panoply of non-neutralities. Removal, by way of tax reform, one element at a time may not in the short run improve the prevalence of distortion. This is what the Second Best Theorem teaches us. A piecemeal reform aimed at creating a set of countervailing non-neutralities might tend to increase complexity and its associated costs of compliance. A comprehensive reform would be aimed at eliminating the set of non-neutralities. Within an organization, such as the EC, a long term goal might be the creation of a neutral corporate tax régime rooted in an agreed harmonious and uniform communitywide system rather than a more complex system that produces a net neutral régime out of a wide range of countervailing non-neutralities. In the medium term the objective would be a more limited end of approximation.

The actual progress towards approximation and/or harmonization has been slow and tortuous. Corporate tax harmonization was not part of the

Single Market programme. The Ruding Committee Report (1992) constitutes the latest small step towards harmonization. The proposals emanating from this report were subject to some degree of concern. The apparent fear was that non-EC capital might be discouraged from entering the EC as a result of relatively punitive corporate tax régimes operating within the EC. Ruding proposed a corporate tax rate of between 30 per cent and 40 per cent. Within the EC only Germany, at 50 per cent on undistributed profits, and Italy, where an equalization tax is applied to high distributions, have rates beyond those particular limits. Political preference appears, as one might expect, to be for a market-led Chown-type route to harmonization.

If an unharmonized corporate tax system within the EC is considered to be no good thing, then by what means or mechanisms can the necessary adjustments come about? The European Commission, the policy initiator of the EC, displays an initial preferred tendency to make things the same throughout the EC by way of a quick rational fix. This is the experience of the story of the progress towards Value Added Tax approximation. If the initial proposals are not well received and get log jammed then the European Commission is prepared to become more flexible and market-led in order that agreement, and progress, become possible. Progress in fiscal matters is made on the basis of unanimous agreement in the Council of Ministers.

Even if, as Chown asserts, an unharmonized corporate tax system exists, within the EC, is not an indicator of an allocative efficiency problem, remember that governments will have made appropriate adjustments such that each remain in line with other governments. Governments do not put themselves in a position where they are forced to attempt to buck market forces. This position can only pertain if governments are able to get inside the heads of enterprises and are able to understand the extent to which distortion has, in the past, and would, in the future, take place. Again we demand of governments a degree of omnicompetence that defies belief.

Placing one's faith in, and reliance on, the marketplace to drive the tax system in the direction of harmonization may be misplaced. As we have seen, nations do tend to operate their corporate tax régimes in such a way as to try to keep funds at home. The incentives to invest abroad are thereby reduced. This activity is designed to operate in the immediate interest of the home nation. But, of course, that behaviour which is beneficial to one will be copied by the rest. As a consequence of the self-seeking behaviour, in a prisoner's dilemma-type context, the common good may be jeopardised. Such is the sorry tale of the 'tragedy of the commons'. Aggregate corporate tax revenues will decline and governments will have beggared each other.

Tax authorities might be advised to load taxes on those factors which are relatively less mobile. One would then wish to avoid taxing portfolio-type investment because of its footloose nature. Such investments might then be the subject to 'tax war activity. Actual outcomes will be dependent on the specific character of the context of the tax changes. So, if the economic desirability of New York compared to Arizona were to be great that Arizona could reduce its tax rates to zero and beyond without tempting any enterprise to up sticks and move to Arizona. If the relocation costs are significant then one might, in effect, be trapped in New York. Being in New York does not mean that one wants to be in New York. In these circumstances the tax war will not produce any winners other than the then existing enterprises in Arizona.

One might imagine that the dream of the European Commission is of a level playing field, whereas the reality is a nightmare where individual member states are busy creating a mine field. In terms of the current example the result, throughout the EC, is a series of inefficient investments made domestically by inefficient domestic enterprises.

A wide variety of possible reforms are imaginable. Governments may wish to exercise sovereignty- in this case to extract tax- over the production and value added that is created within its demesne and over the income that is seen to accrue to those resident within the national borders. A firm operating out of Country A but producing in Country B will be faced by the sovereign claims of both countries, whereas the firm operating wholly within one country will face only one fiscal authority. The competing claims of Country A and Country B will have to be reconciled in some way. Harmonization is more demanding in terms of reconciliation.

A narrower range of possibilities are short list candidates. One could imagine a single corporation tax operating communitywide. The individual member state would be free to choose the rate of income tax imposed on dividend payments. This possibility can be used a bench-mark. It has many appealing qualities.

Devereux & Pearson (1990) consider a variety of other options including corporate tax by location of residence of the shareholder, corporate tax by the residence of the parent company and corporate tax by the location of production. The abolition of withholding taxes are seen as the "simplest way of improving economic efficiency" in the EC. What though of market forces bringing about a 'creeping' harmonization? High tax countries would lose out to low tax countries in terms of investment and jobs. Creeping harmonization will be a long time coming. EC corporate tax systems remain "a long way apart" (Devereux & Pearson, 1990). Again the indirect tax story is instructive where the market forces argument gained ground through the late 1980s into the 1990s. But then the 'approximation' goal was continuously watered down as a result of the need to gain agreement so that forward reform momentum might be maintained.

Conclusions

The situation, with respect to the corporate taxation within the EC, is one of substantial diversity. Whether these differences and non-neutralities actually do significantly distort behaviour is not a settled matter. Rational maximizing entrepreneurs should have their investment decisions distorted. Survey data reveals that often tax differentials do not affect investment decisions.

If it is found that, within the EC as a whole, welfare consuming distortions have been created and are continuing to be created then it is incumbent on the European Commission to come up, for the benefit of the EC as a whole, with plausible solutions. The market-led solution might be working. One would need to investigate the presence of any trends, attributable to market forces, in the degree of diversity of corporate tax régimes of the member states of the EC.

The rational bureaucratic solutions, that tend to emanate from the European Commission, are an understandable response from an organisation that represents the collectivity that is the EC. Individual members states, mindful of their sovereignty, might see such proposals as irrational- preferring a minimalist and gradualist process as their number one preference. Progress in this world is likely to be, at best, slow and halting.

If the member states of the EC operate different corporate tax systems, individual companies will have incentives to arrange their tax affairs to minimize the net impact on their business. In general companies will seek to appear to earn profits in 'fiscal friendly' countries. Strictly 'unnecessary' compliance costs may be incurred arranging affairs in a way that satisfies the tax authorities of relevant member states.

The current complexity of operation and administration of the corporate tax systems of the member states of the EC is substantial. Such a regime is unlikely to generate efficient spatial, sectoral and structural allocations of capital. The welfare of EC collectivity is consequently diminished.

References

Bachtler, J. (1990) 'Grants for Inward Investors: Giving Money Away'. *National Westminster Bank Review*, May, pp. 15-24.

Chown, J. (1991) 'European/British Company Taxation'. In *The State of the Economy* (1991). Institute of Economic Affairs IEA Readings Number 34, London.

Devereux, M. & Pearson, M. (1990) 'Harmonising Corporate Taxes in Europe'. *Fiscal Studies* vol 11, no 1, February, pp. 21-35.

Institute for Fiscal Studies (1991) *'Taxing Profits in a Global Economy'.* OECD: Paris.

Institute for Fiscal Studies (1992) 'The Taxation of Profits in a Global Economy'. IFS Newsletter, Spring.

Musgrave, P. B. (1987) 'Interjurisdictional coordination of taxes on capital income'. In (ed) Cnossen, S. *Tax Coordination in the European Community*. Kluwer Law & Taxation Publishers: London.

Prest, A. R. (1985) 'Implicit Taxation' *Royal Bank of Scotland Review*, Issue 147, September, pp. 10-26.

Ruding Committee (1992) *'Report of the Committee of Independent Experts on Company Taxation'*. Commission of the European Communities: Brussels.

Part III

MULTI-NATIONAL ASPECTS

8 Controlled foreign companies: A general framework for small UK company groups operating in low tax areas

Derek Spratley

Introduction

This chapter is aimed at producing a general framework by reference to which a UK resident company may avoid inadvertently becoming the subject of an Inland Revenue direction under the controlled foreign companies (CFC) legislation. It pre-supposes that existing international or multinational companies already possess adequate internal tax planning and avoidance departments. This may be either as an autonomous unit within the organisation or as part of the central management function.

However, many small company groups do not possess access to such expertise and it is to this audience that the chapter is directed. In this context it should be noted that issues are analysed and discussed in a general way only. There is no substitute for detailed up-to-the-minute advice.

CFC and low tax areas

The original controlled foreign companies legislation was introduced in the Finance Act 1984. The original statutory law plus minor amendments in subsequent Finance Acts was incorporated into the Taxes Act 1988 upon consolidation of the then current tax law. The current law is set out in only ten sections (747-756) and three schedules (24-26) of the Act.

Under the legislation the Board of Inland Revenue are able to direct that a UK resident company shall be charged to tax on the profits of a non-UK resident company (a foreign company). The foreign company concerned is one which is under the control of the UK resident company. It also pays tax in its country of foreign residence (local tax area) at less than three-quarters of the corresponding corporation tax the UK resident company would pay on like profits.

From the above outline it may be deduced that a controlled foreign company (CFC) is a company:

(a) resident outside the UK,

(b) controlled by persons resident in the UK,

(c) subject to a lower level of taxation in the territory in which it is resident.

Despite the small number of sections involved, the legislation is acknowledged to be extremely complex in both its interpretation and operation. This view is reflected by both tax advisers and the Inland Revenue alike, the latter body having established a special team in its Technical Division purely to deal with cases under CFC law.

To give an example of the nature of the complexities involved; nowhere in the specific sections is there a definition of a company. The general definition in the interpretation section of the Taxes Act 1988 is hardly more helpful. However, for the remainder of the chapter the popular notion of a company *i.e.*, a separate legal entity distinct from its owners with ownership established by shares in the company will be used.

Therefore, it may be established fairly early on that activities which are conducted in an overseas territory by a UK resident company by, say, the establishment of a branch or agency are not likely to be taxed under CFC law. Nevertheless, in view of the earlier definitional problem the status of a particular entity may need close scrutiny both as regards documentation and the relevant foreign law. On the other hand, direct exporting without representation in an overseas territory will not fall foul of the CFC law.

The popular perception of a tax haven or low tax area is an overseas territory in which little or no direct local tax is levied upon the profits arising therein. There may or may not be correspondingly high levels of indirect tax such as value added tax or stamp duties. CFC legislation is only concerned with the incidence of direct tax or strictly the lack of it. However, CFC legislation is also concerned with one other form of low tax area. This is an overseas territory where normal tax rates are applied to profits but substantial reliefs are then provided to offset the incidence of the direct local tax. Whereas the latter class of territories may have been able to negotiate double tax agreements with the UK, the former almost certainly will have not. However, while it is clear that the existence or non-existence of a double tax agreement between the UK and the overseas territory may be helpful in recognising a low tax area, it is not conclusive.

Unlike the problems previously mentioned in defining a company, the statutes do provide a definition of a low tax area. Principally, a low tax area is one in which the amount of local tax paid in the overseas territory is less than three-quarters of the corresponding UK tax on like profits. However, care must be exercised because, it is the amount of tax, or actual marginal tax rate, which determines a low tax area, not the nominal marginal rates of tax operative within the system of the overseas territory.

Active tax avoidance operations

Subsequent to UK exchange controls being abolished in 1979, many tax avoidance schemes were set up by UK based multi-national companies.

The Inland Revenue were concerned by this apparent abuse of the existing law by poor corporate tax citizens. The general method by which avoidance of UK tax was being achieved was the setting up of a subsidiary company in a low tax area. This vehicle was then used to shelter diverted and accumulated profits which would otherwise have been subjected to UK tax.

Tax avoidance was being achieved by a number of specific operations *e.g.* money-box, sales, distribution, service, and offshore captive insurance companies. Clearly such operations were active by nature rather than passive, *i.e.*, they were intended or designed rather than created by commercial accident. Unfortunately, the legislation introduced in 1984, designed to stop perceived abuse by active operations, had the potential to penalise passive operations as well.

The way in which passive operations are distinguished from active tax avoidance operations is now considered both geographically and by commercial activity.

Geographical analysis of at risk areas

As a first step towards distinguishing between active and passive tax operations a list of excluded countries was published in 1984. This information was provided in an Inland Revenue press release dated 16th July 1984. Although this document has no statutory force it may be regarded as a statement of practice by the UK tax authorities. In ways similar to the rapidly changing political world map, this tax map of the world also receives fairly regular revisions. There have been amendments in 1985, 1986, 1988 (twice), 1990 and the latest in early 1991.

The list is divided into two parts. The importance of part one of the list is that an assurance is being given to any company resident and carrying on a business in one of the countries listed, that it will be excluded from the CFC legislation.

Part two of the list grants similar exclusions but only where the company concerned does not benefit from certain specified situations. Thus, part two must be examined rather more carefully by any UK group setting up an activity through a CFC.

Given the regularity at which updating the lists occurs only a general geographical analysis will be given. Nevertheless, this form of analysis is seen as critical if an unwanted CFC direction on a passive overseas operation is to be avoided.

Excluded areas.

North America (but not USA)
Northern South America (but not Venezuela)
Australasia and Indonesia
China and Japan
West Africa (parts)
South and South East Africa
Europe (with some notable exceptions)

Excluded but with special restrictions.

USA
Southern South America
East and Northern Africa (parts)
Europe (Belgium, Greece, Luxembourg, Spain)
Europe (Netherlands, Portugal, Ireland)
Middle East (Turkey)
Pacific Basin (Philippines and Solomon Islands)
South East Asia (Malaysia and Singapore)

Certainly there are likely to be some surprises in this second list *e.g.* the number of EC countries where an unexpected tax liability may arise. Probably none of those listed would be thought of as low tax areas as previously defined. An analysis of the specified situations quickly establishes that these countries are in the main ones where normal tax rates are applied but reliefs or incentives are then provided under the tax laws of that country. The situations are wide and varied but the principle is to create a low actual marginal rate of tax in the overseas country on profits earned.

Clearly, any business activity set up in the rather better known tax havens of the Caribbean is going to be at extreme risk to unwelcome attention by the UK tax authorities. Additionally, it is worth noting that Europe contains some 'hot-spots' of its own:

Cyprus	Gibraltar	Guernsey	Liechtenstein
Monaco	Jersey	Isle of Man	Switzerland

So it would seem that there are a number of at risk geographical areas, some rather better known than others. In addition, although not explicitly listed, care might also be advisable where business activities are contemplated by a CFC in Central America and Venezuela, Central and West Africa, most of the Middle East countries and most of South East Asia. At the time of writing, many of these geographical areas are subject to political and other forms of unrest and therefore, perhaps, are unattractive for commercial ventures in the form of a CFC. However, it is necessary to be aware that a high risk, high return venture could be further seriously undermined by an unexpectedly large tax bill.

Company residence

One other important factor to consider at this point is whether the company is resident in an overseas country or not. If it is treated as resident in the UK then clearly the CFC legislation does not apply; after all, the profits will then be assessed to UK corporation tax rules.

A statutory definition of residence is given in the Taxes Act 1988 and subsequent Finance Acts. A company will be treated as resident in a country where it is liable to tax there, by reason of its domicile, residence or place of management. Under the Finance Act 1988, a company incorporated in the UK is treated as resident in the UK no matter where it is managed and controlled, as is a company incorporated overseas but managed and controlled in the UK. Thus, deemed residence in a geographical area is as much a critical issue as the geographical area itself for CFC purposes.

Commercial activity analysis

In a further attempt to avoid unnecessary penalties being imposed on passive operations, the CFC legislation includes a list of so called exempt activities. The law is extremely detailed and complex and it is beyond the scope of this chapter to reproduce the detail here. However, a summary is now provided to illustrate the importance of the issues involved.

Generally, where a company which is a CFC:

(i) maintains a business establishment in the overseas territory in which it is resident; and

(ii) its business affairs are effectively managed in that territory; and either,

(iii) its main business is neither investment business nor dealing in goods for delivery to or from the UK, and further restrictions upon the conduct of wholesale, distributive or financial business are observed; or

(iv) it is a holding company which may be a local holding company or a non-local holding company satisfying certain conditions,

then it is engaged in exempt activities.

The benefit of being identified as carrying on an exempt activity or activities is for a CFC to escape an assessment to UK corporation tax on its profits. Clearly it is necessary for the company to satisfy (i) and (ii) above and either (iii) or (iv).

How the law is seeking to protect passive operations may be demonstrated by further analysis of what it is saying in essence.

(a) A business establishment is taken to be one which is occupied and used with a reasonable degree of permanence. It is expected that the company's business will be carried on from these premises. The types of acceptable premises range from primary to tertiary on the industrial classifications scale (but see (c) below). Some care has to be taken where the premises are construction sites or similar projects.

(b) It is necessary for a company to show that it has an adequate number of persons employed in the overseas territory to deal with the volume of business. There are restrictions upon services provided for non-residents of the overseas territory particularly where they are provided to the UK.

(c) Care must be taken where the main business of the company comprises investment activities *e.g.* the holding of securities, patents or copyrights or is a wholesale, financial or distributive trade *e.g.* shipping or air transport. In this latter class type, where more than 50 per cent of the CFC's gross trading receipts are derived from associated or connected persons (including a company) *i.e.*, closely controlled situations, the operation may be viewed as one of active tax avoidance.

(d) Extreme care must be exercised where a CFC is part of a complex group structure *e.g.* a non-UK resident parent company with a potential CFC which may become an actual CFC if a UK resident member of the group becomes its parent.

Thus the law in (a) and (b) is seen to be discouraging, from a tax perspective, any form of overseas activity which although posing as a genuine commercial activity is really a 'one man and his dog' operation merely set up to take advantage of a low tax area. It is difficult to see how such a company could satisfy the residence rules summarised earlier. Nevertheless, it can be seen that passive operations are not penalised under (a) and (b) but active operations are caught.

However, the law also establishes a number of at risk activities which have been outlined earlier. The reason for this approach is to preclude multi-national corporations creating, in particular, large scale service industry operations (c), which would satisfy (a) and (b) above, but nevertheless be active tax avoidance operations. Unfortunately, genuine passive operations in these service industries may be penalised unless care is taken.

Similar care must also be exercised where the CFC is part of a complex group structure (d), since in these circumstances misclassification as an active rather than a passive operation may inadvertently occur as the result of a technicality. This will occur in a two or more tier group of holding companies where, for instance, a holding company holds shares in its trading subsidiaries indirectly through a subsidiary which is not a local holding company, a local holding company being defined as one which is resident in the same territory as its own trading subsidiaries.

The tax charge and defences

Under the 1984 legislation, a UK resident company may be charged to UK corporation tax where it has an interest in a CFC. This charge will only arise where a direction is activated by the Inland Revenue.

The appendix to this chapter contains a diagram showing the circumstances in which a direction may or will not be issued. This section briefly examines how the charge is calculated and apportioned and then moves on to summarise the automatic defences which may be used to avoid the direction and therefore the tax charge.

Any charge will be based on the chargeable profits of the CFC calculated in the same way as for UK corporation tax except that capital gains of the CFC are specifically excluded from such chargeable profits. Appropriate relief will be given for what is referred to as creditable tax. The chargeable profits and creditable tax are then apportioned to the persons (whether individual or company, whether UK resident or not) who have an interest in the CFC.

Only the part of the apportioned profits which are apportioned to a UK resident company attracts UK corporation tax. The assessment will be raised upon any UK resident company having an interest in the CFC as the CFC cannot be legally assessed; being outside the UK tax laws as a foreign resident company. Principally, apportionment will be pro-rata to shareholdings in the CFC although other forms of interest do exist and the legislation acknowledges this fact.

The legislation contains a rather wide definition of interest, clearly in an attempt to stop a rather obvious form of abuse arising. The main forms of interest in a CFC which attract apportionment are:

(a) any person possessing share capital or persons who have voting rights,

(b) any person who is able to secure that income or assets be applied for their benefit,

(c) any person who, either alone or with other persons has control of the company,and

(d) any loan creditor which the Inland Revenue think appropriate to include.

It is important to acknowledge that not only current interests but also future interests of a similar nature are covered by the legislation.

Finally, this section will give an overview of the further defences which will achieve exclusion from an Inland Revenue direction. These are where:

(a) the chargeable profits of the CFC are £20,000 or less in an accounting period of twelve months.

(b) the public quotation condition is fulfilled. The general idea of this exemption is that the CFC is classified as a public company *i.e.* one in which 35 per cent of the voting equity shares are held beneficially by the public. It is essential that the shares are dealt in and quoted on a recognised stock exchange in the CFC's country of residence. Recognised stock exchanges include the London stock exchange and others outside the UK which are designated from time to time by the Inland Revenue. Such designations appear in the London Gazette at infrequent intervals.

(c) the CFC adopts an acceptable distribution policy. In essence this requires the CFC to remit to the UK resident shareholders a dividend of at least 50 per cent of profits (excluding net capital gains). Profits for this purpose are not chargeable profits but those available for distribution. Where the CFC is a non-trading company e.g. a non-local holding company as defined earlier at least 90 per cent of available profits must be paid as a dividend.

(d) the motive test. As the description suggests this allows a CFC to mount a defence against a direction on the grounds that one of the main reasons for creating the CFC was not to reduce UK corporation tax by diverting profits from the UK. Additionally, the CFC needs to show that where the UK tax is reduced, the reduction is minimal and transactions which gave rise to the reduction was not one of the main reasons.

Clearly, in all these circumstances the legislation contains detailed definitions and rules to prevent abuse.

A general framework

In this section the key issues which have been identified will be summarised. They are not ranked in any particular order but set out those factors which should be incorporated into any general framework which is used to minimize the chance of an Inland Revenue CFC direction being made. A list of these factors and issues follows:

(a) The legal status of the overseas trading vehicle must be carefully checked by scrutiny of the foreign law and resultant documentation. A 'company' may be unintentionally formed.

(b) The tax status of the overseas territory must be established. It is important to be aware of low tax areas and excluded areas.

(c) Commercial activities in certain European countries must be screened with extreme care.

(d) It is essential to establish, where possible, that operations will qualify as exempt activities.

(e) The deemed residence of the company is important. Where at risk activities such as investment, wholesale, distributive and financial services are being offered UK or inter-group transactions are limited.

(f) Group structures must be constantly monitored to prevent exempt activity status being lost.

In addition to the above key issues a further set of defence issues should be actively incorporated into the general model as careful planning may still offset the chance of a direction.

(1) The CFC may be operated as a public company in its country of residence.

(2) Dividend policies may be established which satisfy the acceptable distribution test.

(3) The preparation of a document explaining the motive behind the establishment of a CFC where this is clearly not a series of transactions merely to avoid UK corporation tax.

At this point it must be acknowledged that the general framework, as developed, is normative. Clearly, it is useful to establish what companies should be doing. However, to be of practical use to small UK company groups, it is necessary to not only establish the relative importance of the issues, but also identify other factors which may be of vital importance.

The next section seeks to do this by analysing the responses of companies to a questionnaire.

Survey and findings

Survey

It was decided to invite contributions from a range of relatively large UK international and multinational quoted companies. The list of companies surveyed was drawn from the Sunday Times "Top 100 Companies" as measured by market capitalization. The number of companies contacted was 55 and the lowest ranked company was placed 60 in the list of 100. The relative sizes by market capitalization ranged from just under £2bn to approximately £25bn.

It was considered companies of this size would be representative of all companies with potential overseas tax problems and no doubt have their own internal international tax planning departments to solve them.

Their business operations were also likely to cover the whole spectrum of passive and active tax avoidance operations. For this reason it was made explicit to all potential respondents that their replies would remain confidential, and that no reference to an organization by name would be disclosed in the findings.

The questionnaire consisted of five questions to establish:

(i) in the planning of overseas operations, whether CFC legislation was considered. A simple yes or no response was invited and where this was no, no further questions needed to be answered.

(ii) how the respondents ranked on a five point scale, ranging from 'never' to 'always', the way in which they considered the factors included in the general framework (a) to (f) above,

(iii) whether defence issues were actively incorporated into the planning process,

(iv) further key tax planning factors, if any, to avoid the issue of a CFC direction, and

(v) whether the respondents would like to be forwarded details of the findings,

Findings

In total, 27 completed questionnaires were returned, plus 2 further non-completed forms as a result of company policy, and 1 item which was not delivered. Thus, a positive response rate of 50 per cent was received.

Of the respondent companies, only 3 indicated that they did not consider CFC legislation when planning overseas operations. Therefore, it is felt that some tentative, but useful, conclusions about the value of the model may be made.

The factors included in the general framework were ranked as follows:

		% of respondents	
1.	Established that operations are exempt activities under Sch.25, Part II, Taxes Act 1988.	Always Often	48 26
2.	Legal status of overseas trading vehicle checked carefully.	Always Often	44 15
3.	Emerging group structures carefully monitored for potential loss of exempt activity status.	Always Often	44 15
4.	Commercial activities in European countries are vetted.	Always Often Sometimes	33 22 33

5.	Tax status of overseas territory is checked carefully for excluded status.	Always 33 Often 11 Sometimes 33
6.	The deemed residence of the company is important.	Always 11 Sometimes 22 Rarely 33
7.	CFC-UK inter-group transactions are limited where at risk activities are being offered.	Always 4 Sometimes 19 Never 33

None of the above results are particularly strong but suggest, not surprisingly, that in a complex taxation area such as CFC legislation, there is no one single factor or issue that dominates the planning process. It seems fair to suggest that exempt activity status is checked carefully during the planning stage and subsequent operations. Also, there is evidence to suggest that the majority of respondents saw the close scrutiny of overseas law important in order to avoid an unintentional CFC formation.

Perhaps the one most surprising result was that over half of the respondent companies always or often vetted commercial activities in Europe.

The weakest responses, as to importance, are reserved for factors such as deemed residence of companies and inter-group transactions in the service industries. However, these issues are still important and should be retained in the general model. This conclusion is based upon the very thin response to other tax planning factors. Of the 27 respondents, 6 gave no response and the remainder gave a very wide range of factors and issues which they take into account. There was no clear pattern to suggest further inputs were needed in the model, although transfer pricing was seen to be important by 3 companies.

As regards the incorporation of "defence against direction" factors into the model, only "planning of dividend policies which satisfy the acceptable distribution test" were judged as very important (67 per cent). A public company defence was not seen as at all important. Surprisingly, only 20 per cent of respondents saw the motive test as being very important.

Lastly, as a point of record, 80 per cent of all respondents expressed an interest in receiving information arising from the survey. This suggests the model may be of interest to both large as well as small company groups; small groups being the original target audience.

Conclusions

This chapter has aimed to produce a model by which companies operating outside the UK may avoid finding themselves subjected to UK corporation tax on their full overseas profits as the result of an Inland Revenue direction.

It identified a number of key issues and factors which were presented in the form of a general framework. These key issues were tested for importance by surveying a number of major UK international and multinational companies. The respondent companies confirmed that the identified issues and factors were indeed critical in the forward planning process with perhaps the addition of an acceptable dividend policy.

It was possible to place in rank order the issues and factors so that any UK company or small UK group might identify the relative importance in their planning process.

Finally, it was identified that, in addition to the perceived small company audience, the general framework, as developed, was of interest to major UK international and multinational companies.

Appendix

Will a CFC direction be made by the Inland Revenue ?

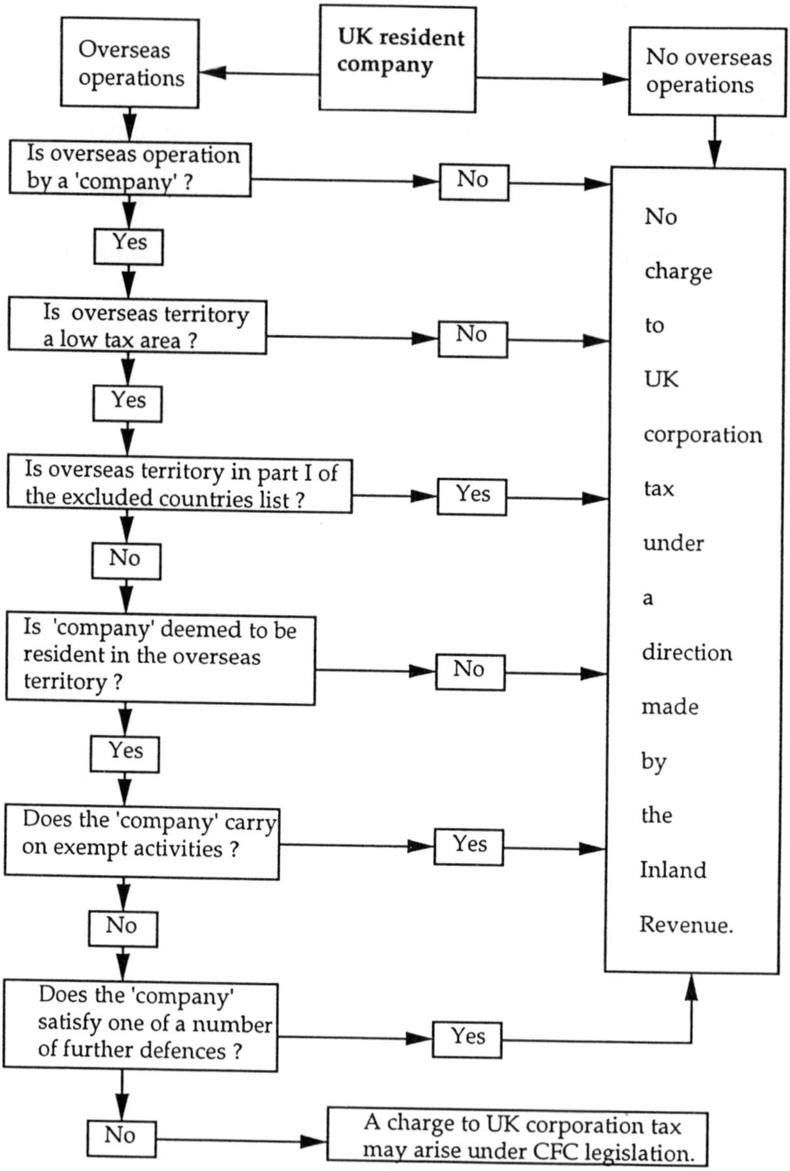

9 Multi-national capital budgeting and finance decisions

Vincent Hooper

Introduction

The financing and capital budgeting decisions of the multinational are distorted by factors including barriers to financial flows such as exchange controls, different national taxation systems, political risks, international capital market segmentation, foreign exchange risks and the organizational structure of the multinational enterprise.

An abundance of literature has been published in the quest to explain the theory of the multinational enterprise. The theory of the multinational is a relatively new concept and has undergone a metamorphosis from risk reduction (Rugman 1979) and internalisation theory (Buckley and Casson 1976), where the multinational is viewed as "internalising" imperfect factor and financial markets to an extent where net benefits to the multinational equate net costs, to Dunning's (1988) eclectic paradigm.

The aim of this chapter is to focus upon the importance that taxation and other factors play in this context.

Background

> "In an ideal world, international investment would be taxed neither more nor less favourably than domestic investment, and flows of capital across frontiers would respond to differences in pre tax rates of return", [OECD (1990)]

Governments around the world have embarked upon a programme of international taxation reform. The objectives of national taxation system reform have been to improve the fairness of the global tax system, to remove tax induced distortions to investment decisions, to discourage tax evasion and avoidance, and to reduce the complexity of the system both for tax administration and for the tax payer.

Many of the reforms to the taxation system in the United States have possibly induced similar action by other governments around the world. For example, Australia has brought about new tax changes by reducing the level of corporation taxation and reducing several tax deductions. The UK has initiated an aggressive set of tax reform proposals.

In the United Kingdom the theory of taxation and corporate finance is led by literature produced by North American academics. It is important to stress that the UK uses the imputation system and the US, the classical system of taxation. Therefore, the literature on capital structure is more orientated towards US multinationals than UK ones. Ashton (1991) argues that if there exists a tax advantage to debt in the UK, it is likely to be fairly small, in the region of 6% of the market value of permanent debt. Within an international context, the capital structure decisions are more complex than in the domestic situation. Therefore there is scope for research which attempts to discover if there are any significant differences between UK and US multinationals. Modigliani and Miller's (1958) and Miller's (1977) capital structure irrelevancy proposition has been subject to great controversy and is yet unresolved; its applicability within a multinational context is subject to even more debate. One of the reasons why their theory may not be upheld within a multinational context is the fact that there are greater market imperfections on a global scale than in a purely domestic situation, hence there are greater opportunities to exploit differences in asset prices. Modigliani and Miller assume that markets are perfect apart from taxation and within a multinational context, added dimensions may tend to negate the applicability of their general theory.

An alternative approach to the financing of a company can be demonstrated when the finance director does not believe that financial markets are perfect. In relation to this assertion, the finance director would attempt to exploit differences in asset prices, including differences caused by taxation systems, in order to maximize the tax shield on debt. This strategy would include attempting to maximize the tax shield on debt and raising finance from countries with high rates of corporation tax.

The capital structure decision of the multinational enterprise can be extensively distorted by non tax factors and other risk considerations, such as political risk. UK and US multinationals often operate in countries with high political risks, which often means that the multinational enterprise will raise finance from the host government in order to get them involved in the running of the subsidiary's operations, in order to minimize the confiscation risk of assets. Multinational theory proposed by Doz and Prahalad (1987), suggests that multinationals need to balance national responsiveness with that of a global vision.

An alternative angle to the traditional theory of capital structure proposed by Modigliani and Miller is that which has its origins in Williamson's transaction cost economics. Williamson (1988) has undertaken a combined treatment of corporate financing and corporate governance, in which debt and equity are treated as alternative "governance instruments" as opposed to "financial instruments". The difference lies in the fact that debt governance works mainly out of rules, but equity governance is a more flexible method of control. This approach can also help to explain why the capital structures in multinational enterprises are different from those in domestic enterprises.

The multinational corporation can finance all or part of its projects by borrowing in the home country or in the country where the project is located. It has been demonstrated theoretically by Madura and Foseberg (1990) that multinationals can have a debt denomination preference even when there are no market imperfections such as corporate taxes. This preference is dependent upon tax rates and other project and country specific variables. There are many underlying risk management policies that govern the allocation of currencies within multinationals. Soenen (1979) has applied portfolio theory to the allocation of currencies within a multinational enterprise and concludes that it is a potential strategy for mitigating foreign exchange exposure.

Research into the effect of multinational operations on the financing of US based multinationals has been investigated by Fatemi (1988) who found that US based multinationals tended to have target leverage ratios significantly below those of their domestic counterpart. Fatemi explained that the lower debt-equity ratio is due to the possibility of a higher level of non-interest tax shields, the higher agency and bankruptcy costs associated with international diversification and the higher risk of foreign currency denominated debt.

Other empirical evidence by Lee and Kwok (1990) has shown that US multinational corporations tend to have different capital structures. The analysis attempted to decide whether multinational and domestic corporations have the same level of agency costs, bankruptcy costs and debt ratios. The foreign tax ratio was used as an alternative measure of multinationality. Results indicated that multinationals do not have lower bankruptcy costs and tend to have lower debt equity ratios than domestic companies.

Multinationals with subsidiaries located in countries with high corporate tax rates can concentrate borrowings in those subsidiaries to generate greater interest deductions which in turn reduce the subsidiaries' taxable income, Kahn (1991).

Research aims and hypotheses

In 1992 the author conducted a survey, a fundamental aim of which was to assess the importance of taxation in relation to a number of issues involved with multinational capital budgeting and financing decisions. These issues relate to:

1 the objectives of the capital structure decision,
2 resource allocation policies,
3 financing considerations in high political risk countries,
4 sources of finance,
5 country-specific considerations in relation to financing,
6 the trend in the centralization of finance functions, and
7 the evaluation of overseas projects and, in particular, the discount rate used to assess overseas operations.

A secondary aim was to discover whether there are any significant differences between UK and US multinational enterprises in relation to the above.

Survey method

A questionnaire survey, addressed to the finance director was sent out in the autumn of 1992. One question to the finance directors was whether they believed raising debt finance increased or decreased the value of the firm. Responses were measured on a Likert-type scale of one to five, one representing of no importance and five of greatest importance.

A total population of 220 UK and 330 US multinationals was identified for this study. Three criteria were used in order to identify the multinational company. First, the market capitalization was greater than £50 million, the multinational was paying tax to an overseas government in excess of £1 million and finally, it had to have overseas production capabilities, in the form of overseas subsidiaries. Similar criteria was used to obtain a sample for the US case. The reason why this study focuses upon UK and US multinationals is because more multinationals are based in these two countries than any other country. A total of 32 US and 42 UK multinationals responded to the survey. Although follow-up telephone calls were conducted, the majority of non-respondents indicated that they were inundated with requests for information and did not have the capacity to satisfy the demands of all surveys.

Objectives of the capital structure decision

The finance directors of UK and US multinational enterprises were asked to indicate the scale of importance of a number of issues as set out in Table 9.1.

For US multinationals, minimizing the cost of capital of the parent company was of highest priority, also maximization of the tax shield on debt was of high importance. Diversification of the investor base was of lowest priority. The ordering of priority was virtually the same for UK multinationals.

Table 9.1
The Capital structure decision

	US		UK	
Factor	**Mean**	**Standard dev.**	**Mean**	**Standard dev.**
Minimize the cost of capital of the parent multinational	4.00	1.28	3.98	1.37
Minimize the cost of capital of the subsidiaries	3.10	1.45	2.85	1.19
Maximize the value of the tax shield on debt	3.61	1.20	3.77	1.31
Conform to the industry and cultural norms of the host nation	2.86	1.33	2.44	1.05
Achieve the target configuration on debt	2.79	1.18	3.27	1.34
Minimize the global cost of capital of the multinational group	3.97	1.30	4.05	1.26
Diversify the investor base	2.45	1.06	2.25	0.98

Policies relating to the configuration of assets and liabilities

In relation to the general principles underlying the allocation of currencies within the multinational enterprise, the finance director was asked to indicate the scale of importance, as shown in Table 9.2.

US multinationals placed most emphasis upon allocating assets and liabilities in an overall tax minimizing configuration and upon allocating debt and equity in a risk minimizing configuration. The allocation of assets and liabilities in a portfolio to maximize expected currency returns was of lowest priority.

UK multinationals placed greater emphasis than US multinationals upon allocating assets and liabilities in an overall risk minimizing configuration than US multinationals. UK multinationals exhibited the least preference for allocating assets and liabilities in a portfolio to maximize expected currency returns.

Table 9.2
The allocation of currencies

	US		UK	
Factor	**Mean**	**Standard dev.**	**Mean**	**Standard dev.**
Allocate assets and liabilities in an overall risk minimizing configuration	3.53	1.36	4.18	0.78
Match values of assets and liabilities in each respective currency	3.30	1.39	4.08	1.05
Allocate debt and equity in a risk minimizing configuration	3.67	1.09	3.38	1.11
Allocate liabilities in proportion to net project cash flows in each currency	2.90	1.01	2.79	1.10
Allocate assets and liabilities in an overall tax minimizing configuration	3.70	0.95	3.65	0.98
Allocate assets and liabilities in a portfolio to maximize expected currency returns	2.53	1.14	2.46	1.07

Financing considerations in relation to political risk

Where multinationals raised finance in countries with a high political risk, directors were asked to indicate the scale of importance of the reasons why they raised finance from these countries.

The results summarized in Table 9.3 reveal that US multinationals placed the most emphasis upon reducing the risk that assets may be expropriated. It was also of great importance to reduce the incidence of exchange controls and to lessen exchange rate risk by borrowing in a weak currency. Achieving the correct portfolio configuration of debt was of lowest priority. UK multinationals emphasised matching assets against liabilities for the overseas subsidiary in the high political risk country. Of lowest priority was the purpose of achieving the correct configuration of debt. Tax appeared to be of modest importance for both US and UK multinationals.

Table 9.3
Political risk and financing

	US		UK	
Factor	**Mean**	**Standard dev.**	**Mean**	**Standard dev.**
To obtain cheap government financing	3.48	1.23	2.93	1.27
To take advantage of higher tax shields on debt	3.46	1.06	3.44	1.25
To decrease the risk that assets may be expropriated	3.96	1.00	3.70	1.30
To lessen exchange rate risk by borrowing in a weak currency	3.72	1.21	3.30	1.56
To match assets against liabilities for the subsidiary	3.63	1.35	3.85	1.10
To reduce the incidence of exchange controls	3.87	1.12	3.74	1.13
To achieve the correct portfolio configuration of debt	2.96	1.19	2.50	1.30

Sources of finance

Further questions were asked regarding the financing of overseas subsidiaries and affiliates. The scale of importance of the various factors is indicated in Table 9.4.

US multinationals place the most emphasis upon local sources of finance from the host country such as host country banks. More emphasis is placed upon local debt markets of the host country and internally generated funds from the subsidiaries reserves rather than international sources such as international equity and bond markets. Finance from the local equity markets was of lowest priority. UK multinationals exhibited similar behaviour in relation to the importance of the various financing sources.

Table 9.4
Financing sources

	US		UK	
Factor	**Mean**	**Standard dev.**	**Mean**	**Standard dev.**
Local debt markets of host country	3.47	1.07	3.25	1.13
Internally generated funds from the parent's reserves	3.23	1.19	2.83	1.15
Internally generated funds from the subsidiaries' reserves	3.43	1.10	3.70	0.94
Local equity markets of the host country	1.60	0.86	1.78	1.10
International equity markets	1.77	1.07	1.73	1.09
International bond markets	2.17	1.26	2.10	1.22
Host country banks	3.77	0.94	3.70	0.97
Other host country financial institutions	2.79	1.18	2.67	1.12
Host country governments	2.59	1.24	1.95	1.05
Co-financing with the World Bank	1.68	1.09	1.20	0.52

The conclusion is that multinational corporations tend to prefer local sources of finance to international ones.

Country specific considerations

For each of the following country specific factors, the finance director was asked to indicate the scale of importance when raising finance from overseas, as shown in Table 9.5.

Table 9.5
Country-specific factors

	US		UK	
Factor	**Mean**	**Standard dev.**	**Mean**	**Standard dev.**
Level of political risk of the host country	3.59	1.12	3.31	1.13
Level of money interest rates of the host country	3.83	0.80	3.69	1.10
Level of real interest rates of the host country	4.04	1.04	3.92	1.11
Host country inflation rate	3.72	1.13	3.21	1.03
Exchange rate between the home and the host country	3.61	1.07	3.05	1.12
Transaction costs	3.00	1.00	2.74	1.03
Taxation treaties signed between the home and the host country	3.79	0.90	3.36	0.96
Exchange controls	3.90	0.77	3.55	0.92
Variability of the exchange rate between home and host country	3.62	1.01	3.44	0.99
Variability of host country interest rates	3.52	1.21	3.37	0.91

The level of real interest rates in the host country is of prime importance to the US multinational, when considering raising finance from overseas. Of lowest priority are the transaction costs. A similar pattern was followed by UK multinationals.

Trend in finance functions

In relation to the trend in centralization, the finance director was asked to indicate the scale of importance for the following functions: financing, hedging, capital budgeting, cash management and tax planning.

From Table 9.6, it is evident that both UK and US multinationals displayed greater decentralization of capital budgeting and cash management than the other functions. Shifts in the decentralization of financing, hedging and tax planning remained limited. Tax planning is thus seen as a centralized function, even more strongly in the US than in the UK.

Table 9.6
Trend in finance functions

	US		UK	
Factor	**Mean**	**Standard dev.**	**Mean**	**Standard dev.**
Financing	4.53	0.68	4.45	0.85
Hedging	4.33	0.80	4.51	0.72
Capital budgeting	3.40	1.22	3.42	1.15
Cash management	4.03	1.03	3.68	1.23
Tax planning	4.60	0.62	4.29	0.90

Overseas project evaluation

An important question is whether the discount rate used to evaluate overseas projects is significantly lower, the same or significantly higher than the domestic rate. A response of one on the scale indicated that the rate is significantly lower than the domestic rate, three indicated the same as the domestic rate and five indicated that it is significantly higher. The results are set out in Table 9.7.

It appears that US multinationals are using higher discount rates to evaluate overseas projects than UK companies, compared with domestic rates. The difference is significant.

Table 9.7
The discount rate in overseas project evaluation

	US		UK	
	Mean	**Standard dev.**	**Mean**	**Standard dev.**
Scale factor for discount rate	3.61	0.69	3.12	0.48

Impact of debt and high tax rates upon the value of the multinational enterprise

In relation to the impact that various financing strategies had upon the multinational enterprise, the finance director were asked what they believe happens to the value of the multinational enterprise when it raises debt finance from countries with high rates of corporation tax.

Table 9.8
Effect of debt and high tax rates upon value (% of respondents)

	US	UK
Value decreases	15.4	8.8
Value remains the same	50.0	58.8
Value increases	34.6	32.3

The results set out in Table 9.8 for UK and US multinationals appear to be similar. The majority of respondents believed that the value of the firm remained constant thus upholding Miller's (1977) general equilibrium theory. However, about one third of all multinationals believed raising finance in countries with high rates of corporation tax increased the value of the multinational.

Significant differences between UK and US Multinationals

A t-test was conducted on the data in order to find out whether there were any significant differences between UK and US multinationals. Although the t-test is a univariate technique, and therefore the variables are considered in isolation, it does give an insight into where the differences lie. The differences are listed in Table 9.9.

In relation to the general policies underlying the allocation of currencies within the multinational enterprise, UK multinationals placed greater importance upon allocating assets and liabilities in an overall risk minimising configuration than US multinationals. This result supports evidence in the literature, that UK multinationals are more risk averse than their US counterparts. In addition, UK multinationals placed greater emphasis than US multinationals upon matching the values of assets and liabilities in each currency supporting an economic "close out" policy, reinforcing a general risk averse profile of UK multinationals.

Table 9.9
The significance of differences between UK and US

Question Reference	US mean scale factor	UK mean scale factor	Value of 't'	Degrees of freedom	Two tailed probab -lity
Allocate assets and liabilities in an overall risk minimizing configuration	3.53	4.18	-2.32	43.19	0.025
Match values of assets and liabilities in each currency	3.30	4.08	-2.66	68	0.010
Finance from host country governments	2.59	1.95	+2.32	67	0.024
Co-financing from the World Bank	1.67	1.20	+2.16	35.54	0.038
Host country inflation rate	3.72	3.20	+1.97	66	0.053
Exchange rate between home and host country	3.60	3.05	+2.04	65	0.045

Table 9.9 (continued)

Taxation treaties signed between home and host country	3.79	3.35	+1.91	66	0.063
Centralization of tax planning	4.60	4.29	+1.70	68.80	0.094
Scale of discount rate used to assess overseas projects	3.60	3.11	+3.19	46.80	0.003

US multinationals indicated greater importance of finance from host country governments and cofinancing with the World Bank than UK companies. However, the importance of the World Bank was of low priority for both UK and US multinationals.

As to the importance of country specific factors involved in raising finance from overseas countries, US multinationals indicated greater emphasis upon the host country inflation rate and exchange rate than UK companies. This result is consistent with the assertion that UK companies tended to stress greater importance upon allocating assets and liabilities in a portfolio as to minimize risk than US companies, since the exchange rate would be largely irrelevant. This type of configuration of assets and liabilities is termed a zero net exposure. US multinationals stress greater importance than UK multinationals upon taxation treaties signed between the host and the home country.

With regard to the trend in centralization of tax planning, UK multinationals tended to be moving towards greater decentralization. However the difference was fairly tenuous.

US multinationals tended to assess overseas projects by using a higher risk-adjusted discount rate than UK companies, who tended to use the same discount rate as in the domestic situation. This result supports evidence in the literature, which suggests that US multinationals are more sophisticated than UK companies in their capital budgeting or US multinationals are subjected to greater risk from overseas diversification than UK multinationals.

Summary

In relation to the objectives of capital structure decisions, the maximization of the tax shield on debt was not the overriding concern for both UK and US multinationals. However, about one third of multinationals believed that raising finance in countries with high rates of corporation tax, increased the value of the firm. Generally, however, there was much more support for Miller's general equilibrium theory of tax and capital structure.

In the management of risk, UK companies stressed greater importance than US companies upon the allocation of assets and liabilities in an overall risk minimizing configuration. In addition, UK companies tended to place greater emphasis than US multinationals upon matching the values of assets and liabilities in each respective currency, which supports evidence in the literature that UK multinationals are more risk averse than their US counterparts. Overall, US multinationals believed that allocating assets and liabilities in a portfolio to minimize tax liabilities was of primary concern.

US companies place greater importance on local sources of finance than UK companies. Supporting this, US companies tended to place greater emphasis upon the host country inflation rate, when raising finance from overseas than UK companies. This is consistent with financing overseas subsidiaries on a localised basis, and perhaps a more sophisticated approach to financing. Also, US companies tended to emphasise the exchange rate between the home and the host country, compared with UK companies. Remembering that UK companies believed that matching was an important policy, then under such a policy, consideration of the exchange rate would be irrelevant.

There were significant differences between US and UK companies in relation to the discount rate used to assess the cash flows of foreign projects. The US tended to use a greater discount rate than the domestic situation, which would reflect a higher risk profile than UK companies which are more risk averse. UK companies tend to use the same discount rate, to assess foreign cash flows, as the domestic situation. This is an interesting result since it has been demonstrated in the literature that UK companies are less sophisticated in their capital budgeting than US companies. However, this may be explained by evidence that supports a risk averse stature of UK multinationals. The literature on multinational theory has implied that risk reduction can be achieved through international portfolio diversification of operations [Rugman (1979)]. Nevertheless, the fact, that in general, multinational finance managers are using the same or higher discount rates than in the domestic situation supports a shift in paradigm towards internalisation and eclectic theories of the multinational enterprise, where risk reduction is not emphasised.

References

Ashton, D. J. (1991), `Corporate Financial Policy: American Analytics and UK Taxation'. *Journal of Business Finance & Accounting*, vol 18, no. 4, pp. 465-482.

Buckley, P.J. and Casson, M. (1976), `*The Future of the Multinational Enterprise*'. London: Macmillan.

Doz, C.K. and Prahalad, Y.L. (1987), `*The Multinational Mission: Balancing Local Demands and a Global Vision*'. Free Press.
Dunning, J.H. (1988), `The Eclectic Paradigm of International Production: A restatement and some possible extensions'. *Journal of International Business Studies*, vol 19, no. 1, pp. 1-31.
Fatemi, A. M. (1988), `The Effect of International Diversification on Corporate Financing Policy'. *Journal of Business Research*, vol 16, no.1, pp. 17-30.
Kahn, S (1991), `Corporate Financing: When the Operating Sub Should Be the Fund-Raiser'. *Global Finance*, vol 5, no. 5, pp. 15-16.
Lee, K. C. and Kwok, C. C. Y. (1990), `Multinational Corporations vs. Domestic Corporations: International Environmental Factors and Determinants of Capital Structure'. *Journal of International Business Studies*, vol 30, no. 4, pp. 331-352.
Madura, J and Foseberg, R. H., (1990), `The Impact of Financing Sources on Multinational Projects'. *Journal of Financial Research*, vol 13, no. 1, pp. 61-69.
Miller, M. (1977), `Debt and Taxes'. *Journal of Finance*, vol. 32, no. 2, pp. 261-75.
Modigliani, F and Miller, M. H. (1958), `The Cost of Capital, Corporation Finance and the Theory of Investment'. *American Economic Review*, vol 48, no. 3, June, pp. 261-297.
OECD (1990), `*Taxation and International Capital Flows: A Symposium of OECD and Non-OECD Countries*'. June.
Rugman, A. (1979), `*International Diversification and the Multinational Enterprise*'. Lexington, MA.
Soenen, L. (1979), `*Foreign Exchange Exposure Management: A Portfolio Theory Approach*'. Sijthoff and Noordhoff.
Williamson, O.E. (1988), `Corporate Finance and Corporate Governance'. *Journal of Finance*, vol 43, no. 3, pp. 567-591.

Conclusions

A number of domestic and international issues in business taxation have been examined. Part One focused upon particular issues in the UK context, Part Two widened the horizon to Europe and specific multinational aspects were investigated in Part Three.

The impact of taxation on the capital investment decision was the first issue for analysis. Significant tax incentives were found in plant and machinery investments. The tax-free rates of return required for the level of risk are greater than the equilibrium rates of return in a post corporate and personal tax model. As far as industrial buildings are concerned, there are disincentives to invest in average risk projects, where companies pay the full corporate tax rate, although there is a neutral tax effect for the company with small profits. High profit companies investing in low risk industrial building projects are in a tax neutral position. However, for low profit companies investing in low risk industrial building projects there are tax incentives. For both high and low profit companies investing in high risk industrial building projects there are incentives to invest. But there are disincentives to invest in commercial buildings regardless of the level of risk.

From an empirical study of the lease or buy decision it was shown that most respondents take tax into account and it is normally considered to be an important factor. Although the after-tax cost of debt is popular as a discount factor many respondents do not account for the full effects of taxation. The disclosure requirement under SSAP 21 is not normally considered important in the finance lease decision. However, there is a relationship between the level of gearing and whether finance lease contracts affect a firm's borrowing capacity.

Recognition of the interdependencies of projects, caused by the tax constraints, is the motivation behind the mathematical programming model which has been presented. In particular, the model incorporates the tax rules relating to the setoff of advance corporation tax and losses, as well as constraints relevant to lease evaluation. The model provides a basis for the assessment of the post-tax net present value of a single incremental project or a combination of projects in the context of the firm's overall tax situation.

In Part Two, European issues were examined, beginning with comparisons of the tax treatment in different European countries of dividends, depreciation, capital gains, losses, stocks, interest, foreign source income and value added tax. Discrepancies between non-deductible items in different countries were also itemized.

From a simulation study of investment, risk and the EC tax systems, it was shown that each system can create tax incentives to invest in plant and machinery projects of low and medium risk and disincentives to invest in building projects of medium and high risk. For high risk investments there are significant variations in the ranking of relative incentives between countries under different asset categories. Low risk investment rankings are positively related. Also, for the same type of buildings under different risk categories there is normally a strong positive correlation. There is a negative correlation in country rankings between low and high risk investments in plant and machinery. Overall, the strongest investment incentives were found in Ireland and Portugal and the weakest in Belgium and Greece.

The simulation exercise extended to the evaluation of the tax incentives to debt finance, under both active and passive debt management policies. Wide variations were found. In some countries, for example in Greece and Italy, the gains are negative, although very small. The French and German systems are also approximately neutral, although the gains are positive, but small. By contrast, in Portugal, Luxembourg, the Netherlands and Spain, the gains are large. These gains are smaller under an active debt management policy and reduce further as the unlevered rate increases, although the gains for these four countries are still significant. The UK system was examined in more detail, demonstrating that the gains can range from zero to very substantial values, depending upon the marginal personal and corporate tax rates and whether the marginal investor borrows or lends.

Research conducted on capital structure data reveals significant differentials in the mean debt-equity ratios of firms across European countries, which may partly be explained by institutional factors. Apart from extreme cases, the countries whose firms have higher debt-equity ratios employ imputation or tax credit systems, which is counter-intuitive. The general lack of bimodality of European capital structure distributions questions the usefulness of the Miller general equilibrium model in explaining European capital structures. Intra-country capital structure differences appear to be explained by differences in dividend policy, profitability, earnings and bankruptcy risk.

It has been established that there is a wide diversity of corporate tax systems within the European Community. The current complexity of administration and operation of the corporate tax systems is substantial. Although preliminary data suggests that tax differentials may not affect investment decisions, further research into corporate and personal decision-making is needed. The sceptic would expect it to be unlikely that efficient allocations are generated. As to harmonization, it will be necessary to investigate the presence of any trends, attributable to market forces, in the degree of diversity of corporate tax regimes of the member states. Individual member states, mindful of their sovereignty, might see bureaucratic solutions as irrational and prefer a minimalist and gradualist process as a first preference. Progress has been and may remain slow.

In Part Three the controlled foreign company legislation was a particular issue for scrutiny. In the planning process companies, in practice, carefully check for exempt activity status and the close scrutiny of overseas law is seen as important, in order to avoid an unintentional formation of a controlled foreign company. Perhaps one of the most surprising results is that over half of the respondent companies always or often vetted commercial activities in Europe. To defend against a controlled foreign company direction, companies consider it very important to plan dividend policies that satisfy the acceptable distribution test. Surprisingly, only one-fifth of respondents see the motive test as being very important.

The final study was based upon a survey of the capital budgeting and financing decisions of UK and US multinational companies. It is shown that the maximization of the tax shield on debt is of importance for both US and UK multinational companies, although not the overriding concern. US multinationals place emphasis upon the allocation of assets and liabilities in an overall tax minimizing configuration, although UK multinationals place more emphasis upon the allocation of assets and liabilities in an overall risk minimizing configuration. When considering raising finance from overseas, for both US and UK multinationals, the level of real interest rates of the host country are of prime importance, although taxation treaties signed between the home and the host country are of some importance. Tax planning is seen as a centralized function. About one-third of multinationals believe that raising finance in countries with high rates of corporation tax increases the value of the firm. Generally, however, there is much more support amongst US and UK multinationals for Miller's general equilibrium theory of tax and capital structure.

UNIVERSITY OF BRISTOL

UNIVERSITY
OF BRISTOL
LIBRARY